939.21
T

BaT  3/05
Re

# THE TROJAN WAR

**Greenwood Guides to Historic Events of the Ancient World**

# THE TROJAN WAR

Carol G. Thomas and
Craig Conant

Greenwood Guides to Historic Events of the Ancient World
Bella Vivante, Series Editor

GREENWOOD PRESS
Westport, Connecticut • London

**Library of Congress Cataloging-in-Publication Data**

Thomas, Carol G., 1938–
   The Trojan War / Carol G. Thomas and Craig Conant.
      p.  cm.—(Greenwood guides to historic events of the ancient world)
     Includes bibliographical references and index.
     ISBN 0–313–32526–X (alk. paper)
     1. Trojan War.  2. Civilization, Aegean.  3. Aegean Sea
Region—Antiquities.  4. Homer—Criticism and interpretation.
I. Conant, Craig, 1947–  II. Title.  III. Series.
BL793.T7T47   2005
939'.21—dc22      2004017660

British Library Cataloguing in Publication Data is available.

Library of Congress Catalog Card Number: 2004017660
ISBN: 0–313–32526–X

First published in 2005

Greenwood Press, 88 Post Road West, Westport, CT 06881
An imprint of Greenwood Publishing Group, Inc.
www.greenwood.com

Printed in the United States of America

The paper used in this book complies with the
Permanent Paper Standard issued by the National
Information Standards Organization (Z39.48–1984).

10 9 8 7 6 5 4 3 2 1

**Copyright Acknowledgment**

The authors and publisher gratefully acknowledge permission for the use of the
following material:

Excerpts from *The Aeneid* by Virgil, translated by Robert Fitzgerald, copyright © 1980,
1982, 1983 by Robert Fitzgerald. Used by permission of Random House, Inc.

# CONTENTS

*Photo essay follows Chapter 5.*

# SERIES FOREWORD

As a professor and scholar of the ancient Greek world, I am often asked by students and scholars of other disciplines, why study antiquity? What possible relevance could human events from two, three, or more thousand years ago have to our lives today? This questioning of the continued validity of our historical past may be the offshoot of the forces shaping the history of the American people. Proud of forging a new nation out of immigrants wrenched willingly or not from their home soils, Americans have experienced a liberating headiness of separation from traditional historical demands on their social and cultural identity. The result has been a skepticism about the very validity of that historical past. Some of that skepticism is healthy and serves constructive purposes of scholarly inquiry. Questions of how, by whom, and in whose interest "history" is written are valid questions pursued by contemporary historians striving to uncover the multiple forces shaping any historical event and the multilayered social consequences that result. But the current academic focus on "presentism"—the concern with only recent events and a deliberate ignoring of premodern eras—betrays an extreme distortion of legitimate intellectual inquiry. This stress on the present seems to have deepened in the early years of the twenty-first century. The cybertechnological explosions of the preceding decades seem to have propelled us into a new cultural age requiring new rules that make the past appear all the more obsolete.

So again I ask, why study ancient cultures? In the past year, after it ousted that nation's heinous regime, the United States' occupation of Iraq has kept that nation in the forefront of the news. The land base of Iraq is ancient Mesopotamia, "the land between the rivers" of the Tigris and Euphrates, two of the four rivers in the biblical Garden of Eden (Gen. 2). Called the cradle of civilization, this area witnessed the early development of a centrally organized, hierarchical social system that utilized the new technology of writing to administer an increasingly complex state.

Is there a connection between the ancient events, literature, and art coming out of this land and contemporary events? Michael Wood, in his educational video *Iraq: The Cradle of Civilization*, produced shortly after the 1991 Gulf War, thinks so and makes this connection explicit—between the people, their way of interacting with their environment, and even the cosmological stories they create to explain and define their world.

Study of the ancient world, like study of contemporary cultures other than one's own, has more than academic or exotic value. First, study of the past seeks meaning beyond solely acquiring factual knowledge. It strives to understand the human and social dynamics that underlie any historical event and what these underlying dynamics teach us about ourselves as human beings in interaction with one another. Study of the past also encourages deeper inquiry than what appears to some as the "quaint" observation that this region of current and recent conflict could have served as a biblical ideal or as a critical marker in the development of world civilizations. In fact, these apparently quaint dimensions can serve as the hook that piques our interest into examining the past and discovering what it may have to say to us today. Not an end in itself, the knowledge forms the bedrock for exploring deeper meanings.

Consider, for example, the following questions. What does it mean that three major world religions—Judaism, Christianity, and Islam—developed out of the ancient Mesopotamian worldview? In this view, the world, and hence its gods, were seen as being in perpetual conflict with one another and with the environment, and death was perceived as a matter of despair and desolation. What does it mean that Western forms of thinking derive from the particular intellectual revolution of archaic Greece that developed into what is called rational discourse, ultimately systematized by Aristotle in the fourth century B.C.E.? How does this thinking, now fundamental to Western discourse, shape how we see the world and ourselves, and how we interact with one another? And how does it affect our ability, or lack thereof, to communicate intelligibly with people with differently framed cultural perceptions? What, ultimately, do we gain from being aware of the origin and development of these fundamental features of our thinking and beliefs?

In short, knowing the past is essential for knowing ourselves in the present. Without an understanding of where we came from, and the journey we took to get where we are today, we cannot understand why we think or act the way we do. Nor, without an understanding of historical development, are we in a position to make the kinds of constructive changes necessary to advance as a society. Awareness of the past gives us the resources necessary to make comparisons between our contemporary world and past times. It is from those comparisons that we can assess both the advances we have made as human societies and those aspects that can still benefit from change. Hence, knowledge of the past is crucial for shaping our individual and social identities, providing us with the resources to make intelligent, aware, and informed decisions for the future.

All ancient societies, whether significant for the evolution of Western ideas and values, or whether they developed largely separate from the cultures that more directly influenced Western civilization, such as China, have important lessons to teach us. For fundamentally they all address questions that have faced every human individual and every human society that has existed. Because ancient civilizations erected great monuments of themselves in stone, writings, and the visual arts— all enduring material evidence—we can view how these ancient cultures dealt with many of the same questions we face today. And we learn the consequences of the actions taken by people in other societies and times that, ideally, should help us as we seek solutions to contemporary issues. Thus it was that President John F. Kennedy wrote of his reliance upon Thucydides' treatment of the devastating war between the ancient Greek city-states of Athens and Sparta (see the volume on the Peloponnesian War) in his study of exemplary figures, *Profiles in Courage*.

This series seeks to fulfill this goal both collectively and in the individual volumes. The individual volumes examine key events, trends, and developments in world history in ancient times that are central to the secondary school and lower-level undergraduate history curriculum and that form standard topics for student research. From a vast field of potential subjects, these selected topics emerged after consultations with scholars, educators, and librarians. Each book in the series can be described as a "library in a book." Each one presents a chronological timeline and an initial factual overview of its subject, three to five topical essays that examine the subject from diverse perspectives and for its various consequences, a concluding essay providing current perspectives on the event, biographies of key players, a selection of primary documents, illustrations, a glossary, and an index. The concept of the series is to provide ready-reference materials that include a quick, in-depth examination of the topic and insightful guidelines for interpretive analysis, suitable for student research and designed to stimulate critical thinking. The authors are all scholars of the topic in their fields, selected both on the basis of their expertise and for their ability to bring their scholarly knowledge to a wider audience in an engaging and clear way. In these regards, this series follows the concept and format of the Greenwood Guides to Historic Events of the Twentieth Century, the Fifteenth to Nineteenth Centuries, and the Medieval World.

All the works in this series deal with historical developments in early ancient civilizations, almost invariably postdating the emergence of writing and of hierarchical dynastic social structures. Perhaps only incidentally do they deal with what historians call the Paleolithic ("Old Stone Age") periods, from about 25,000 B.C.E. onward, eras characterized by nomadic, hunting-gathering societies, or the Neolithic ("New Stone Age"), the period of the earliest development of agriculture and hence settled societies, one of the earliest dating to about 7000 B.C.E at Çatal Höyük in south-central Turkey.

The earliest dates covered by the books in this series are the fourth to second millennia B.C.E. for the building of the Pyramids in Egypt, and the examination of the Trojan War and the Bronze Age civilizations of the eastern Mediterranean. Most volumes deal with events in the first millennium B.C.E. to the early centuries of the first millennium C.E. Some treat the development of civilizations, such as the rise of the Han Empire in China, or the separate volumes on the rise and on the decline and fall of the Roman Empire. Some highlight major personalities and their empires, such as the volumes on Cleopatra VII of Ptolemaic Egypt or Justinian and the beginnings of the Byzantine Empire in eastern Greece and Constantinople (Istanbul). Three volumes examine the emergence in antiquity of religious movements that form major contemporary world systems of belief—Judaism, Buddhism, and Christianity. (Islam is being treated in the parallel Medieval World series.) And two volumes examine technological developments, one on the building of the Pyramids and one on other ancient technologies.

Each book examines the complexities of the forces shaping the development of its subject and the historical consequences. Thus, for example, the volume on the fifth-century B.C.E. Greek Peloponnesian War explores the historical causes of the war, the nature of the combatants' actions, and how these reflect the thinking of the period. A particular issue, which may seem strange to some or timely to others, is how a city like Athens, with its proto-democratic political organization and its outstanding achievements in architecture, sculpture, painting, drama, and philosophy, could engage in openly imperialist policies of land conquest and of vicious revenge against any who countered them. Rather than trying to gloss over the contradictions that emerge, these books conscientiously explore whatever tensions arise in the ancient material, both to portray more completely the ancient event and to highlight the fact that no historical occurrence is simply determined. Sometimes societies that we admire in some ways—such as the artistic achievements and democratic political experiments of ancient Athens—may prove deeply troublesome in other ways—such as what we see as their reprehensible conduct in war and in brutal subjection of other Greek communities. Consequently, the reader is empowered to make informed, well-rounded judgments on the events and actions of the major players.

We offer this series as an invitation to explore the past in various ways. We anticipate that from its volumes the reader will gain a better appreciation of the historical events and forces that shaped the lives of our ancient forebears and that continue to shape our thinking, values, and actions today. However remote in time and culture these ancient civilizations may at times appear, ultimately they show us that the questions confronting human beings of any age are timeless and that the examples of the past can provide valuable insights into our understanding of the present and the future.

Bella Vivante
University of Arizona

# PREFACE

Within the series, the Greenwood Guides to Historic Events of the Ancient World, the present volume is perhaps singular in that it attempts to describe an event whose reality is by no means certain. Although the Trojan War was very real to the Greeks and Romans of antiquity and to educated people during the Middle Ages, the development during and after the Renaissance of the scientific method with its insistence on critical inquiry cast a shadow of doubt on the factual basis of the legend of Troy. By the nineteenth century, these doubts had turned to out-and-out disbelief. Nonetheless, in 1870 Heinrich Schliemann, who did not share the skepticism of contemporary historians and archaeologists, began excavating the Hill of Hissarlik in northwest Turkey, a site he felt sure hid the ruins of Homer's Troy.

In the century since Schliemann's death in 1890, developments in archaeology and many allied fields have borne out the truth of his faith. Today most scholars are reasonably sure that the ruined Bronze Age town discovered at Hissarlik is in fact Troy. This is not to say, however, that having found Troy, we have also found the Trojan War. Nor will we attempt to demonstrate the reality of such a war, for the evidence does not yet allow for such a demonstration. However, a good deal of circumstantial evidence has been found, which we will examine during the course of this book: Troy seemingly did exist; so also did the city of Agamemnon, Mycenae, the ruins of which have always been visible. With Troy and Mycenae we have, as it were, the *corpus delecti*. More circumstantial evidence, and possibly a motive, are supplied by the discovery and decipherment, also in the twentieth century, of the records of the Hittite archives found at Boğazköy and the Linear B tablets from Knossos on Crete and Pylos in southwest Greece.

The first half of the book will survey all this evidence, while the second half will focus on the Epic Tradition that grew up around the tale of the Trojan War. We will attempt to discern the beginnings of this tradition in the middle second millennium B.C.E.,[1] how it culminated in the poems of Homer in the eighth century B.C.E., and finally how the tradition was spread and popularized throughout the Mediterranean world during the later centuries of antiquity.

In Chapter 1 we recount the legend of the Trojan War as the Greeks knew it. We then provide a brief survey of the rise and development of Bronze Age culture which forms the historical context of Troy and the Trojan War.

The archaeological discoveries that brought Troy, Mycenae, Pylos, and many other Bronze Age sites to light are surveyed in Chapter 2. We also examine a few of the pertinent Hittite documents of the Late Bronze Age and consider their intriguing references to such little known lands or states as Ahhiyawa, Wilusa, and Millawanda. The antiquity and nature of the Epic Tradition that gave rise to Homer's poems, the *Iliad* and the *Odyssey*, will be discussed in Chapter 3. We investigate some of the evidence, both internal to the epics and external deriving from nonliterary sources, which indicate that Homer was inspired by a tradition already many centuries old. Also in this chapter we look at Homer's contribution to the Epic Tradition and examine arguments for identifying him as an oral poet within a largely nonliterate society newly exposed to alphabetic writing.

Chapter 4 inquires how the tales surrounding the Trojan War spread outward from Greece and the Aegean, first to the new Greek settlements on the west coast of Anatolia (modern Turkey), and then northwestward up the Adriatic and over to Italy and Sicily. Special attention is paid to such sites as the Cave of Polis on Odysseus' island of Ithaca and the grave of a young boy discovered on the island of Pithecoussae (modern Ischia) outside the Bay of Naples. We also survey the adoption of elements of the Trojan War Cycle, and the uses to which they were put, by non-Greek Italians, particularly the Romans, as well as by later Greeks, including Alexander the Great.

Chapter 5 provides a brief summary of the book and discusses the enduring popularity of Homer's epics and the legend of the Trojan War generally. Also discussed in this final chapter is the ancient Greeks' perception of their own history and the impact of their belief in a Trojan War on their ideas of the past.

The narrative of the book is followed by a number of sections that may be of use to those readers unfamiliar with the Bronze Age of the Aegean and the Near East or the story of the Trojan War. The biographies include both those of real persons alive at the time a Trojan War would likely have occurred and those who exist, so far as we know, only in legend. A range of primary sources, in translation, is included to provide readers with a sampling of the kinds of evidence that must be interpreted to answer even the most basic question about a Trojan War; namely, did such a war take place? Illustrations, too, help to make it easier to visualize Bronze Age places, objects, and people. A glossary of terms has been added as an aid to the nonspecialist unfamiliar with Bronze Age archaeology or culture. In the Annotated Bibliography we list mainly books and articles easily obtained and accessible to the nonspecialist reader. However, we have also included a number of more specialized writings that we consider most illuminating, both to us and to those readers interested in further inquiry into this complex and rewarding subject.

## NOTE

1. Unless otherwise indicated, all dates are Before the Common Era (B.C.E.).

# Chronology

| Dates BCE | Greece | Crete | Troy | Anatolia | Egypt | Dates BCE |
|---|---|---|---|---|---|---|
| 8000 | Neolithic | | | Neolithic | | 8000 |
| 7000 | | | | | | 7000 |
| 6000 | | Neolithic | | | | 6000 |
| 5000 | | | | | Neolithic | 5000 |
| 4000 | | | | | Pre-dynastic states | 4000 |
| **Bronze Age** | | | | | | **Bronze Age** |
| 3000 | Early Helladic I (EH I) | Early Minoan | Troy I | | Unification of North and South Kingdoms | 3000 |
| 2900 | | | | | Old Kingdom Dynasties I, II | 2900 |
| 2800 | | | | | | 2800 |
| 2700 | EH II | | | | Dynasties, III-V | 2700 |
| 2600 | | | Troy II "Treasure of Priam" | Indo-European speakers enter Anatolia | | 2600 |
| 2500 | | | | | | 2500 |
| 2400 | | | | | | 2400 |
| 2300 | | | Troy III | | | 2300 |
| 2200 | EH III | | Troy IV | Indo-European Hittites in Central Anatolia | First Intermediate Period, Middle Kingdom Dynasties XI, XII | 2200 |
| 2100 | Middle Helladic (MH) (early) | Middle Minoan | | | | 2100 |
| 2000 | MH (middle) | First Palace Period | Troy V | | | 2000 |
| 1900 | | | Troy VI | Assyrian Trading Stations | | 1900 |
| 1800 | MH (late) | | | | | 1800 |
| 1700 | Late Helladic I (LH I) | Second Palace Period | | Hittites: Old Kingdom | Hyksos, Second Intermediate Period | 1700 |
| 1650 | Thera Volcano | | | | | 1650 |
| 1600 | | | | | | 1600 |
| 1550 | LH IIA | Late Minoan | | | New Kingdom, Dynasty XVIII | 1550 |
| 1500 | | | | | | 1500 |

## Chronology (cont.)

| Dates BCE | Greece | Crete | Troy | Anatolia | Egypt | Dates BCE |
|---|---|---|---|---|---|---|
| 1450 | Mycenaean expansion to Cyclades, Crete; LH IIB / LH IIIA1 | Mycenaean domination at Knossos, Third Palace Period | | | Egyptian Empire | 1450 |
| 1400 | | Destruction of Knossos | | New Kingdom (Hittite Empire) | Amarna Period | 1400 |
| 1350 | LH IIIA2; Mycenaean koine / LH IIIB1; Destruction of Thebes | | Troy VIh | | | 1350 |
| 1300 | LH IIIB2 / Monumental tholos tombs; fortification of Mycenaean citadels | | Destruction of Troy by earthquake? | Mursili II / Destruction of Millawanda; Muwatalli II / Millawanda an Ahhiyawan vassal | Dynasty XIX | 1300 |
| 1250 | Trojan War? | | Trojan War? | Hattusili III, Piyamaradu / Tudhaliya IV; Hittite control of Millawanda | Ramses II, Kadesh | 1250 |
| 1200 | LH IIIC / Mycenaean destructions; Pylos Linear B tablets | Post Palatial | Troy VIIa | Hittite collapse | Merenptah repulses Sea Peoples / Dynasty XX; Ramses III repulses Sea Peoples | 1200 |
| 1150 | Sub-Mycenaean | Sub-Minoan | Troy VIIa destroyed / Troy VIIb | | | 1150 |
| 1100 | Dark Age (end of Bronze Age) | Dark Age (end of Bronze Age) | Site abandoned? | | End of Egyptian Empire | 1100 |
| Iron Age 1000 | | | | | | Iron Age 1000 |
| 900 | Cave of Polis | | | Neo-Hittite States | Libyan Dynasties, XXII-XXIII | 900 |
| 750 | Alphabet, Homer | | Troy VIII | | | 750 |

# CHAPTER 1

# TROY AND THE WORLD OF THE LATE BRONZE AGE

Even without taking a course or watching a documentary describing ancient Mediterranean history, most people are aware of the wealthy and powerful civilizations of Egypt and Mesopotamia that were flourishing 5,000 years ago. The waters of the Nile in Egypt and the Tigris and Euphrates rivers in Mesopotamia propelled the development of the earliest complex, urban societies on the face of the planet Earth. Initially, this complex way of life was relatively compressed to the land on either side of the Nile and to that between the two Mesopotamian rivers. But the complexity spread steadily to other regions of the ancient Near East as newcomers were drawn into the regions and as inhabitants of the original civilizations expanded their visions whether by trade, by creation of new settlements similar to their own, or by force of arms.

By the middle of the second millennium B.C.E., the eastern Mediterranean sphere was an interconnected world encompassing the Levant (the eastern coast of the Mediterranean now divided among Syria, Lebanon, Palestine, and Israel) as well as the offshore island of Cyprus, Anatolia (essentially the territory of the modern Turkish nation), the Aegean islands, the peninsula of Greece, and Crete, the island straddling the Aegean and the Mediterranean seas. Egypt continued to be a major power. During this phase, known as the New Kingdom, Egyptian power was well established in the Levant and was expanding even further northward. The other major power was a newer kingdom: that of the Hittites, a people who had immigrated into Anatolia as recently as approximately 2000 B.C.E. Though newcomers, they quickly learned the art of creating a complex, powerful state in the northeast of the peninsula from which they began to expand westward and south. Increasingly, rulers of these two kingdoms gained control over much of the rest of the region through trade, force of arms, and diplomacy.

In spite of their superior power, the Egyptians and Hittites not only tolerated lesser kingdoms and even small states but relied on them for the resources and skills these minor states might possess as well as securing allies to use against one another. Troy was one of these small states, situated in the northwest corner of Anatolia. The epic of the Trojan War is the site's major claim to fame: the *Iliad* and *Odyssey* are among the world's greatest poems. In addition, the likelihood that a war did occur at the site of Troy in the Late Bronze Age is an important demonstration of the network of ties that characterizes the entire period. Recent archaeological investigation at the site indicates that Troy may well have been the northernmost center in the coastal trading system that reached beyond the eastern Mediterranean Sea into the Black Sea in the north and into the central Mediterranean in the west.

Consequently, the title of this volume—*The Trojan War*—is well suited to provide the pivot of an account of this International Age. As remembered in the Homeric epics, it was the Age of Heroes when mortals could hoist a stone that three men could barely lift in later times. The tale of the Trojan War is the subject of the *Iliad* and the *Odyssey*. It was fleshed out, even in antiquity, by other accounts that describe events not remembered in the two Homeric epics. So powerful were these tales to the Greeks that a whole cycle of stories became attached to the epics. Thus, deep roots anchor this famous war to earlier times and spheres, particularly that of the gods, while its later consequences also merited tales of their own.

The poets and mythographers say that when Peleus, the father of Achilles, wed the sea goddess Thetis, all the gods and goddesses of Olympus attended the wedding save one. Through some oversight, Eris, or Strife, was not invited. Untroubled by her lack of an invitation, Eris came anyway and, aiming to cause some small mischief, presented a golden apple bearing the inscription "For the Fairest" to the goddesses Hera, Athena, and Aphrodite. Unable, or unwilling, to choose, the gods charged Hermes, the wiliest of the gods, to solve this puzzle. Thinking it only fitting that the fairest of mortal men should decide who was fairest among the immortal goddesses, Hermes escorted the three to the slopes of Mount Ida where Paris, fairest son of King Priam of Troy, was tending his flock. Paris promptly awarded the Golden Apple to Aphrodite, but only after she had promised him that the most beautiful of women would be his for the taking.

Either Aphrodite failed to inform Paris, or he thought it of slight importance, that Helen, the most beautiful of women and the daughter of King Tyndareus of Sparta, was already married to Menelaus, the brother of King Agamemnon of Mycenae. In any case, some time later, Paris finagled an invitation to Menelaus' halls in Sparta, and as soon as her husband was away on some errand or other, Paris seized his opportunity and fled taking Helen with him. Discovering what had occurred, Menelaus made his way with all haste to Mycenae where he begged Agamemnon to raise forces from all the cities of Greece and go in pursuit of Paris and Helen. This was not as difficult as it might seem, for before she married Menelaus nearly every Greek prince or warrior of any account had sought Helen's hand in marriage, and they had all sworn an oath to defend whomever would be chosen as her husband against anyone intent on doing him harm.

Soon a great host and fleet had gathered at Aulis in Boeotia in east-central Greece ready to sail for Troy with the first favorable wind. Among the many renowned captains who assembled there was Diomedes fresh from his victory over Thebes, Idomeneus who levied a large force from the ninety cities of Crete, Odysseus eloquent and crafty in council though his kingdom of Ithaca was small, old Nestor of Pylos, the wisest of the Greeks, and Great Ajax, the most formidable warrior save one. That one was Achilles who, though hardly more than a boy, was unsurpassed in war craft.

All these together with their armies and their ships gathered in Aulis, but to no avail, for days and weeks passed and still there was nothing but contrary winds. Finally, the seer Calchas informed Agamemnon that only by sacrificing his most beautiful daughter to Artemis could he gain a favorable wind. At first Agamemnon refused to listen to this grim advice, but as the days lengthened and the winds stubbornly refused to change, the army threatened to mutiny if Agamemnon did not summon his daughter to Aulis. At last Agamemnon relented, and Iphigeneia, the most beautiful of his three daughters, arrived in Aulis some days later. Some say that the girl was indeed sacrificed, while others insist that Artemis appeared just as the blade was placed to her neck and carried Iphigenia off to serve the goddess as her priestess in the land of the Taurians in what is now southern Russia. In any case, a favorable wind sprang up the following day, and the great fleet finally set sail for Troy.

The city proved to be a powerful foe and not easily conquered no matter how large the army sent against it. For one thing, Troy was possessed of numerous allies among the islands near the Asian shore and among the cities of the region around Troy, or the Troad, and even further afield. Even if all these could be reduced, then there was the city itself whose mighty walls had been constructed by Apollo and Poseidon. But of course the Trojans would not be satisfied to cower behind their walls and wait for the Greeks to devise some means of taking the city, for they themselves were a warlike people commanded by Priam's son Hector, who was himself a great warrior and more than a match for any of the Greeks save Achilles.

But although Priam and Paris were determined never to return Helen, Agamemnon and Menelaus were just as determined to win her back. The result was years spent in capturing the towns allied to Troy and many months fighting before the city walls. In the ninth year of the war, disaster nearly overtook the Greeks when a bitter quarrel broke out between Agamemnon and Achilles over the division of spoils. We will not retell here what Homer has recounted so masterfully in the *Iliad*, but suffice it to say that this quarrel resulted in Achilles absenting himself from the fighting, threatening to return home at the first opportunity. Although Agamemnon relented and begged him to return to battle, offering him rich gifts if he did so, Achilles' injured pride would not allow him to set aside his wrath, with the result that Hector and his forces were soon among the Greek ships setting them afire.

Achilles' boon companion, Patroclus, convinced his friend to allow him to don Achilles' armor and take the field just long enough to drive the Trojans from the ships. Having accomplished this object, Patroclus could not resist the temptation to pursue the fleeing Trojans all the way to the gates of the city. But once there Apollo would allow him to go no further, and smote him between the shoulder blades; Patroclus fell senseless in the dust where he was soon dispatched by Hector who stripped him of Achilles' armor.

Nearly mad with grief, Achilles vowed vengeance against Hector and rejoined the battle with new armor cunningly devised by the smith-god Hephaestus. Routing the Trojans with great slaughter, Achilles succeeded in trapping Hector outside the city walls, slew him, and, tying the corpse to his chariot, dragged it all the way back to the Greek camp.

The death of Hector was a sore blow to the Trojans, but they were far from finished. Another of Priam's sons, Deiphobus, took command of the troops, while Priam called in allies from farther afield. These included Penthesileia, queen of the Amazons, and Memnon the Ethiopian who arrived with a large army from India and a Phoenician fleet. Penthesileia was a stout warrior and even succeeded in driving Achilles from the field a number of times before he himself slew her. Memnon was also a great warrior and drove the Greeks back to their ships before falling to Achilles' spear in single combat. But this was Achilles' last triumph, for shortly afterward he was slain when Paris shot an arrow that struck him in his heel. This was his only vulnerable spot, for his mother Thetis had held her infant son by his heel when attempting to burn away his mortal body in order to make him immortal.

Although the Trojans had lost two great allies, the Greeks had lost their best warrior and seemed no closer to taking the city. The situation was made worse for the Greeks when Agamemnon awarded Achilles' armor to Odysseus instead of Ajax who had carried Achilles' body from the field though beset by a host of enemies. Ajax went mad at the insult to his honor and killed himself.

And so, despairing of conquering the city by main force, Odysseus devised a plan whereby Troy might be taken by trickery. Following his plan, a great wooden horse was built and made hollow and fitted with a trap-door so that twenty or thirty hand-picked warriors could be housed within for a short time. The whole structure was then placed on wheels so that it might be dragged into the city. When it was completed, Menelaus and Odysseus and a number of other warriors entered the horse, while Agamemnon and the rest of the army embarked in their ships and sailed to a spot on the far side of the Island of Tenedos, out of view of the Trojans. They left behind one man who explained to the Trojans that the Greeks had given up and sailed home leaving the horse as an offering to Athena in hopes of a safe voyage.

In spite of the warnings uttered by his daughter Cassandra who was a seer, Priam believed this tale and ordered that the horse should be dragged into the city to honor Athena for her deliverance of Troy. That night the Trojans, hardly believing their good fortune, gave themselves up to wild celebration, and as the moon rose high and even the sentries slept in a wine-soaked slumber, Odysseus and Menelaus and their small force crept out of the horse, signaled to Agamemnon's fleet from the walls, and opened the gates of Troy to his forces when they arrived soon after.

The Trojans who had not been slaughtered in their beds awoke to find their city ablaze and marauding bands of Greek warriors roaming the streets. It is said that the Dardanian prince Aeneas tried to organize a defense, but after a while as the situation grew plainly hopeless, he broke off the fight and, with his lame father perched on his shoulder, escaped the doomed city with a small band of followers. Priam's cousin Antenor and his sons are also said to have survived the sack. Antenor had long argued that Helen must be returned or the city would face destruction, and during the last few months a peace party had formed under his leadership. Some say that Antenor and his sons were allowed to escape through a prior arrangement with Agamemnon.

By the dawn of the next day, Troy lay a smoldering ruin. Priam and nearly all his sons had been slain, and Hector's child Astyanax had been cruelly thrown from the battlements. Priam's queen Hecuba, his daughter Cassandra, Hector's wife Andromache, and many other Trojan women were led away in chains.

After thoroughly despoiling the city of any treasures they could find, Agamemnon gathered his forces back at the Greek camp. It was his aim to spend a brief period in offering up sacrifices and prayers of thanksgiving to Athena for their final success, but Menelaus, impatient to return home with Helen, set sail immediately. Athena, angered by this lack of piety, sent a storm that blew Menelaus' fleet off course to Phoenicia and then to Egypt. It would be eight years before the goddess relented and finally allowed Menelaus to return to Sparta. On the other hand, Agamemnon's piety earned him a swift return home only to be murdered by his wife Clytemnestra and her lover Aegisthus. Aegisthus was Agamemnon's cousin and had long thought that the throne of Mycenae should be his. As for Clytemnestra, she harbored a bitter enmity toward her husband for his sacrifice of Iphigenia. The return of other Greek captains were equally hazardous or lengthy. Diomedes returned also to find that his wife had played him false and the throne of Argos occupied by a usurper. He eventually made his way to Italy where he founded many cities, but was murdered by King Daunus in a fit of jealousy. Idomeneus returned to Crete to find his wife and daughter dead at the hands of another usurper. Unable to dislodge this tyrant, Idomeneus also went to Italy where he died in obscurity. But of all the tales concerning the return of the Greeks from Troy, the most famous is that told of Odysseus who was forced to wander for another ten years before reaching his home on the island of Ithaca to the west of the Gulf of Corinth. Those wanderings and his eventual return are told in the *Odyssey*.

Initially blown off course to the Island of the Cyclopes, Odysseus earned the ill will of Poseidon when he blinded the Cyclops Polyphemus who was the god's son. Poseidon's anger, like that of Athena against Menelaus, would keep Odysseus from reaching home for ten years. During his wanderings, Odysseus visited the land of the cannibalistic Laestrygonians where many of his ships were destroyed and their crews slain and devoured; thence to the Island of Aeaea ruled by the witch Circe who changed Odysseus' men into hogs and would have done the same to Odysseus had it not been for the aid of Hermes; then on to the Land of the Dead where the shade of Teiresias foretold to Odysseus many long years of wandering and that when finally he reached Ithaca there would be more trouble waiting for him. Odysseus then arrived in Sicily where his starving crew slaughtered and devoured the cattle of Hyperion, sacred to the Sun. Hyperion complained to Zeus who hurled a thunderbolt that destroyed Odysseus' last remaining ship, drowning all save Odysseus himself.

Devising a crude raft from the wreckage, Odysseus paddled to the Island of Ogygia where the nymph Calypso dwelt. She fell in love with Odysseus, and he stayed with her some say seven years, others five. But at last he told Calypso he must try again to find Ithaca where his wife Penelope and young son Telemachus awaited his return. Sailing away in another raft, this one better built with Calypso's help, Odysseus had not gone far before Poseidon spied him and upended his raft with a huge wave. With the aid of the goddess Leucothea, Odysseus was washed ashore on the island of Drepane, the home of the Phaeacians, where he was discovered by Nausicaä who escorted him to the palace of her father, King Alcinous. There Odysseus was entertained royally as was befitting one returned from the sack of Troy, and many days later he was given a ship piled high with gifts and in due course disembarked on Ithaca. There he was met by the goddess Athena who transformed his appearance to that of an old beggar. This was necessary because the land had become overrun with spoiled and violent young aristocrats who, convinced that

Odysseus was dead, were intent on marrying Penelope and thereby be-coming king.

All these years, these young hooligans had imposed themselves on Odysseus' household, slowly bringing it to ruin. And all the while they continued to insist that Odysseus would never return and that Penelope must choose one among them for her husband. Penelope put them off by begging them to wait until she finished weaving a shroud for Odysseus' aged father Laertes who had not many more years to live. Each night Penelope would unravel all that she had woven the previous day and in this manner was able to forestall the suitors. Even so this ruse did not keep them from descending each night on Odysseus' halls where they would drink his wine, devour his herds and flocks, and seduce his serv-ing girls.

Finally, just as Odysseus was landing on Ithaca, the suitors discovered Penelope's ruse and demanded that she choose one among them. Pene-lope at last relented, but having one more trick to play, she insisted that only the man who could string Odysseus' bow and shoot an arrow through the rings of twelve ax heads placed in a row would be her husband. The suitors agreed to this test that was to take place the following day.

The next day not only did the suitors arrive, but also Odysseus, still disguised as an old beggar. One by one each of the suitors attempted the test in vain, for not one could so much as bend the bow to string it, much less send an arrow through the twelve rings. When the last suitor tried and failed, they had decided to come back and try again the next day, but just then Odysseus stood up in his rags and to the sneering delight of the contestants asked to attempt the bow. But their jeering laughter died on their lips when to their horror and astonishment Odysseus bent the bow easily, strung it, and sent a lightning-swift shaft through all twelve rings. The next arrow he trained on the suitors, and one by one he, with the help of his son Telemachus, the faithful swineherd Eumaeus, and the goatherd Philoitius, slew them all. Later on the kinsmen of the slain suitors, hearing of what had just transpired, swore to have revenge and marched on Odysseus' palace. But Odysseus and his companions were ready for them and Athena gave youthful strength to the aged arm of Laertes who launched his far-shadowed spear, slaying one of the ring-leaders. At this stroke, both Odysseus and Telemachus waded into the ranks of kinsmen striking them down with spear and sword until Athena and Zeus called a halt. Speaking in a commanding voice, Athena let it be known among all the warring factions that further bloodshed would only serve to anger Zeus. Fearful of the goddess in her wrath, the kinsmen threw down their weapons and fled home, while Odysseus, reunited at last with Penelope, Telemachus, and Laertes, again took up the rule of Ithaca and returned home indeed.

While these stories may recall Grimm's Fairy Tales for the reader, archaeologists have provided a new kind of evidence. The determination of men like Heinrich Schliemann (1822–1890), who believed that Greek history reached far earlier than 776 B.C.E. (the date of the first Olympic Games), has shown that Homer did not sing of a fictitious time and place. Evidence throughout the Aegean region and beyond establishes a real past at many of the places made famous in the *Iliad* and *Odyssey*: material remains now exist for Mycenae, the kingdom of Agamemnon; Pylos, home of garrulous Nestor; Knossos, the home of the labyrinth of Minos; and Troy, the doomed city of Priam. Joining the material evidence uncovered by archaeologists with the epic tradition enables us to reconstruct an account of the glorious Bronze Age and the godlike race of heroic men, demigods who fought over Thebes and at Troy as the early Greek poet Hesiod described them in his poem known as *Works and Days* (lines 156–173).

## THE ROOTS OF BRONZE AGE COMPLEXITY IN THE AEGEAN

The story of human life in the Aegean stretches back far earlier than this heroic age that dates to the second millennium B.C.E. Village life existed in Anatolia by 7000 B.C.E. and shortly thereafter spread to northern Greece. Crete was inhabited by 6000, while people settled in the less hospitable islands of the southern Aegean by about 4300. Movement of people and the settled agricultural way of life spread westward out of Anatolia, a connection that is visible in common features among individual cultures: language, technology, farming, and animal husbandry. As generations passed, villages grew larger in size and population and multiplied in number. And with closer proximity to one another, certain common traits emerged in larger regions of the Aegean sphere. Bordering on the Aegean Sea itself four cultural spheres took shape: on the mainland of Greece, on the island of Crete, among the inhabitants of the Cycladic islands in the southern Aegean, and along the western coast of Anatolia, commonly termed Asia Minor. We will begin with Anatolia since so much of the impetus for complexity in the Aegean cultures derived from this great peninsula.

Inland from the coast, the vast interior of Anatolia could accommodate a variety of separate cultural spheres. Mountains that ring an upland plateau hamper communications with the western, northern, and southern coastline, while mountains on the eastern land mass are a formidable barrier. Spurs of the mountains with their steep slopes divide the land into smaller units. Although there are several rivers in Anatolia, many of them inhibit communication rather than fostering it. The location of several major language groups by approximately 2000 B.C.E. supports the picture of the regionalism that geography encouraged. In spite of this natural fragmentation, an Anatolian presence in the Aegean sphere was an ongoing stimulus.

Despite the natural barriers, routes into the interior do exist, some of which are relatively trouble-free. Coupled with the resources of fertile soil for agriculture, timber, and minerals Anatolia has attracted immigrants from prehistoric times to the present. Consequently, the spacious peninsula came to be home of varied populations. Of the immigrants, one group played a prominent role in the Age of Heroes, namely, the Hittites who had settled into the bend of the Halys River in the northeast of Anatolia by the start of the second millennium. By language they are identified as Indo-Europeans, speakers of a language related to Greek. Their accomplishments made them one of the two major eastern Mediterranean powers during the second half of the second millennium as they drew much of Anatolia under control from their capital at Hattusa and then engaged in extending their sway southward into the Levant and westward toward Asia Minor and the Aegean. By 1500, the nature of life in the Aegean sphere had moved well beyond the world of small villages to one of the lively interaction—peaceful and militant—between major kingdoms described at the start of this chapter.

Even earlier, the role of Anatolia was instrumental in planting the seeds for later complexity. In fact, actual seeds were the instrument by which Anatolia became a region from which the foundation of ancient economic life spread in what is called the agricultural revolution. While the domestication of plants and animals in the ancient Near East began in the fertile crescent that forms an arc in the highlands around the Euphrates and Tigris river valleys, settled farming villages soon emerged in southern Anatolia in the eighth millennium. From this southern region the practice of farming and husbandry of domesticated animals opened out into other regions of Anatolia and then westward to the Aegean and, later, to the whole of Europe. Movement of people may well have been the means of dispersion: as population density rises in farming communities (it is calculated as doubling every eighteen years), additional land is needed. Thus, movement would be slow and random, depending on the nature of environment.

Farmers made their way to northern Greece and to the island of Crete early in the seventh millennium, places where the soil was suited to farming. One of the earliest villages in northern Greece dates to approximately 6200 B.C.E., while settlement at Knossos in central Crete may be two centuries later. More difficult conditions prevail on the islands of the Aegean that are, after all, the peaks of submerged mountains; on many of those islands, rainfall is the only source of water, and for much of the year rains are few and far between. Thus, farmers came to them later, in approximately 4300 B.C.E. The spread of an established way of life has immense implications: it permitted, even necessitated, a settled existence that allowed for the storage of goods over longer periods of time than a few days; it created a way of life that could support far greater numbers as well as conditions that required new tools and skills that, in turn, demanded increased specialization. And, as numbers grew within the small villages, the size of the villages themselves increased. Such expansion brought communities into closer proximity with one another, a situation that encouraged both peaceful links, for example, through trade, and conflict when contention arose over boundaries and/or valuable resources.

## EMERGENCE OF COMPLEX CIVILIZATIONS: CYCLADIC, MINOAN, AND MYCENAEAN

Physical evidence from the fourth millennium demonstrates the results of the steady spread of the agricultural revolution in the Aegean sphere. The revolution accelerated with the domestication of olive trees and grape vines, enlarging the subsistence base of the community and drawing more marginal land into production. The new products required new tools and technologies, fueling specialized skills and techniques. Small villages became large towns, often well fortified to protect the greater wealth within the walls. Some structures also increased in size, suggesting a diversity of wealth, function, and status for some of the community's members.

That new towns were located on or near the coast is proof of another major development: trade was occurring not only over land but also by sea. Natural resources are widely and unevenly dispersed; thus, essential resources will be required by peoples without close access to them. For instance, obsidian—the natural black glass found in volcanic areas—is plentiful on the Cycladic island of Melos. Because of its sharpness, it was sought out before bronze technology became widespread. Even before Melos was permanently occupied, the availability of obsidian drew visitors to it as early as the seventh millennium. It was by ships that the first settlers reached the island of Crete and the Cyclades. Colonizers in both places continued to rely on the sea for purposes of trade and not only in their immediate vicinities. The Carmel mountain ridge in the Levant has a number of incised pictures of boats of various forms and sizes. One boat, dated to the Neolithic period, is an Aegean type of vessel.[1]

The Cycladic islands may claim credit for development of the type of vessel that made longer-distance travel possible. Their longship painted or inscribed on objects by 3000 B.C.E. was more trustworthy and efficient than previous vessels had been. Surely the inhabitants of these islands had a strong motive to perfect their navigational ability: living on their rocky islands, they were forced to travel—obviously by sea—to obtain not luxuries but basic necessities of life. Another innovation may have given impetus to their seafaring: evidence of the domestication of both the olive and the grape has been found in these same islands in the late fourth/early third millennia. The creation of the polyculture of grain–olive–grape production along with animal husbandry transformed the basic economy. The material record shows technology to produce new tools and utensils required by the products of olive trees and grape vines; specialized skills of craftsmen and producers; diversity in production; creation of luxury products suited to trade; and more precise ordering of communal affairs. Also clear is a rise in populations: the population leapt from an estimated 3,000 in the Neolithic period to more than approximately 34,000 in the third millennium.

Inhabitants of Crete not only followed the Cycladic propensity for trade by sea but expanded that activity in scope and quantity. In fact, the Cretans' seafaring success during the Bronze Age has bestowed the title of "thalassocracy"—strength by sea—on their civilization, known as Minoan after the legendary ruler, Minos. Aegean sites, as expected owing to their proximity to Crete, witness heavy and sustained contact with Crete: not only have sites yielded large quantities of Cretan vases but even locally made wares imitate Minoan prototypes. Anatolian sites and islands off its southwest coast also have imports from Crete, while Egypt experienced two periods of intensive contact with the Minoan Cretans: the first beginning in the nineteenth century and the second in the sixteenth. Recent discovery of frescoes at the ancient settlement of Tell el-Dab'a on the northeastern border of Egypt is striking evidence of the penetration of Minoan skills and arts. Egyptian objects found on Crete are most dominant during c. 1600–1350. The Near East, especially but not exclusively northern Syria, was also familiar with Minoan products and perhaps artists as well since frescoes at several important cities appear particularly Minoan in character and technique.

Inhabitants of the Greek mainland, the third regional culture in the Aegean, involved themselves in this intensive network of trade but somewhat belatedly: activity of the Mycenaean Greeks escalated from about 1500 at the expense of Minoan Cretan interests. The increasing presence of mainland goods, and surely mainlanders, extended eastward from the Aegean islands to the Anatolian coast and neighboring islands, southward to Crete particularly at Knossos, and on to Egypt and the Levant. Discovery and excavation of a shipwreck off the southern coast of Anatolia dating to the end of the fourteenth century is dramatic evidence of the breadth of trade. The products recovered from the sea derive from cultures on the littoral of the eastern Mediterranean and even beyond; the travelers on that vessel are likely to have been as mixed as the crews of cargo ships pictured in Egyptian burial places at Egyptian Thebes.

Involvement with the more complex civilizations of the eastern Mediterranean brought a major change to the social, political, and economic nature of the Aegean participants. Not merely basic products such as olive oil and wine but also specialized goods and crafts including finely woven textiles, fine jewelry, perfumed olive oil, and elegant vases of stone, metal, and pottery were important exports. The tempo of trading activity produced a demand for other kinds of specialists, ranging from those who constructed the means of transport to those who coordinated the activity. Specialization and control of production is the substance of written documents that began to be kept in the second millennium. The emergence of writing in the Aegean sphere in itself illustrates the force of internationalism. The Cretan system seems to have been influenced by Egyptian writing; adapted to convey the language of the Minoan Cretans, which remains uncertain, it took the form of a combination of pictograms, linear signs for certain sounds, and a system for calculation. It is known as Linear A. The mainland, in turn, was influenced by the Minoan writing system. Adapting the same combination of pictograms, linear signs for sounds, and numerical signs to their own language—which has been deciphered as Greek—produced a variant called Linear B. The records, their contents, and the scribes who wrote them were under the eye of powerful figures who coordinated the activities of tens of thousands of people from impressive palace centers. To assist in the coordination was a multilayered administrative structure responsible to the kingly heads of the several realms on Crete and, somewhat later, the mainland. Major centers on Crete were—from east to west—Zakro, Gournia, Mallia, Knossos, Phaistos and its neighbor Ayia Triada, and Khania. On the mainland, important centers were—from southwest to northeast—Pylos, Mycenae, Tiryns, Athens, Thebes, Gla, Orchomenos, and Iolkos. To tie these realms together and to facilitate communication beyond the borders of the individual kingdoms, transportation was improved by road construction as well as by the establishment of port sites equipped with ship sheds and large storage facilities.

A common attendant of trade is diplomacy. That the Mycenaean centers were part of the network of relations in the Bronze Age is suggested by a group of Egyptian imports found at Mycenae in the decades on either side of 1400. Nine objects carrying the cartouche of either the Pharaoh Amenhotep III (1405–1367) or his queen, Tiy, reached Mycenae at approximately the same time that similar inscribed objects found their way to five other sites in the Aegean. It is not coincidental that these five places are among fourteen names of Aegean sites that can be read on a statue base found in the Valley of the Kings at the Temple of Amenhotep III. This combination of written and material evidence prompts the sensible conclusion that "Egypt was taking a particular interest in the Aegean" at this time, perhaps "to woo a potential ally, to establish trade relations or diplomatic ties with a new Aegean power."[2]

Although trade was a major objective, the Mycenaean expansion also had a pronounced warlike character. Some element of compulsion seems certain in the Mycenaean presence in Knossos in the fifteenth century.

Destructions at several sites in the Cyclades divide the earlier, dominant Minoan cultural influence from the later Mycenaean influence at those sites. Similar scenarios occurred on other islands and at Anatolian sites. Perhaps the most famous account of prolonged war is the ten-year siege of one Anatolian site as remembered in the Homeric epics of the battle over Troy. It is this Mycenaean "Age of Heroes" that the *Iliad* and *Odyssey* purport to describe. We will examine the nature of the Epic Tradition (Chapter 3) and consider physical evidence that may document its historical reality (Chapter 2). If the account is discovered to be grounded in reality, it offers a broader description of the internationalism represented by Troy. As we shall see, in their push to expand, the Hittites seem to have become involved in struggles with the Mycenaean upstarts in the territory of western Anatolia.

## THE ROLE OF THE HITTITES

Strong centralized states such as the Late Bronze Age palace centers that arose on Crete and the Greek mainland did not develop in isolation. Bronze Age Crete and mainland Greece were influenced by the older civilizations of Egypt and the Near East, which, in turn, were influenced by the newer cultures. As we have seen, a large body of evidence indicates a lively trade between the Minoan and Mycenaean palace centers, the islands of the Aegean, the west Anatolian shore, and, with one major exception, the great powers of the Near East. That one exception is the central Anatolian kingdom of the Hittites. The Kingdom of Hatti, as the Hittites called their land, is the one great Near Eastern power with which the peoples of the Aegean seemingly had little, if any, sustained trading arrangements. And yet it is possible that from the late fifteenth to the late thirteenth centuries the Hittites and Mycenaean Greeks were very much aware of each other.

The Kingdom of Hatti arose from a complex of small central Anatolian states scattered up and down the valley of the Halys River. Sometime during the first half of the seventeenth century, the Kingdom of Hatti under the leadership of the semilegendary King Labarna (or Tabarna in some texts) began an ambitious program of imperial expansion. He succeeded in uniting under his rule many of the petty states in the Halys Valley, and under his grandson and successor Hattušili I a capital was established at Hattusa, the modern village of Boğazköy.

Over the next 500 years the successors of Labarna and Hattušili built an empire based in central Anatolia, which, at its height during the fourteenth and thirteenth centuries, maintained direct control over most of Anatolia and northern Syria. The Hittites dealt on an equal footing with the other great powers of the Near East: Assyria, Babylon, and, particularly after the Battle of Kadesh (1276), Egypt. In addition to this extensive realm, the Hittites developed, through dynastic intermarriage and military conquest, a system of vassal states through which they were able to control large areas of southern and western Anatolia, thus giving the kingdom access to both the Aegean and eastern Mediterranean seas.

It was in this west coastal region of Anatolia that the Hittites came into contact with a power whom they refer to in their records as Ahhiyawa. The flash point lying at the heart of the Hittites' western policy, the name *Ahhiyawa* (or Ahhiya in earlier texts) has become the flash point of a modern scholarly debate over who, what, and where Ahhiyawa was. Since the 1920s when the first references to this shadowy power were discovered among the Hittite records, the debate has centered around the proposition that the name *Ahhiyawa* was the Hittite rendering of the Greek *Achai(woi)*, familiar to readers of the *Iliad* as Achaeans. If Achaeans had indeed been found in the Hittite records, then it would have been the same as saying that Mycenaeans had been found, for only Mycenaean Greeks were contemporaneous with the Hittite records. The debate between those who accept this proposition and those who do not has raged off and on over the past eighty years. However, with the discovery of new evidence and the reinterpretation of old evidence, particularly since the late 1980s, the proponents of the equation Ahhiyawans = Mycenaeans have gained a substantial, perhaps decisive advantage.

We will save for a later discussion (see Chapter 2) a more detailed analysis of this evidence and of Hittite–Ahhiyawan relations generally. For now let us just state that this evidence favoring the Ahhiyawans = Mycenaeans equation consists of much more than a rough similarity of names or the fact that Ahhiyawa is somewhere in the west. For one thing references to Ahhiyawa are often associated with references to another state or city somewhere on Anatolia's west coast, which in the Hittite texts is called Millawanda or Milawata. For much of its history, Millawanda appears to have been a Hittite vassal state, but for a period of perhaps fifty years between c. 1300 and c. 1250 this state was controlled by Ahhiyawa. Now Millawanda or Milawata is almost certainly Bronze Age Miletus, and for those who prefer to identify Ahhiyawans with Achaeans or Mycenaeans, the archaeology of this site shows increasing Mycenaean influence from about 1450 on. Miletus was destroyed shortly before 1300, a date that conveniently coincides with the destruction of Millawanda by the Hittite king Muršili II. Millawanda, it should be noted, was destroyed in reprisal for its rebellion against Hatti and its subsequent alliance with Ahhiyawa.

To further our argument in favor of the Ahhiyawans = Mycenaeans equation, we must note that at various times during the fourteenth and thirteenth centuries the Hittites referred to Ahhiyawa as a great power and of equal importance in the counsels of Hittite foreign policy as Assyria, Babylon, and Egypt. With the Hittites' own characterization of Ahhiyawan power in mind, the question arises: if, as the Hittite texts seem to indicate, Ahhiyawa lay somewhere in the west, and if Ahhiyawa was in fact a great power, who else but a state or confederacy of states in the Mycenaean world would fit this description? If, as some scholars have suggested, Ahhiyawa was on the south or west coast of Anatolia or in Thrace, where are the archaeological finds to support such a contention?

The short answer, of course, is that there are no serious contenders outside of Mycenaean Greece for the location of Ahhiyawa. Why any of this should matter in a book about the Trojan War will be more fully developed further on. But if the Ahhiyawans are Mycenaeans and Mycenaeans attacked Troy and Troy was Hissarlik in northwestern Anatolia, then our likeliest place to look for something approaching documentary evidence for such a conflict must come from the records of the Hittites. As we will see, whereas there is no "smoking gun" in this mystery, there is a good deal of circumstantial evidence, which we will examine in Chapter 2.

## COLLAPSE OF BRONZE AGE INTERNATIONALISM

Whoever the Ahhiyawans were, they presented a challenge to the Hittites on their western frontier. But during the thirteenth century, Ahhiyawa was not the only challenge, nor were the Hittites alone in experiencing problems from internal as well as external sources. The challenges were widespread throughout the eastern Mediterranean and sufficiently calamitous to bring down the flourishing, complex civilizations of the Bronze Age as well as the connections between them. Recovery would require three or more centuries.

Evidence for the magnitude of the troubles is plain to see and read. Egyptian records describe the "conspiracy" of foreign countries that all at once were on the move, scattered in war. No country could stand before their arms. Although modern scholars call these attackers "the Land and Sea Peoples" (see Glossary) they do not seem to have been a unified body of people. One group is quite certainly identified as Libyans; others are possibly identified as people from southern Anatolia, the Lukka or Lycians mentioned in connection with the Hittites and later located in southwest Anatolia; new settlers in the southern Levant, the Peleset or Philistines; and even Aegean peoples, the Denyen and Ekwesh. But Aegean states were affected by the difficulties as well as possibly causing them. Evidence on the Linear B tablets from the Mycenaean Kingdom of Pylos describing the dispatch of rowers and watchers to the coast, for instance, may well date to the time that the Egyptian pharaoh was expecting the arrival of the foes. Other written records reveal that enemies were active in northern Syria, in the waters off Cyprus and in Anatolia. Records of the last Hittite king tell of campaigning, desertion by his army, royal bodyguard, and the people, and the capture of some of the king's men. In seeking aid from the king of Ugarit, a major center in the northern Levant, the Hittite king described how ships came up against him and gave battle, three times out at sea and later on dry land.

So great was the crisis for the Kingdom of Hatti that the Kingdom disappeared. Egypt was fragmented into small villages strung out along the Nile; the once-mighty kingdom is described in the Old Testament as "that broken reed, Egypt." Tiny survival communities of forty or fifty people replaced the Aegean kingdoms, each of which previously had united 50,000 or more people. Population plummeted as did the level of existence, to the extent that the last two centuries of the second millennium and the first two centuries of the first are justly titled the "Dark Age" for most of the eastern Mediterranean.

Evidence for the magnitude of the troubles is plain to see and read; causes are hotly debated. Until recently, the favored explanation was destruction by invaders. Although vast movement did accompany the collapse, as demonstrated in the "Land and Sea Peoples," that movement may have been a result, rather than the cause, of the difficulties. Rather than several, almost simultaneous attacks by groups of aggressive migrants, we should look for an answer that explains the situation for the entire, interlocked region. The trade network may have been damaged, or it may have been overextended, or several years of poor agricultural productivity may have weakened its foundation. Natural disasters may well have been agents: earthquakes, volcanic eruptions, and climatic change that are regular occurrences in Mediterranean lands have serious repercussions. Palace centers controlled the life of a large subservient population, and it is not unlikely that some internal unrest focused on those centers. We have noted the complaints of the last Hittite ruler. War between kingdoms was also part of the international environment during the Bronze Age, and, as history shows, warfare exhausts resources and populations. People fleeing from any of these experiences at home may well have sought better conditions elsewhere, thereby becoming members of the Land and Sea Peoples.

Whatever the causes of the collapse, its repercussions were immense: entire kingdoms vanished, and those that managed to carry on were limited to a much reduced level of existence. In the Aegean sphere, survival from one day to the next was uncertain as the kingdoms collapsed and the tools of their organization—including the art of writing—disappeared. As the decades and then centuries of the Dark Age dragged on, memories of the glorious Bronze Age would grow dimmer. It is perhaps not surprising that the memory of a Trojan War, preserved only in oral poetic form, would later seem to belong to the world of myth or legend rather than that of historical reality. The following chapters explore the means of restoring the Age of Heroes to a Bronze Age context.

## NOTES

1. M. Artzy, "Routes, Trade, Boats and 'Nomads of the Sea'," in S. Gitin, A. Mazar, and E. Stern (eds.), *Mediterranean Peoples in Transition Thirteenth to Early Tenth Centuries BCE* (Jerusalem: Israel Exploration Society, 1998), pp. 444–445.

2. Eric Cline, "Egyptian and Near Eastern Imports at Late Bronze Age Mycenae," in W. V. Davies and L. Schofield (eds.), *Egypt, the Aegean and the Levant: Interconnections in the Second Millennium BC* (1995), pp. 91–115: quotes from p. 94 and p. 95.

# CHAPTER 2

# FINDING TROY AND THE TROJAN WAR

For the ancient Greeks, Homer was, in the words of Plato, "the best and the most divine of poets." They doubted neither his existence nor the reality of the events he described. In the nineteenth and early twentieth centuries C.E., on the other hand, that view was replaced by the verdict expressed confidently by J.A.K. Thomson: "That Homer is no more than a type, the representative of all the minstrels who preserved the poetry passing under his name, must I think, be accepted by any one who gives the most obvious interpretation to certain things which we know to be true of the ancient Greek epos."[1] The debate was infused with anger and, on the basis of existing evidence, seemed impossible of resolution.

Evidence of a more concrete nature was necessary to demonstrate the actuality of an Age of Heroes, a period occurring well before the Classical world, which dated to the advent of the Olympic Games in 776 B.C.E. The fledgling science of archaeology offered that evidence, although the methods utilized during the youth of the discipline would not immediately convince doubters. Only in the eighteenth century C.E. did archaeology develop from antiquarianism to a quasiscientific discipline with the discovery of early tools associated with extinct animal and human bones. The understanding that humans had created tools well before the once accepted date of 4004 B.C.E. for the beginning of human existence pushed the human past so much earlier that many agreed with the nineteenth-century scholar John Lubbock that "The first appearance of man in Europe dates from a period so remote that neither history nor tradition can throw any light on his origin or mode of life."[2] Since recognition of the great depth of the human story emerged with the aid of physical objects, artifacts from the past, serious study of material remains from the past would likely yield further answers. The discipline of archaeology is rooted in this belief. During the first half of the nineteenth century C.E., new evidence emerged and finds were consolidated. Upon that base the great discoverers of the nineteenth century sought evidence in regions such as Egypt and Mesopotamia where the earliest civilizations were documented, at first largely through biblical references. The techniques of uncovering evidence gained sophistication, although, by modern standards, they often were primitive.

In the second half of the nineteenth century, the search for physical evidence of the early story of humankind spread further. One area thought to be promising was the Aegean sphere, where those who would be great discoverers of early Greek civilization began to excavate in the last third of the century. One believer in the Age of Heroes sought to establish the reality of the Trojan War through excavation. His name is Heinrich Schliemann.

The story is told that when he was a boy, Schliemann saw a picture of Troy burning in a universal history book by Ludwig Jerrer which sparked a desire to find the remains of the destroyed city. After a difficult youth both with respect to his family and to lack of funds for education after the age of fourteen, Schliemann advanced himself to the point that he was able to retire from his business activities as a wealthy man in 1863. After a world tour from 1864 to 1866, he devoted his attention to planning his search for Troy and for sites on the Greek mainland where the conquerors of Troy had lived. By now he was competent in ancient and modern Greek in addition to a raft of other languages, and he had married for a second time, to a young Greek woman named Sophia. By no means was he well trained as an archaeologist; in those days, one became an archaeologist simply by digging. However, Schliemann did have what he considered a crucial guide to the location of sites that would demonstrate the reality of the Age of Heroes—the Homeric poems. Homer's description of the springs at Troy was decisive in Schliemann's decision that Hissarlik rather than another site nearby would prove to be the citadel of King Priam, ruler of Troy in the *Iliad.*

How did Schliemann proceed in the excavation, and what did his efforts from 1870 to 1890 reveal? Quite simply with the help of a great many hired workmen he dug into the mound that he believed covered the remains of Troy. In his determination to reach the earliest remains, Schliemann directed the digging of a trench that bisected the mound from north to south to a depth of more than 50 feet in some places. But realizing the importance of expertise, he attracted skilled personnel to his team; particularly valuable was the aid of anthropologist Rudolph Virchow and archaeologist Wilhelm Dörpfeld who would continue Schliemann's work at Troy after Schliemann's death.

In the end, seven major levels were revealed, each of which had several strata. Their chronology extended from c. 3000 to 1100 B.C.E. From the start, the site had been a fortified stronghold; finds indicated that its occupants were wealthy. A treasure associated with the level known as Troy II contained gold diadems, a fillet, gold earrings, bracelets, rings and buttons, as well as golden goblets. Discovered packed together on the citadel wall, Schliemann judged that he had found the treasure of King Priam, treasure taken by a member of the royal family who was fleeing the burning citadel. We now realize that Troy II was too early by more than a millennium to have been the site of the Trojan War. Yet the treasure is impressive for the importance of the site in the early Bronze Age.

It was just as necessary to uncover evidence of a contemporary civilization on the mainland of Greece in order to restore to history the Achaean attackers of Troy. For this goal, Schliemann could again rely on the *Iliad* and *Odyssey* since they allotted specific kingdoms to the Achaean leaders. In addition, the account of Greece written by Pausanias in the second century C.E. also provided helpful clues of features that could be seen in Pausanias' own day, such as Mycenae's Lion Gate, Cyclopean Walls, and great tombs commonly thought to house the remains of Agamemnon and his wife Clytemnestra. Traces of the gate, walls, and tombs remained for Schliemann to see, and on inspecting them, he wrote,

> I never doubted that a king of Mycenae, by name Agamemnon . . .
> had been treacherously murdered . . . and I firmly believed in the
> statement of Pausanias that the murdered persons had been interred
> in the Acropolis. . . . My firm faith in the traditions . . . led to the
> discovery of the five tombs, with their immense treasures.[3]

Schliemann excavated at other mainland sites connected by tradition with the Age of Heroes and was rewarded by discoveries at Tiryns and Orchomenos, although the palace of Odysseus on the island of Ithaca eluded him, as it continues to evade other seekers.

All the same, Schliemann had demonstrated his main point: sites long buried revealed the existence of flourishing civilizations in the Aegean sphere centuries earlier than the Classical Age. But Classical scholars were not impressed—one stated that Schliemann had simply misjudged Byzantine finds for prehistorical[4]; others claimed that he had manufactured the treasure in order to prove his theory. Even Schliemann and his associates had their doubts about what they had discovered: Which level was associated with the Trojan War? What were the causes of the destruction of the major levels? Was there any connection between inhabitants of this citadel site and people living on the Greek mainland—a necessary connection if one were to argue the historical validity of a Trojan War? Equally difficult was the location and small size of the site. Schliemann himself was sorry to admit that it was only some $225 \times 175$ yards and that it lay four miles from the sea. No ship could anchor or be beached within sight of the fortress, as Homer portrayed the situation.

The site has continued to draw archaeologists. Dörpfeld continued the work after Schliemann's death, and a major new investigation was carried out in the 1930s under the direction of the University of Cincinnati archaeologist, Carl Blegen. In the four decades since Schliemann's work had stopped, techniques of stratigraphy had been considerably refined. Thus, forty-nine major and minor catastrophes and reconstructions were detected in the site. Careful attention was paid to seemingly insignificant finds: animal bones—large numbers of sheep bones demonstrating the importance of sheep raising, the sudden appearance of horse bones; pottery techniques; examples of pottery that represent foreign, rather than local, cultures; and inordinate numbers of spindle whorls. All of these developments had important ramifications, but they pale in comparison to the most recent study of Troy.

In 1988, the Turkish government extended a permit to Manfred Korfmann of the University of Tübingen in Germany to excavate at Troy in connection with the University of Cincinnati. The efforts of an international team of seventy scientists and ninety local workers have been repaid with stunning finds. At the base of the small citadel stretches a large city projected to have been home to 5,000 to 10,000 people. Troy is now ten times larger than was previously suspected. Schliemann did not discover this lower city because the most important tool was not then available: a magnetometer—a geophysical remote sensing device that passes energy through the soil to read what lies below the surface from the anomalies encountered by the energy, or by measuring the intensity of the earth's magnetic field. Magnetometers function both underwater and on land. At Troy the perimeter of the lower settlement has been detected, and individual streets and structures have been revealed. Very little excavation has taken place in the most recent survey at Troy. However, drilling has produced new objects that are being studied by specialists: archaeobiologists are working with the bones and carbonized plant remains; archaeometallurgists are examining the metal finds to determine, for example, the mines in which the copper was once worked; dating is being determined through carbon 14 and dendrochronology; and analysis of pottery is being conducted to detect the source of the clay.

Beyond enlarging Schliemann's Troy, another scientific tool has done much to validate the epic picture of Troy and its environs. We have mentioned that the site is now four miles from the sea. Consequently, a reconstruction of a Greek camp site bore little relation to the picture that emerges from the *Iliad*. How could the Greeks camp near their beached ships and in sight of the Trojan citadel if the sea was as much as four miles distant? However, since 1980, hydrologists have been working to reconstruct the configuration of the ancient site. Subsurface stratigraphy by means of deep core boring has provided evidence of major, though gradual, change in the character of the Trojan plain. Since the samples contained material datable by radiocarbon, an absolute time frame has emerged for the stages of the transformation.

Over the past 10,000 years, a major marine embayment stretching 15 kilometers (c. 10 miles) south of the Dardanelles has been gradually filled in by silting. The bay between the two points where the Greek fleet was traditionally anchored was considerably deeper and larger in the second millennium B.C.E. than it is at present. The coastal plain around the bay was narrow but was expansive enough near the site of Troy to accommodate a landing for ships immediately west of the citadel or north of it. In fact, a paved ramp extending from a gate of the second settlement of Troy is a candidate for a path to that landing. Given these findings, a new reconstructed configuration places the Greek camp across the bay from Troy, instead of along the coast north of the citadel as most earlier plans had imagined. It also makes a great deal more sense of the Homeric references.

This combination of Homeric description with increasingly precise archaeological investigation has convinced most students of pre-Classical

Greek history that Hissarlik is correctly identified as the site of ancient Troy. J. V. Luce, for instance, creates a stunning painting of Troy and Ithaca that is so carefully tied to the Homeric epics that his landscapes seem to be peopled with figures from the poems.[5]

Yet the perceived reinforcement that archaeological evidence has given to the Homeric tradition has never convinced everyone. As we have mentioned, opinion was divided in Schliemann's own lifetime. While William Gladstone could write in his preface to Schliemann's *Mycenae* of "the splendid services which he [Schliemann] has conferred upon classical science," a satirical "telegram from Troy" in the German *Kladderradatsch* "announced" the discovery of Achilles' grave, with Schliemann's assistant Virchow recognizing the ankle bone (the bone would have shown that it was pierced by an arrow), although the body between the head and ankle was missing. The mean-spirited article concluded, "Achilles stuck in pocket. All well. Schliemann." Although it had to be admitted that Schliemann's efforts had uncovered something, many scholarly detractors refused to accept an identification of Hissarlik as Troy. One critic, Ernst Bötticher, declared that Schliemann's Troy is in no way a settlement; rather, the evidence of burnt ashes deposited in urns demonstrates that it is a great burial place, a Necropolis. A contemporary archaeologist, W. J. Stillman, stated in the *London Times* of January 9, 1889, "I hope before long to put all the evidence . . . in such a shape that no one can doubt reasonably that 'Troy' is the Troy of Croesus" (i.e., the sixth century B.C.E.). Most members of the Berlin Archaeological Society also stood against Schliemann and his conclusions.

The reaction is understandable when set in the proper context of the late nineteenth century, a time in which the discipline of archaeology was struggling to develop proper methods. Even by comparison with excavation in Egypt and the Near East, Aegean archaeology was only just underway and, thus, few known sites existed to confirm the accuracy of Schliemann's finds. Personally, too, Schliemann was the sort of "colorful" figure who attracts attention, often hostile. He was irascible, temperamental, unsure at times and full of conceit at others. Many of his finds were shipped secretly out of Turkey, and he has been charged with "creating" the treasure of Troy II. For some of these personal characteristics and his actions, Schliemann has been castigated as a man who could not tell right from wrong, and, thus, he could and did deliberately distort the archaeological record. It is important to keep in mind both the nature of the discipline of archaeology in his day and the type of person attracted to it in order to understand Schliemann's role in the search for the Trojan War. In his favor, Schliemann admitted that he made mistakes and was willing to reevaluate conclusions; he knew the value of intrinsically worthless finds; he traveled extensively to understand the regional character of his sites; he drew on the expertise of specialists; he published and publicly displayed his finds as quickly as possible. On the basis of his beginnings, others have tested his excavations for more than a century, adding to as well as altering the evidence and its interpretation.

In the ongoing process, an important new dimension of archaeological research has become essential in understanding the larger importance of individual sites. Survey archaeology focuses attention on large regions—the Troad instead of just "Troy"—in order to learn the relationship between the land and its use over long periods of time. Thus, survey archaeology can provide a composite picture of environmental, social, and economic developments of all levels of the region's population. Because its scope is so broad, it requires a variety of specialists: ethnologists, epigraphists, metallurgists, civil engineers, geologists, historians, geographers, and agricultural economists along with archaeologists.

Such diversity is a sign of another new feature of archaeology, namely, the use of scientific technologies that began to be employed about the middle of the twentieth century. As the most recent investigation at Troy has shown, the current tools of archaeologists include magnetometers that reveal features beneath the earth's surface and objects buried in the seafloor; robots for investigating caves inaccessible to humans; tools of aerial reconnaissance; and, of course, computers. Dating of artifacts is far more precise through techniques such as radio carbon dating, dendrochronology, and analysis of charged atoms. Even the source of clay in pottery can be learned. These are the tools currently employed in the study of Troy to produce more precise knowledge of the site and its artifacts.

Consequently, it is ironic that the most recent investigations at Hissarlik have been greeted by a response akin to that which Schliemann received. In each case, the methods employed have sparked much of the controversy. An article in the *London Times* of February 25, 2002, noted that "A NEW Trojan war only slightly less vicious than the original has broken out among archaeologists over the size of the fabled city of Homer's *Iliad*." A major figure in this debate is professor and ancient historian Frank Kolb, also of the University of Tübingen, who believes that the picture presented by the team directed by Manfred Korfman is a fiction, that the new Troy with its lower city accommodating 5,000 to 10,000 inhabitants is a myth. He bases his charge on the fact that the area is estimated to be small, having no room for so large a population; it is loosely built up; and the buildings and activities carried on in the area are unimpressive. This current wave of criticism concludes that the site is a small country estate without a port whose connections are with the northern Aegean and the Balkans rather than with the widespread trade centered in the great ports of the eastern Mediterranean.

## SUPPORTIVE EVIDENCE: BRONZE AGE TRADE BY SEA

All the criticism notwithstanding, we should keep in mind the larger picture that has emerged. Mycenaean imports found at Hissarlik attest to contact between Bronze Age Greeks and their contemporaries at Troy–Hissarlik in the last half of the second millennium. Mycenaean trade expanded in the late fifteenth century, as we have seen in the pattern of development discussed in Chapter 1. By the thirteenth century, Mycenaean pottery found its way to many Aegean locations as well as Syria, Palestine, and Egypt in the eastern Mediterranean. Evidence of this trade reminds us of yet another legend: that of the voyage of Jason and his Argonauts in search of the Golden Fleece protected by a dragon at the ends of the known world.

This distant place, called Colchis in the legend, has been located on the eastern shore of the Black Sea. To reach it requires a voyage through the Dardanelles into the Propontis and then into the Black Sea by way of the treacherous Bosporus Straits where, as Circe warns Odysseus as he returns to his seafaring:

> There stand the jutting rocks and before them resounds
> The mighty wave of dark-browed Amphitrite.
> The blessed gods call them the Clashing Rocks.
> No birds not even timid doves who bring
> Ambrosia to father Zeus can pass them by.
> But the sheer face of rock always catches them
> And the Father must add another to fill the cohort.
> (*Odyssey* 12:59–66, translated by Carol Thomas and Tristan Goldman)

Only one passed through those rocks: the famous Argo carrying the Argonauts. Only the help of the goddess Hera made the feat possible, an element that enhances the mythical quality of the tale.

On the other hand, recent archaeological investigation has moved the tale of the voyage closer to the realm of actual memory of the nature of the Aegean Bronze Age. An increasing number of Aegean goods has been discovered in the Propontis and Black Sea: stone anchors; ingots—one of which bears an incised mark comparable to the linear signs used in the Cretan and mainland Greek scripts; harnessing equipment with cheek pieces virtually identical to some discovered at Mycenae; swords comparable to Mycenaean examples. Moreover, the boars' tusk helmets worn by the Homeric heroes, arrow smoothers, horse burials, and gold akin to that deriving from the Bulgarian coast of the Black Sea indicate reverse contact from the Black Sea to Greece.

The kingdom from which Jason and his companions purportedly sailed has also emerged from legend through the identification of a place known as Iolkos—near modern Volos—possessing Mycenaean remains that suggest the site was the northernmost citadel-centered kingdom in the late Bronze Age. The find of an unplundered Mycenaean tomb was announced in early 2004. Iolkos is situated in a region that offers good land for agriculture and animal husbandry; it also overlooks a bay with a fine harbor that is still important today. Inhabitants of the region had a fondness for decorating their pottery with many-oared boats; they had access to goods brought by others; and they possessed the resources to trade their own products in return. Thus, we can be reasonably certain that Mycenaeans from this part of Greece traveled by sea in the second millennium.

One of the destinations could well have been Troy, a relatively easy journey, to what the most recent investigations at Troy indicate was a prosperous, thriving trade center. The Propontis is also manageable and even the Prowling Rocks of the Bosporus could be traversed. Recent understanding both of the nature of the winds and currents of the Bosporus and of the construction of Mycenaean ships has considerably strengthened the case for a voyage similar to that portrayed in the tale of Jason. In sum, Troy becomes more than the unfortunate victim of war; it symbolizes the lively interaction that characterized the northern appendage of the Mediterranean as well as the better-known eastern waters of that sea.

Indeed, a number of ancient writers made a connection between Troy and the voyage of the Argo. One reason stated for Jason's choice of a northerly route, skirting the Thracian coast, was to avoid any encounters with the Trojan fleet of King Laomedon, the father of Priam. It was also said of Laomedon that he would allow no foreign shipping through the Hellespont without exacting a heavy toll.

Another tale is told of Heracles who, in addition to his many other exploits, was an Argonaut. Either on the voyage out or on the return trip from Colchis, Heracles is said to have stopped at Troy just long enough to bring down a terrible vengeance on the city by slaying Laomedon and all his sons save Priam. It seems that Laomedon, a notorious cheat, had failed to pay Heracles his promised reward for saving his daughter Hesione from a sea monster. It should be added that Poseidon had sent this creature to ravage Troy because Laomedon had cheated him and Apollo of their wages for building Troy's great walls.

These tales should be borne in mind when we consider the realities of Mycenaean and Trojan trade. Troy might have been a tempting target in part because of its strategic position at the point where the Black Sea and Aegean trade routes met. To judge by the military nature of their culture, the Mycenaeans traveled not only as peaceful traders but also as soldiers. Production of armor, weapons, and chariots was a prominent activity in the citadel centers; most of the citadels were heavily fortified by massive walls. One of the most important figures in the administration of the kingdoms documented by the Linear B tablets was the *lawagetas* who can probably be defined as leader of the host. In addition, the archaeological evidence reveals a discernible pattern in the rise and fall of individual Mycenaean kingdoms: destruction at Knossos, Thebes, Pylos, and other sites is not accompanied by evidence of foreign agents. In other words, the instrument of destruction seems to have come from within Greece itself. With two of the above-named sites, again we note a remarkable convergence of myth and archaeology. The legends of the Seven Against Thebes and the successors of the original heroes in that struggle recount the tale of two assaults on Thebes by Argos and its allies, of which the second was successful. Indeed, the city's destruction was so substantial that it alone of all the major Greek palace centers failed to provide a large contingent to the effort against Troy. The other site, Pylos, is said to have been destroyed by Heracles (again) in revenge for some insult paid him by its king Neleus. Of all Neleus' house only Nestor survived to rebuild and enlarge his father's kingdom and, in old age, provide invaluable advice and ninety ships to the Trojan War.

## EVIDENCE FROM THE HITTITE RECORDS

As ongoing study at Hissarlik reveals, Troy was a lucrative target and as we have suggested in the Chapter 1, the Hittite records provide evidence about the situation in western Anatolia in the Late Bronze Age.

Archaeological evidence reveals the presence of Greeks in the area during the period. The site later named Miletus and almost certainly to be identified by the name Millawanda in the Hittite records figures prominently in the difficulties of the second half of the second millennium. As we have seen, a Mycenaean character replaced the city's earlier Minoan features during the fifteenth century. A burnt layer indicating destruction accords with Hittite records that the army of the Hittite king Muršili II destroyed Millawanda toward the end of the fourteenth century. Mycenaeans and Hittites may have interacted in more peaceful ways further north, that is, at the site now commonly known as Troy. Although there is little evidence of direct trade between Mycenaeans and Hittites, large quantities of Mycenaean goods have been found at Troy and Hittite goods also are present. Troy then offered a center for peaceful trade, a trade that may have drawn the envy of those who personally knew its importance and wealth.

But while the archaeological evidence found at Troy for the most part indicates peaceful trading contacts with both Mycenaeans and Hittites, the Hittite archives found at their capital of Hattusa often reveal a more warlike relationship. In fact, the first likely mention of Troy comes from the record of a military expedition conducted by the Hittite king Tudhaliya I against the *Confederacy of Assuwa* sometime in the late fifteenth century. Listed among the many towns and cities comprising the confederacy are Wilusiya and Taruisa. Assuwa, the region in which the confederacy arose, is almost certainly to be identified as Asia, known in Greco-Roman times as a province in northwest Anatolia. Wilusiya, or Wilusa, is also well known from later Hittite texts and is thought to be the same as (W)Ilios, the archaic Greek rendering of Ilios, another name for Troy. More problematic and yet equally striking in this context is the name Taruisa which some scholars have equated with Greek Troia—Troy itself.

It is an odd fact that in Greek myth and legend the city of Priam and Paris is known alternatively as Ilios (or Ilion) and Troy. The Greeks themselves seem to have been sufficiently confused by the two names that they invented two mythical founders—Tros who gave his name to the Troad and thence to Troy, and Ilus who founded the city of Ilios. Unfortunately, the Hittite reference does not clarify the matter except to indicate that the two names referred to two different places.

Our next reference to Wilusa/Ilios is equally martial in character. This reference appears in the *Manapa-Tarhunda Letter* dated most likely to the reign of the Hittite king Muwatalli II (1295–1272). The background of this letter appears to be the following: Manapa-Tarhunda, the king of the Šeha River Land, also in northwest Anatolia and south of Assuwa, has attacked, possibly with Muwatalli's blessing, a rebel Hittite chieftain named Piyamaradu who has made himself overlord of Wilusa. The result of this attack was a resounding defeat for Manapa-Tarhunda. As Manapa's letter makes clear, Piyamaradu was not content merely to ward off the attack, but he apparently, if temporarily, removed Manapa from power and placed the Šeha River Land in the hands of his son-in-law Atpa, the ruler of Millawanda and at this time a vassal of the king of Ahhiyawa. Furthermore, Piyamaradu followed up this coup with an invasion of the Land of Lazpa, a dependency of the Šeha River Land. This news must have caused some alarm at Hattusa, for all three regions were vassal states and Wilusa was highly prized for its unswerving loyalty to the Hittite Crown. In response to this emergency, Muwatalli sent out an army, and after securing the Šeha River Land his intent was to defeat Piyamaradu and capture him. In this endeavor Muwatalli hoped for assistance from Manapa-Tarhunda, but he excused himself, saying "[But with me] it goes ill, I am grievously sick; the sickness has [ . . . ] prostrated me." Whether his illness was real or feigned, Manapa took no part in the operations against Piyamaradu, the conclusion of which is unknown owing to a break in the text. The assumption is that Piyamaradu escaped, and as another text makes clear, Wilusa returned to its old relationship with Hatti.

One of the more interesting aspects of the *Manapa-Tarhunda Letter* is its allusion to the new status of Millawanda. It appears that sometime during the first half of the thirteenth century this state succeeded in escaping from the Hittite orbit and attached itself to Ahhiyawa. It will be recalled from the brief discussion in Chapter 1 that Ahhiyawa may be identified with a single Mycenaean state, or perhaps a confederacy of states, and that Millawanda almost certainly is Bronze Age Miletus. It appears that during the late fourteenth and early thirteenth centuries Ahhiyawan influence in Millawanda increased dramatically, just as we know that Mycenaean influence at Miletus increased during the same period. By the early thirteenth century, the Hittites may have simply accepted Ahhiyawan (or Mycenaean) overlordship of Millawanda as a *fait accompli* in part because by the 1280s Muwatalli's foreign policy was increasingly focused on Syria where the Egyptians were actively seeking to expand their empire. It has been suggested that a deal was struck, most likely informally, with Hatti acknowledging Ahhiyawan interests in Millawanda if in turn Ahhiyawa ceased further provocative acts elsewhere in western Anatolia. As we shall see, if such a deal was ever made, it was founded on a vain hope.

Having chased Piyamaradu from Anatolia's shores, or at least to Millawanda, Muwatalli set about ordering Wilusa's affairs. In the treaty drawn up between Muwatalli and the new vassal king of Wilusa, Alaksandu, the Hittite king, spells out the conditions under which his vassal is expected to provide military support to Hatti (this document is known to Anatolian scholars as the *Alaksandu Treaty*):

> If I, the Sun, am called to the field from your direction, either towards Karkisa, Masa, Lukka, or Warsiyalla, then you must march out on my side with infantry and chariotry. . . . Also the following campaigns are obligatory on you: the kings who are of equal rank with the Sun, the King of Egypt, the King of Sanhara [Babylon], the King of Hanigalbat [Mitanni in northern Mesopotamia], or the King of Assyria.
>
> (translated by O. R. Gurney)

This text is important not only as a demonstration of renewed Hittite power in the region but of the absence of Ahhiyawa or Millawanda from the list of possible foes. Perhaps this omission was an effect of a new understanding between Hatti and Ahhiyawa. One other item of possible interest is the name Alaksandu. The name looks and presumably would have sounded like the Greek Alexandros, or Alexander, and Alexander Paris, the son of Priam and abductor of Helen, is a principal character in

Trojan legend. Despite scholarly objections, it seems eminently reasonable that Mycenaeans and later Greeks might have confused the foreign *Alaksandu* with the more familiar *Alexandros*.

Another reference to Wilusa comes from the *Tawagalawa Letter* addressed to an unknown Ahhiyawan king by Muwatalli's brother and successor, Hattušili III (1267–1237). Again the context is of Piyamaradu's depredations, this time carried out from Millawanda where he has the protection of his son-in-law and the Ahhiyawan king's vassal, Atpa. Hattušili leads an army against Piyamaradu, who escapes to Millawanda and from there by ship goes to parts unknown. The Hittite king in frustration addresses a letter to the Ahhiyawan king, asking that he exercise some control over Piyamaradu who is continually using Ahhiyawan-controlled territory to raid Hittite vassal states. Toward the end of the letter, Hattušili hints that he and the Ahhiyawan king are friends and that it is not right for Piyamaradu, a vassal of the Ahhiyawan king, to commit violence against the vassals of Hattušili. In this spirit, the Hittite asks the Ahhiyawan to remind Piyamaradu that "The King of Hatti and I—in that matter of Wilusa over which we were at enmity, he has converted me and we have made friends; . . . a war would not be right for us." The reference to *"that matter of Wilusa"* appears to be an allusion to Piyamaradu's activities during the previous reign, the phrase *"he has converted me"* implying that the designs of Ahhiyawa were defeated. It should also be noted that Millawanda is still firmly under Ahhiyawan control.

Another point of interest in this document occurs when Hattušili, in reference to Piyamaradu's depredations, asks the Ahhiyawan king, "Are you now, my Brother, favorably disposed to this conduct?" The phrase *my Brother* is to be taken neither literally nor as base flattery, but instead as the diplomatic language used between the great powers of the Bronze Age Near East when the king of one country addressed the king of another whom he considered to be his equal. When Hattušili used this expression in addressing the king of Ahhiyawa, we can only assume that the Hittite considered the Ahhiyawan to be his equal and a great king.

The *Millawanda Letter* provides us with a final reference to the relationship between Hatti and Wilusa/Ilios. This letter, dating probably from early in the reign of Hattušili's son and successor Tudhaliya IV (1237–1209), reveals a revolution in Hittite/Ahhiyawan affairs, for Millawanda is now back in the Hittite sphere of influence. Indeed, in part of the letter Tudhaliya instructs the addressee (whose name is not known) regarding the proper boundary of Millawanda. "When we, My Majesty, and you, my son, established the border of Millawanda for ourselves . . . I did not give you [such and such a place] within the territory of Millawanda."

Apparently, the previous ruler of Millawanda, the addressee's father, had always been hostile to Hittite interests and had embarked on a campaign of raiding the western states allied to Hatti. This precipitated a war in which the Millawandan king's son joined forces with the Hittites. Tudhaliya and his new ally succeeded in deposing this king, and the king's son was placed on the Millawandan throne. Although the deposed king is never named, it is quite likely that he was Atpa, the Ahhiyawan vassal ruler of Millawanda for many years and the son-in-law of Piyamaradu.

Further on in the letter, mention is made of a king of Wilusa named Walmu. Tudhaliya prized this Walmu for his loyalty, and it was perhaps for this reason that he was deposed. At any rate he fled to Millawanda where the new ruler gave him shelter. With an ally now in control of Millawanda, Tudhaliya was in a better position to further Hittite interests throughout the west, and he instructs the Millawandan king to send Walmu to him and he will see that he is restored to the Wilusan throne.

This is the last mention of Wilusa in the Hittite archives. Shortly after Tudhaliya's death the Hittite Empire, already showing grave signs of weakness, collapsed under the attacks of enemies from the north and rebellion from within. As for Wilusa/Ilios, the thirteenth century was also a critical period. Even if Wilusa cannot be equated with the ruins at Hissarlik, we know from those ruins that Troy VI attained its height of prosperity during this century and was destroyed sometime during the decades either side of 1250. Judging from the archaeological remains, Troy VIIa, built on the ruins of Troy VI, was a much smaller and less prosperous town, its rude buildings huddled against the hastily patched walls as if sheltering from a storm. Again assuming that Troy or Hissarlik can be equated with Wilusa, then the latest phase of Troy VI, Troy VIh, was probably the town of Alaksandu whereas the Walmu mentioned in the *Millawanda Letter* may have ruled Troy VIIa.

With the Hittite references we have enough material to sketch out the rudiments of a thirteenth-century Wilusan chronology. During the earlier part of the century, the Hittite rebel and adventurer Piyamaradu, with backing from Ahhiyawa, assumed control over Wilusa. His depredations on nearby Hittite vassal states aroused the ire of the Hittite king who forced Piyamaradu to flee overseas or to Millawanda, then an Ahhiyawan vassal state. The Hittites then installed Alaksandu as king of Wilusa and a vassal to the Hittite Crown. Decades later, probably around 1230, King Walmu of Wilusa who was possibly Alaksandu's son was deposed, perhaps by internal rebels or possibly by Atpa, king of Millawanda and son-in-law of Piyamaradu. Walmu was subsequently restored to his throne by the Hittite Tudhaliya IV with the aid of Atpa's own son who had been installed as king of a new, pro-Hittite Millawanda.

Little of the above chronology is evocative of the great conflict recounted in Homer's *Iliad*. But one element is of more than passing interest, and that is the involvement of Ahhiyawa with Wilusa at one certainly, and perhaps two, points in the thirteenth century, the century in which the Trojan War is most likely to have occurred. It is almost certain that Ahhiyawa provided support to Piyamaradu in the first instance recounted in the *Manapa-Tarhunda Letter*, and if the Ahhiyawan vassal, Atpa of Millawanda, was instrumental in deposing Walmu, then he likely had Ahhiyawan support as well.

It is important to emphasize, however, that, with the possible exception of Millawanda, we have no evidence of direct conflict between Hittites and Ahhiyawans anywhere in the West. Nor do we have incontrovertible evidence of *direct* Mycenaean conflict with Wilusa. Based on the records we do have, however one-sided and imperfectly understood though they are, it would seem that Ahhiyawa, though wishing to avoid direct hostilities with Hatti, was nevertheless more than willing to provide support and protection to proxies and clients regardless of whether they were renegade Hittites like Piyamaradu, native west Anatolians, or Mycenaeans such as Atpa may have been. Their immediate purpose in pursuing this policy was to destabilize the Hittites' western vassals by taking advantage of local anti-Hittite sentiment and, where possible, detach as many of these states from their allegiance to the Hittite Empire as they could without risking direct engagement. As we have seen in the case of Millawanda, this policy was successful for a period of perhaps as long as seventy years and was nearly so in the case of Wilusa and the Šeha River Land.

As for Ahhiyawa's long-term designs in west Anatolia, their interest was very likely of a material nature, consisting most probably of horses, metals, and slaves. Metals, particularly copper and tin from which bronze is made, would have been a strategic resource. Horses also would have had strategic value since chariots, the Bronze Age equivalent of tanks, are useless without them. In Homer's time, the Troad was legendary as a horse-breeding region, and much of Priam's wealth may have been based on metals. As for slaves, the Linear B tablets found at Pylos mention women and children whose points of origin appear to be Lesbos, Miletus, and Knidos, all three locales on or near the west Anatolian coast. Lesbos (Lazpa in the Hittite archives) in particular was close enough to Troy to act as an *entrepôt* for captives taken during a conflict there. The tablets are silent on the circumstances of their enslavement, but it is tempting to believe that some at least came originally from Troy.

All this is of course most unsatisfying if one is looking for substantial evidence of a conflict between a confederacy of Mycenaean states and Troy and its allies. All one can point to is the interesting circumstantial evidence that whatever Mycenaean power or powers Ahhiyawa represented took a keen interest in the affairs of Wilusa and other west Anatolian states during much of the thirteenth century. Although the Hittite records indicate that native kings at Wilusa were deposed twice, at least once by an Ahhiyawan client, no mention is made of destruction of the city. On the other hand, Greek legend informs us that Troy was destroyed, and we know from the archaeological remains at Hissarlik that the site, depending on which chronology of Troy VIIa one accepts,[6] was destroyed twice in that century. After weighing this evidence, we must admit that the reality of a Trojan War remains a tantalizing, but elusive, phantom.

Let us close this chapter with two more fragmentary bits of evidence. The first is a broken section of an incised stone bowl from the Hittite capital of Hattusa. The incised decoration shows the helmeted head and upper torso of a warrior about to plunge his round pommeled sword into an unseen victim. The round pommel together with the spiral-decorated cuirass and plumed helmet are common Aegean motifs. And finally there is a single line of poetry, written in Luwian that was most likely the language of Troy, and also found in the Hittite archives. The line could be the beginning of an epic, and indeed it sounds Homeric: "They came from steep Wilusa . . ."[7]

## NOTES

1. J.A.K. Thomson, *Studies in the Odyssey* (Oxford: Clarendon Press, 1914), p. 189.

2. John Lubbock, *Prehistoric Times as Illustrated by Ancient Remains and Manners and Customs of Modern Savages by Lord Avebury* (New York: Henry Holt, 1913; first published 1865), p. 1.

3. *Mycenae: A narrative of researches and discoveries at Mycenae and Tiryns* (New York: Scribner, Armstrong & Co., 1878), p. 335.

4. Byzantine finds would have been far later even than the Classical period. The Byzantine or Eastern Roman Empire lasted from the fourth to the fifteenth century C.E.

5. *Celebrating Homer's Landscapes: Troy and Ithaca Revisited* (New Haven, CT: Yale University Press, 1998).

6. Some scholars have suggested an early twelfth-century date for the destruction of Troy VIIa.

7. See Sarah P. Morris, "A Tale of Two Cities: The Miniature Frescoes from Thera and the Origins of Greek Poetry," AJA 93 (1989): 532.

# CHAPTER 3

# HOMER AND THE EPIC TRADITION

As we have noted previously, the Troad and indeed all of western Anatolia and the neighboring islands were in a highly unsettled state during the fourteenth and thirteenth centuries B.C.E. This should come as no surprise, for the region was a borderland on the fringes of both the Hittite Empire and the Mycenaean states. Sometime around 1400 the Hittites under Tudhaliya I conducted their first serious operations against an alliance of western states, which included both Wilusa (Ilios) and Taruisa (Troy?). Meanwhile, during the fifteenth century the Mycenaeans were extending their influence and dominance south through the Cyclades to Crete and east over the Aegean to the southern Dodecanese and other islands close to the Anatolian shore. By 1400 there was already a sizable Mycenaean community at Miletus (Millawanda), although the city was probably tributary to the Hittites at this time. Unsettled conditions can readily be attributed to the meeting of these two opposing forces in west Anatolia. If there is any reality to the legend of the Trojan War, it should most likely be seen within this context of these East-West tensions.

The purpose of this chapter, however, is not to argue for or against the Trojan War as an historical event. We have already examined some of these arguments and found that, although there is much evidence in favor of the Hissarlik = Troy equation, with more evidence accumulating year by year, there is little in the way of unchallenged evidence for a Trojan War, and what evidence exists is largely circumstantial.

But if there was no Trojan War, what was the origin of the tale told in the poems of the Epic Cycle? Was Homer simply making it all up? Was he, in effect, a verse novelist? As we have seen in discussing the career of Heinrich Schliemann and the criticism leveled at him, such notions were not uncommon. However, modern research in the ways in which epic poets work and the place of epic poetry in nonliterate societies have rendered such opinions rare. Epic poetry is simply too conservative an enterprise to allow individual poets the freedom to simply "make things up." Instead, epic poets, Homer included, would have been constrained to treat traditional lore. No doubt such treatments would have varied widely in terms of both manner and quality, but the story that was told would have been a familiar one. This is not to say that epic poetry deals in historical fact as we have come to understand it. The poet is neither a historian nor a journalist, although poets in nonliterate societies do assume some of the functions of both. Rather, Homer, who was telling a tale already old at the time of the telling, was recounting a story that he and his audience assumed to be true.

Again we return to the same question: how old is the Epic Tradition, and what is its origin? If archaeology has so far been unable to find the Trojan War, might we not at least gain a little more circumstantial evidence by examining the Tradition itself—performing, as it were, an archaeological excavation of the epic? We will begin by asking a further question: what, stripped of its poetic finery, is the tale of the Trojan War?

## THE ANTIQUITY OF THE EPIC TRADITION

Simply put, the tale of Troy is a story of an assault, siege, and sack of a seaside town by a sea-borne army. Within this barebones framework there is plenty of opportunity for an imaginative storyteller to introduce and develop characters who, like Hector and Achilles, are both heroic and tragic. Such a tale would also allow plenty of latitude for presenting folk tale themes, adventure, romance, and, in the case of Thersites (*Iliad* ii.211–277), even a little rough humor.[1] But looming over all is the great theme of a city doomed, forsaken by its gods and under attack by alien forces.

From the attackers' point of view, however, there is another, crucial element to the story. However tragic the fate of the besieged city, it is nevertheless a fate brought about by the actions of its own people. The besieged are guilty of a grievous crime—kidnapping and breach of hospitality—for which the besiegers intend to exact a heavy punishment. The besiegers see themselves as the aggrieved party, and if justice is to prevail in the world, making war on the city of the besieged is both nec-

essary and noble. Thus, in addition to the elements of tragedy and warfare, the story harbors a moral element of crime and punishment.

There is every reason to believe that tales of naval attacks on sea-girt
towns such as Troy were familiar ones not only in Homer's time but during the Late Bronze Age as well. We have seen how during the fifteenth
and fourteenth centuries Minoan influence at Miletus gradually gave way
to Mycenaean influence. This process had been repeated numerous times
during the same period both in the Cyclades and at Knossos on Crete.
In a few instances at least, this change from Minoan to Mycenaean influence was accompanied by violence: at Phylakopi on the Cycladic island of Melos there is a destruction level coinciding with material
indications of Mycenaean dominance. The same may be said of Knossos
where the palace was destroyed in about 1450. Meanwhile at Agia Irini
on the island of Kea, the Mycenaeans apparently took advantage of a ruinous earthquake to impose their dominance.[2]

No doubt much of this Mycenaean expansion was carried out through
trade; in fact, trade seems to have been their chief interest throughout
this period. But historians can point to many instances both ancient and
modern in which trade, piracy, and warfare went hand in hand. The same
observation might be made about the sometimes peaceful, sometimes
truculent, relations between Ahhiyawa and the west Anatolian states.
Some scholars have suggested that the Hittites imposed a trade embargo
against Ahhiyawa during much of the fourteenth and thirteenth centuries. If this were true, then peaceful trade might very quickly have de-
generated into piracy.

In any case, Mycenaean poets would not have had to look far for inspiration if their aim was to tell a story of a sea-borne attack on a coastal
town. Such things were known to happen in real life. Indeed, a number
of scholars have argued for a Bronze Age poem or poems, which led in
time to the development of the Homeric epics. M. L. West[3] argues from
linguistic evidence internal to the Homeric poems, which he feels indicates a Bronze Age original. Linguistics aside, it is more difficult to argue
against seemingly genuine Bronze Age artifacts present in the poems. The
problem with these artifacts, however, is that their presence does not necessarily indicate a memory of thirteenth-century warfare. In some instances they may be much older. E. S. Sherratt[4] has identified several
inconsistencies concerning the length of spears, the size and shape of
shields, and the use of iron in the poems. Hector in two passages (*Il.*

vi.318–320; viii.493–495) possesses a spear 11 cubits, or about 4 meters, in length. Such a spear, more like a Macedonian *sarissa* or Swiss pike, was not a proper weapon for throwing but would have been used for thrusting while simultaneously keeping the enemy at a safe distance. But that does not stop Hector from throwing his spear at Achilles (*Il.* xx.438) who, of all the Greeks, was the one Hector would most wish to be kept at bay.

As for Ajax's shield, this artifact has long been considered a genuine revenant of the Bronze Age. The shield is a body shield and huge, capable of sheltering both Great Ajax and Lesser Ajax, the son of Oïleus. It also would have been extraordinarily heavy, composed as it was of seven layers of bull's hide and an eighth of bronze. As if this were not enough, the shield is surmounted in the center with a great metal boss (*Il.* vii.267). Hector also at *Iliad* vi.117 has a great shield that reaches from his neck to his ankles, but later on at *Iliad* vii.250 his shield is described as circular. By contrast, most other shields are described as circular and of a size consistent with eighth-century usage.

Perhaps the most interesting inconsistency involves the use and value of iron. At *Iliad* xxiii.826–835 during Patroclus' funeral games, Achilles offers as a prize a sizable lump of unworked iron. The hero obtained this treasure after killing its previous owner, King Eëtion, the father-in-law of Hector, and ruler of Thebe, a city near Troy. In case the contestants at the games do not properly appreciate the value of a lump of iron with a royal pedigree, Achilles goes on to explain that with possession of such an object a man's plowman will not need to visit the city to obtain iron for plowshares for five years! Homer has apparently become confused regarding the nature of the value of iron—is its value to be found in its rarity or in its utility?

The oddest thing about this jumble of spears, shields, and lumps of iron is not only Homer's inconsistency in describing these objects and their use but the fact that they are all, or nearly all, anachronistic if one holds to a thirteenth-century date for the Trojan War. Both long, pike-like spears and body shields protecting from neck to ankles are antiques—artifacts of the sixteenth and fifteenth centuries. So also are boars' tusk helmets too early, appearing in seventeenth-century representations, but not to be found in the thirteenth century. On the other hand, spears short enough for throwing belong, at least in a military context, to the thirteenth century or later, while circular shields would not be common before the ninth century. Metal bosses, however, are artifacts of the eleventh century. As for iron, offering it as a valuable prize would be consistent for nearly any time between 3000 and 1200, but would not be put to so utilitarian a use as making plowshares until the eleventh century or later. The point of all this is to underscore the fact that, except for short, throwable spears and iron as an intrinsically valuable commodity, these items are either too old or too recent to play a meaningful role in a thirteenth-century Trojan War.

Yet Sherratt has overlooked one item of military gear that is close to the proper chronology. A number of warriors in the *Iliad* are said to possess horned helmets. Agamemnon himself owns such a helmet:

> Upon his head he placed a helmet, double-ridged, with
> four horse-hair crests, and the plumes nodded terribly above it.
>
> (*Il.* xi.41–42)

The Warrior Vase from Mycenae and dated to around 1200 shows a troop of warriors marching off to some unknown conflict, each one wearing a helmet with horns projecting from the front. The helmets are crested and plumed, although the crest appears to be leather with silver or bronze studs. But when we look at the rest of Agamemnon's panoply, we again encounter some familiar inconsistencies (*Il.* xi.32–35; 43–44). His shield is circular with a metal boss at the center. He takes up two spears, thus indicating that one at least will be used as a javelin. In any case, it is doubtful that he would wish to lug around two 11-cubit spears.

Sherratt's conclusion is that the *Iliad*, and the *Odyssey* perhaps to a lesser degree, at certain points betray elements deriving from three separate accretions or layers of epic material. He feels that the long spears, body shields, and boars' tusk helmets belong to an original treatment of the Trojan War composed sometime in the late fifteenth or early fourteenth century. A second layer including shield bosses, throwing spears, and horned helmets belongs to the era of Mycenaean decline and collapse and the first century or so of the ensuing Dark Age (c. 1200–1000). The third layer would feature the circular shield and crested helmet (without horns or plumes) and be roughly contemporaneous with Homer himself (ninth and eighth centuries).

Clearly, there is no room in Sherratt's scheme for a thirteenth-century Trojan War, and indeed he believes that if there ever was a Trojan War it is most likely to have occurred around 1400. He supports this dating by referring to a destruction at Troy at around this time, asserting along with others that the destruction was the result of violence and tied in with a wave of destruction caused by Mycenaean expansion into the Cyclades, Crete, the Dodecanese, and the Anatolian coast (*supra*, p. 39). The date of 1400 is interesting, for it is at about this time that we first find reference in the Hittite archives to Ahhiyawa, or in this case Ahhiya, in the document known as the Indictment of Madduwatta. This document makes mention of "the man of Ahhiya" named Attarssiyas (Attarssiyas has been identified by some as Atreus, the father of Agamemnon) who, with 100 chariots, engaged a Hittite force. Certainly we know from finds at Miletus that the Mycenaeans were active in west Anatolia at this time, but it is a far cry from activity at Miletus to being the cause of destruction at Troy. In any case, the damage to Troy appears to have been limited to two buildings destroyed by fire. It seems to us that the culprits could have been anyone or anything from a band of raiders to an overturned oil lamp.

## ANCIENT EPIC NARRATIVE AND THE FRESCOES OF THERA

Sherratt has based his argument on artifacts both literary and archaeological. Sarah P. Morris[5] has made a similar argument for the antiquity of epic thematic material based on two frescoes found in an upper story room of a house at Akrotiri on the island of Thera in the Cyclades. In the mid-second millennium, Thera was the home of a prosperous town of one- and two-story houses and a people who had a well-developed taste for art. The frescoes under discussion are only two of several found in other rooms and buildings depicting people engaged in a variety of activities and showing signs of both Minoan and Mycenaean influences. Unfortunately, the Therans built their town on the slopes of an active volcano that, sometime around 1625, erupted with extraordinary violence burying the town, much as Pompeii was buried by Vesuvius many centuries later. Luckily for the islanders, they were forewarned by a series of earthquakes and apparently escaped the main eruption.

The two frescoes, one on the south and another on the north wall of Room 5 of the West House, present what might be interpreted as a pictorial narrative, including a number of epic tropes or formulas. The fresco on the south wall shows an expanse of water where sails a fleet of ships of various sizes, some fairly small, almost canoelike, while others are quite large, their rigging festooned with flowers. All save the one that is under sail are propelled by oarsmen. Framing this scene at left and right and representing what could be points of departure and arrival for the fleet are two land masses, perhaps islands. On each land mass or island there is a walled port town, a smaller, more modest town at the left and a much more substantial settlement on the right.

The smaller town on the left consists of a number of two- and even three-story buildings situated on a mountainous promontory. The town and its harbor are encircled by a river beyond which the landscape suddenly becomes rugged and wild. On the forested peaks above the river a lion chases a deer. The world of men in the town maintains a tenuous connection to the wild world of the lion and deer by means of a shepherd who, from his encampment on the wild side of the river, seems to be carrying on a conversation with a townsman standing between river and town. Except for these two, the attention of all in the town appears to be fixed on the fleet sailing in its leisurely way toward the city to the right.

This town is a hive of activity with lines of men marching toward the harbor, men and women watching from the windows and roofs of houses, all eyes to the left, the opposite direction of those watching from the smaller town across the water. Meanwhile, other groups of men appear to be watching from the hill country inland from the town, and messengers appear to be running back and forth between the town and a small building situated on a forward peak just above the harbor.

Many attempts have been made to explain the nature of this scene and to identify its location. Some have referred to it as a Ship Procession in celebration of the opening of the sailing season. These are by no means empty suggestions, for cultures from the ancient Mediterranean to ancient China are known to have conducted nautical processions and races to celebrate the return of sailing weather. The flowers decorating the rigging of some of the vessels would seem to argue for a time in early spring, perhaps April, when many such festivals occurred. As for location, arguments have been made for Crete and various islands of the Cyclades including Thera itself. Morris suggests that this scene may be a product of the imagination but is ultimately rooted in epic narrative. In whatever way the smaller town to the left may fit into this scene—it may be that the flotilla is bypassing rather than departing from it—the larger town to the right does seem to be the ships' destination. Two or three of the foremost vessels appear to be about to put into the harbor. The men marching in a line toward the harbor are leading an animal, perhaps for a welcoming feast or a sacrifice in thanksgiving for a safe homecoming. Seen in this way the fresco may represent a *nostos*, or homecoming, of which the most famous are those of Odysseus, Menelaus, and Agamemnon returning from the Trojan War, all of which are recounted in the *Odyssey*. Looked at in a more sinister light, the town on the right might be identified as Nauplia, the port of Mycenae, and the messengers racing back and forth between the town and lookout (*scopiei*) on the forward peak might be the spies of Aegisthus bringing word to their master of Agamemnon's return.

Ancient pictorial representation, however, is by nature ambiguous. For instance, both land masses might be identified as Ithaca. The one on the left has close contact between urban and rural life. Perhaps the shepherd is Eumaeus, one of the few servants who remained loyal to Odysseus through his long absence. The one on the right, like Ithaca, has two harbors. But perhaps the right-hand scene is not a destination at all but a stopover in an itinerary. The line of men leading the animal, perhaps for sacrifice, is reminiscent of Telemachus' voyage to Pylos where he arrived to find Nestor and the whole town on the shore conducting the sacrifice of a black bull to Poseidon (*Odyssey* iii.31ff.).

One might wonder why the fresco must contain any narrative content at all. Taken by itself it might be a nautical festival or simply a scene from Bronze Age Aegean life. However, the argument that the South Wall fresco forms part of a narrative makes more sense when it is considered in relation to the fresco from the North Wall.

Just as the South Wall fresco seems to present a peaceful, even festive world, the fresco on the opposite wall shows a world at war. Unfortunately, this fresco is heavily damaged, and large sections are missing. Enough of the fresco survives, however, to give us a general impression of what is happening. The lower border of the fresco shows some sort of battle at sea happening with ships damaged and men falling overboard and drowning. Directly above the ships and drowning men there is what appears to be a bit of wall positioned seemingly right on the shore. Above this wall and to the left is the most substantial structure to be seen in this fragmentary fresco—an ashlar masonry structure with a flat roof and what appear to be three entryways, in one of which a young boy, perhaps a shepherd, can be seen. Sitting and standing on (or beyond) this roof are four other boys or young men gazing into the distance to the left. Meanwhile, marching off in the opposite direction is a line of at least eight warriors armed, like Ajax, with ox hide body shields; like Hector they have long pikes easily twice as long as the warriors are tall; and like Odysseus they each wear a boars' tusk helmet. Where they are marching we cannot say owing to the fragmentary state of the fresco.

In striking juxtaposition to the warlike nature of this scene are two lines of animals—goats, cattle, and sheep—with their herders. One herd is being driven out to pasture, while the other is returning to the fold. Another domestic scene appears above the ashlar structure. Beneath two trees and surrounded by a low stone wall is a well with water jar. Striding off in the same direction as the marching warriors are two women, water jars perched on their heads.

In a separate fragment off to the left we see a group of men of different heights clothed in kilts and cloaks. They are standing on a hill and seem to be taking counsel together. We cannot of course know the intent of their consultation, but the boys or young men perched on the roof of the ashlar structure seem to be watching them with great interest.

So what does all this mean, and if it is a pictorial narrative, what story is it telling? If it does tell a story, it is likely both synoptic—that is, summarizing a story containing several episodes—and asynchronous—meaning that not all episodes are happening at the same time. Otherwise we would find ourselves in the unenviable position of having to explain all these elements—the hilltop council, the women carrying water from the well, the drovers herding their animals to and fro, the marching soldiers, and the sea battle—as happening simultaneously. The fresco makes even less sense if we view it as a series of nonnarrative, unrelated representations or icons. Instead, if we view the fresco as both synoptic and asynchronous, we can perhaps make better sense of it.

The gathering of men on the hilltop may be a council of war held by the defenders before battle is joined. The differences in height and clothing may be explained as referring to differences in age and social position among those participating: the tall men clothed in cloaks may be elders past the age of active combat—the Priam and Antenor of this scene; the shorter men in kilts might be younger men and warriors—Hector and Aeneas perhaps. The hilltop itself is a close analog to the look-out or *scopiei* seen in the South Wall fresco. Only the peak shrine is missing. Such a hill is noted in the *Iliad* at ii.811–815 where "the Trojans and their companions were marshaled in order." It is interesting in relation to the South Wall *scopiei* that the gods knew this hill as "the burial mound of dancing Myrina," a name that implies a dual purpose to the place. The peak lookout shown in the South Wall fresco could be both sacred ground and a part of the town's defenses. Again the *Iliad* (*Il.* ii.790–794) provides a parallel in referring to Priam's son Polites, who kept watch for the Trojans atop the burial mound of Aesyetes. Of course, the council meeting does not have to be between leaders of the defense: the invaders having landed after the sea battle might have a council of their own like that held by the leaders of the army displayed on the Shield of Achilles (*Il.* xviii.510–512) who are debating whether to destroy the city or divide up its property and goods. Or the gathering might not be a council at all, but an embassy between defenders and attackers. Various non-Homeric legends tell of one or two embassies sent by Agamemnon to negotiate Helen's return. The tale most closely matching the fresco is told in a later summary of events that occurred before those of the *Iliad*, in which an embassy is sent to the Trojans immediately following the first battle after landing.

So the council takes place either before or just after the sea battle. This *naumakhia*, or sea fight, is echoed in the boast of Achilles (*Il.* ix.328–329) who claims to have sacked twelve cities by ship and eleven by land. What appears to be a bit of wall, mentioned above, gains in importance when seen in relation to the ships just below. So close to the shore, indeed right on the shore, such a wall would likely have been erected by the attackers immediately after landing. Such a wall plays a prominent role in the *Iliad*, for it is the breach of this wall, allowing the Trojans to attack the Greek ships, that convinces Achilles that he must let Patroclus enter the battle in his stead to prevent the burning of the ships (*Il.* xv.592–xvi.130). It should be noted here that accompanying the drowning men are one or two objects that appear to be long poles with curved ends, rather like shepherds' crooks. They are perhaps grappling hooks or pikes such as that mentioned at *Iliad* xvi.677–678 wielded by Ajax against the Trojans trying to burn the ships. This pike, however, is said to be 22 cubits in length, or twice the length of Hector's spear, and the objects floating in the water near the drowning men are only a

fraction of that length. Perhaps a closer parallel is provided by a stone
rhyton from Epidauros in the Peloponnese showing men in warships
wielding pikes, with warriors above them marching presumably toward a
city or some other military target.

This brings us back to the eight (at least) marching warriors with their
early Mycenaean, and yet oddly Homeric, panoply. This image is arresting both as silent testimony in support of Sherratt's argument and as possible evidence for the antiquity of Mycenaean influence on Cycladic art.
Judging from long-established pottery sequences, the destruction of the
site at Akrotiri should date to sometime between the late sixteenth and
mid-fifteenth centuries. However based on revised carbon 14 dating, dendrochronology, and ice core chronology, the eruption of the Thera volcano has been dated to the last quarter of the seventeenth century.
Inasmuch as mainland culture was only beginning to gain greater complexity in the seventeenth century, it would be surprising to see Mycenaeans, or anyone dressed like Mycenaeans, in the Cycladic frescoes at
this early date.

Be that as it may, the eight warriors are marching toward the one element the absence of which is most regrettable. Although we cannot be
sure, most likely the goal of the warriors is a city. To refer again to a
Homeric parallel, it could be Aeneas' city of Lyrnessos where Achilles
nearly captured Aeneas himself and did manage to sack the town. According to Aeneas, this engagement started out as a cattle raid (*Il.*
xx.86–92). Although cattle rustling might seem to be the somewhat triv-
ial stuff of which westerns are made, it was in fact epic material for many
ancient peoples from the *Iliad* and *Odyssey* (*Od.* xii.260–390) to the Irish
*Táin Bó Cuailnge* (The Cattle Raid of Cooley). It is in fact possible that
the object of the marching warriors is not a city, or only a city, but the
livestock shown being driven back and forth to the right of the well.
Whether or not a cattle raid is proper epic material, an army engaged in
a ten-year siege would require many such raids to keep from starving.

But this observation about warriors and livestock takes us to the most
peculiar aspect of the North Wall fresco. The two drovers herding their
animals to and fro and the women striding away from the well, water jars
poised on their heads, form a strange counterpoint to the marching warriors just below and the sea battle with drowning men at the bottom of
the fresco. The fact that the women, their jars full after visiting the well,
are headed in the same direction as the warriors provides mute, internal

evidence that the warriors themselves are heading toward a settlement of some sort. But more importantly, the odd pairing of mundane and martial activities in the fresco presents an image of a world at peace and a world at war. The fact that both the women and the herdsmen seem to be oblivious to the marching warriors might seem to rule out the simultaneity of the two elements, but this observation is of little import since cities the world over are apt to experience both the blessings of peace and the curse of war at some point in their histories. In this fresco we seem to be witnessing the beginnings of that perception of the tragic nature of life peculiar to Aegean peoples. The North Wall fresco is in some sense an expression or inflection of the scene on the South Wall. There the two towns are at peace and indeed appear to be in a festive mood. But even in their apparent happiness not all violence is banished, for the lion chases after the deer just as many a Greek or Trojan warrior in numerous Homeric similes pursues his enemy with spear and sword. Even the flower-bedecked ships of the flotilla show boars' tusk helmets dangling from the mast and yardarm. The two frescoes relate to each other as war relates to peace, but within the confines of each individual representation we see that peace does not exist without the threat of war, nor war without the promise of peace.

The opposite and related themes of a city at war and a city at peace are also found in Homer. The Shield of Achilles (*Il.* xviii.478–607) shows the whole world surrounded by Ocean just as the small town of the South Wall fresco is surrounded by a river. Within the world represented on Achilles' shield there are two cities, one at peace and one at war, but even the city at peace is tinged darkly by violence, for there is a case of manslaughter proceeding in the courts at the same time that a marriage festival is underway elsewhere in the city. Peace is at best a relative thing, and in time all wars must come to an end.

Finally, the women at the well bring to mind another passage from the *Iliad*, in which Achilles is chasing Hector to his doom about the walls of Troy:

> They raced along by the watching point and the windy fig tree
> always away from under the wall and along the wagon-way
> and came to the two sweet-running well springs.
>     There there are double

springs of water that jet up, the springs of whirling
    Scamander.
One of these runs hot water and the steam on all sides
of it rises as if from a fire that was burning inside it.
But the other in the summer-time runs water that is like hail
or chill snow or ice that forms from water. Besides these
in this place, and close to them, are the washing-hollows
of stone, and magnificent, where the wives
    of the Trojans and their lovely
daughters washed the clothes to shining, in the old days
when there was peace, before the coming
    of the sons of the Achaeans.
(xxii.145–156, from *The Iliad of Homer*, R. Lattimore, translator. The
    University of Chicago Press. Reprinted with permission.)

## THE CONTRIBUTION OF HOMER TO THE EPIC TRADITION

We have examined two arguments supporting the proposition that the epic themes found in Homeric poetry are in fact quite ancient. In the case of the Thera frescoes, not only does this material predate Homer by around 900 years, it also predates a thirteenth-century Trojan War by perhaps as much as 400 years. We must now turn from this discussion of the antiquity of the Epic Tradition to the contribution Homer himself made to that tradition.

Of all the questions that bedevil Classical scholarship, surely one of the most enigmatic and intractable is that of the identity of Homer and the circumstances under which the two great poems attributed to him attained their present form. The debates concerning these questions have a long history—indeed, an ancient history, for they were controversial even in antiquity. Over the last two centuries or so the arguments over the authorship of the *Iliad* and the *Odyssey* have actually intensified, with every new theory engendering a hornet's nest of subordinate questions and problems. A glance at a few of these questions leads to an appreciation not only of the difficulty of the issues involved, but also of the sometimes extraordinary lengths to which scholars will go in order to explain the very real peculiarities of the two great epics.

Beginning with the most basic example, was Homer a real person or not? This question was being asked at least as early as the Hellenistic period. Even were we able to answer this first question, other questions would follow. If Homer was real, did he write both poems (also an ancient question)? If not, which poem did he write, and who wrote the other? Was the author of the *Odyssey* a man or a woman? This question is founded on differences of style, language, emphases, and subject matter between the two poems. Perhaps Homer was not one or two poets, but an editorial committee charged with the task of stitching the epics together out of a number of individual shorter ballads and lays current during the Dark Age. This theory reflects the inconsistency of dialect found in the poems and the assumption that an oral poet would be incapable of retaining such lengthy poems in his memory. A related question asks, assuming that Homer was an individual poet, did he write down the poems himself or did he dictate them to a scribe? If the poems were dictated, would not this very mode of transmission alter the nature of the epics? Is there even any certainty that Homer was alive when the poems were first written down?

Our difficulties center on our ignorance of Homer. His references to himself in the course of the poems are exceedingly rare and tend to be of a formulaic nature. Nor does he refer, except indirectly, to his audience whom we can only suppose consisted in the main of aristocratic men and women such as those who gathered in Alcinous' hall to listen to the blind bard Demodocus (*Od.* viii.44–95).

### South Slavic Oral Epic

But we are not as confined to the realm of speculation and guesswork as we might suppose. In the 1930s, the American scholar Milman Parry conducted a series of studies of South Slavic oral epic poetry and poetic performance. During his years in Yugoslavia, Parry recorded many tens of thousands of lines of epic poetry—a few of the poems nearly equal in length to the *Iliad* and the *Odyssey*—and had many more lines dictated. The powers of some of the oral poets appear to have been prodigious, and one poet in particular, Avdo Međedović, stood out in Parry's regard as a genius. Međedović had fifty-eight epics in his repertoire. During the summer of 1935, Parry recorded nine of them and had the poet dictate four others for a total of nearly 80,000 lines of poetry sung from memory.

The phrase "from memory," however, is misleading. One of the peculiarities noticed by both Parry and his student Albert Lord was that these poems, some of them running to 13,000 lines, are not memorized as we might memorize a short poem for recitation. Lord maintains that what happens in the oral recitation of an epic is more a matter of composition in performance. What the poet memorizes is the plot, characters, and sequence of events of the epic tale. To this he adds a store of traditional stock phrases, or formulas, lines and whole stanzas, all set to a specific and undeviating meter which the poet learned and internalized during his apprenticeship, much as we learn the alphabet or the multiplication tables.

This process sounds somewhat mechanical, and perhaps it is for many oral-traditional poets. But in the hands of a truly gifted poet these nuts and bolts of oral composition become transformed and elaborated into inspired epic. Lord recounts an experiment that Parry conducted with Međedović's permission in which the poet heard an epic that was unknown to him sung by another poet. This epic ran to about 2,300 lines, but after hearing it once (and after apologizing to his colleague), Međedović repeated the epic and lengthened it with the elaborate use of formulas and extended similes to just over 6,300 lines.

Now Međedović was an unusual poet, a genius in Parry and Lord's estimation. So also was Homer, not simply in the opinion of antiquity but among modern critics as well. Homer has set the standard by which all other epic poets have been and will be judged. It was Milman Parry's great gift to Homeric studies to demonstrate that, by analogy with South Slavic epic, the *Iliad* and the *Odyssey* were the products, indeed the end products, of an oral epic tradition. Homer stood at the confluence of an ancient oral tradition, with the new world of literacy just then having an impact on Greek society and culture. One might argue that all our surviving oral epics—*Beowulf*, the *Kosovo Epic*, the *Kalevala* are a few other examples—are by definition the products of such interaction. Each had to be written down by someone; otherwise, we would not know them hundreds of years later. But they had to be written down before the oral society that produced such poems had passed from the scene. Such societies as early twentieth-century Yugoslavia, early nineteenth-century Finland, eleventh-century England, and Greece of the eighth century B.C.E., provide the proper mix of a largely nonliterate society interacting with the new tools of literacy to produce great epic poetry.

Parry's student, Albert Lord, has followed his mentor's logic a step or two further to argue that the Homeric poems were a good deal more than the literate residue of an oral epic tradition. True enough, the *Iliad* and the *Odyssey* bear many of the hallmarks of oral epic, including formulaic phrases finely honed to fit a hexameter line, exact repetition of speeches, and elaborate use of extended simile. But beyond these conventions, both poems possess elements that seem to betray an exposure to the analytical habits of mind commonly associated with literacy. The lines quoted above from *Iliad* xxii represent one such passage. In these lines we see an everyday task, a mundane chore, transformed into a brief reverie of peace. It is indeed difficult to imagine a scene of such arresting and tragic beauty juxtaposed as it is with the horror of the two heroes' fatal race as the product purely of oral performance. But a number of such episodes are scattered throughout both poems, and we are left with the question of how the two epics, which most scholars now agree are essentially oral poems, achieved this final refinement.

Lord has answered this question in a most interesting manner. He believes that a single oral-traditional poet, whom we may as well call Homer, was responsible for the *Iliad* as we have received it. Furthermore, judging from the formidable powers of Avdo Međedović, he sees no reason to deny that this Homer might have composed the *Odyssey* as well. Finally, Lord argues that the poems attained their high degree of refinement through the process of dictation. While Parry was in Yugoslavia he had several poets dictate their epics. All observed that it was a slow, laborious process, for no one can write as fast as a poet can sing. A few complained of, and indeed were incapacitated by, the repeated interruptions in meter upon which the oral poet, much more so than his literate counterpart, is dependent. But others, Međedović included, used these same difficulties to their advantage. These poets used the numerous and sometimes lengthy pauses to think more deeply about what they would sing next, to vary slightly formulaic phrases, to elaborate on similes, and—most importantly—to make use of the one great advantage possessed by the literate poet—time and leisure for thought and analysis. When, after dictating a poem, Parry asked a singer what he thought of the end result, his reply was, "Sung songs are truer, dictated songs are finer!"

## Homer and Oral Poetry

So let us assume for the sake of argument that Homer, like Avdo Međedović, was a supremely gifted poet working within the context of an already established oral poetic tradition. Let us further assume that he flourished during the eighth century, just when Greek literacy was providing poets with the tools for rendering, through dictation, ever finer creations. What does this tell us about the poems we are now assuming Homer to have dictated? Unfortunately, it does not tell us very much. Saying that Homer drew on a tradition of oral poetry tells us nothing about the age of the tradition or its provenance. These difficulties can be illustrated by the example of the *Theogony*, a long poem attributed to the Greek poet Hesiod who was perhaps a younger contemporary of Homer. This poem, written, or perhaps dictated, in an epic style but much shorter than either of Homer's poems, recounts the genealogy of the gods. We know from Linear B evidence that many of the gods who appear in the poem were part of the Mycenaean pantheon. It is also safe to say that many of the stories about the gods told in the *Theogony* predate the poem, which was written in the late eighth or early seventh century. As to the poem's provenance, apparently some elements in it were borrowed from, or inspired by, originals current among the Hurrians of northern Mesopotamia in the Late Bronze Age. Does this mean that the *Theogony* is a first millennium Greek rendering of a second millennium Hurrian original? Not necessarily: for one thing the material most closely resembling a supposed Hurrian original is the story of Cronos' revolt against the sky god Ouranos, and there is much else besides this episode in the *Theogony*. For another the Greeks need not have become acquainted with this material as early as the Bronze Age. Our best evidence indicates that Hesiod flourished at the beginning of a period of heightened interaction between East and West. So substantial was Near Eastern influence on Greek artistic sensibilities that the seventh century is often referred to, after the ancient Orient or Near East, as the Orientalizing Period.

So at present we cannot say with any certainty whether the tales told in the *Theogony* were inspired by Near Eastern archetypes, or if so, whether that inspiration occurred during the Late Bronze Age or the Dark Age or even later. We are only on slightly firmer ground with the

*Iliad* and *Odyssey*. Unlike the *Theogony*, which deals almost exclusively with the gods who exist on a plane clearly outside the concerns of historians and archaeologists, the characters of the Homeric poems are for the most part flesh and blood mortals engaged in the very human activities of warfare or picking up the threads of their lives after the war is over. In addition, although some scholars have attempted to draw connections between Near Eastern tales and the Homeric corpus, most notably drawing parallels between the character and exploits of Odysseus with those of the Babylonian hero Gilgamesh, there is as yet no convincing evidence to demonstrate that the *Iliad* and *Odyssey* are anything other than Greek in conception. Again with regard to the date at which the Trojan War first became the subject of poets working in an oral tradition, we have discussed both evidence internal to the poems and external, nonpoetic evidence that shows the likely Bronze Age origin of the epics. But even aside from this evidence, we can state that the world to which the poems refer must be the Late Bronze Age. This must be true even if the Greeks and Trojans never fought so much as a skirmish. We can be certain of this because only in the Bronze Age did Mycenae and Troy have the requisite wealth and power to be believable as antagonists in such a conflict. Had the poet of the *Iliad* been referring to Dark Age Mycenae or Troy, his audience would have been confused to say the least, since by the ninth and eighth centuries Mycenae had dwindled to the status of a poor country town and Troy may not even have been inhabited.

But although the poems refer to a Bronze Age event, the cultural context of the poems—the material culture referred to—appears to be decidedly late Dark Age or early Archaic. In other words, an old tale is told in a manner that is comprehensible to the poet and his audience. Let us consider this last notion briefly. Oral poetic performance in nonliterate cultures serves a number of purposes: depending on the occasion of the performance, the nature of the audience, and the status of the poet, oral song or recitation can instruct the community in the law and the origin of customs and taboos, its history and place in the world, and in religion and the nature of the gods as well as glorifying the exploits of kings and heroes. But whatever the occasion or immediate purpose of the performance, the singer must command the attention of his listeners, and to do that he must entertain.

This matter of entertainment is of greater import than one might think upon first consideration. If the oral recitation of the deeds of gods or heroes, or the genealogy of a king, or even the law is not in some sense entertaining, then it will quickly be forgotten. Although a forgettable hero might not seem a great mishap, consider what might happen if the king's genealogy, which is his claim to legitimacy, were forgotten. What might happen if people forgot the law because the reciter failed to present it in rhyme, or as a simple, easy to remember list such as the Ten Commandments or Hammurabi's Code?

Simplicity, like entertainment value, is another hallmark of oral recitation. By simplicity we are not implying that the poets and audiences in oral cultures are incapable of understanding anything more complex than nursery rhymes or fairy tales. The *Odyssey* is a complex tale making frequent use of flashbacks, while in the *Iliad* the political strife on Olympus mirrors the bloodier strife on the battlefield before Troy. But the characters in these tales tend to be two-dimensional. What is Achilles without his wrath and prowess in battle, or Odysseus without his craftiness or eloquence in council? For an audience possessing no text to which they might refer and who will never hear the same tale told the same way no matter how often it is heard, it is unreasonable to expect them to be presented with complex characters who are torn by self-doubt and inner conflict. In an oral society dependent on memory, such characters would simply not be memorable.

Let us now return to the question of the dating of the Homeric poems. If the cultural reference of the *Iliad* and *Odyssey* is Late Bronze Age, why is so little of that period recalled in the poems' cultural context? Despite the number of references to Bronze Age shields, spears, and helmets discussed previously, such objects are relatively few when compared to other, later artifacts. The cultural elements that can be confidently assigned to the second millennium are indeed thin. Aside from the anachronistic importance of such sites as Mycenae, Pylos, Knossos, and Troy itself, the Bronze Age artifacts include Ajax's body shield, Odysseus' boars' tusk helmet, Agamemnon's horned helmet, Hector's spear, Nestor's cup, and the use of chariots in warfare. Even this short catalog of Bronze Age relics has not gone uncontested. For instance, Homer displays some confusion regarding the proper use of chariots in battle. Instead of being used, like modern tanks, as mobile platforms for launching missiles (spears and arrows) and breaking up infantry formations, Homer has them being used rather like the French used taxi-cabs in the opening days of World War

I, as a means of transporting troops to the front, after which they would alight and fight on foot. Questions have also been raised about the validity of Nestor's cup as a Mycenaean artifact since Homer's version is an enormous, four-handled affair with doves perched on the handles, while the gold cup found in the Shaft Graves at Mycenae boasts only two handles surmounted by what appear to be hawks, not doves, and is much smaller.

In any event, these Bronze Age remnants are more than offset by Homer's descriptions of town and house plans, temples, and religious practice, all of which seem more in keeping with a late Dark Age or early Archaic cultural milieu. The reasons for this prejudice take us back to our discussion of the problems faced by oral epic poets in presenting their material to a nonliterate audience. A small amount of exotic or archaic material references, such as the boars' tusk helmet or chariot warfare, in an otherwise familiar landscape may actually make a tale more memorable, but constant references to unfamiliar artifacts from a long dead culture would only lead to confusion. How might a poet convey the intricate maze of Nestor's palace at Pylos and his elaborate and at least partially literate bureaucracy upon which he depended to keep his kingdom in good order? How might he explain Helen's heavily flounced and open-breasted attire to an audience that quite possibly would have been shocked by such things? As for Ajax's shield, to be historically accurate, Homer would have had to abandon both the sixteenth-century body shield and the round eighth-century hoplite shield. Judging from its appearance on the thirteenth-century Warrior Vase, describing such a shield as Ajax might realistically have borne within the confines of a hexameter line would be a neat trick.

Even if Homer had known all there was to know of Mycenaean material culture, it is doubtful he would have used this knowledge in order to give a more accurate rendering of the tale. It is not so much a case of epic poetry and historical accuracy being sworn enemies. Rather, it is simply that Homer's audience would have had no such knowledge and most likely would have been shocked, confused, and probably *not* entertained by constant references to authentic Mycenaean artifacts in the poems. The epic hero must have larger-than-life qualities—he may even have superhuman or magical qualities. Odysseus' craftiness is larger-than-life, his bow to which no other man can draw arrow is superhuman, and his ability to enter the Land of the Dead and return unscathed is magical.

But everything else about him, from the clothes he wears to the weapons he uses to his house on Ithaca, would be recognizable to an eighth-century audience.

With the *Iliad* and the *Odyssey* we are witnessing the end product of a centuries-long tradition. During this process of development, many new elements have been added and many old ones have been edited out. If the Trojan War cycle originated in Mycenaean times, it is natural to assume that Mycenaean cultural references would abound in the earliest phases of that development. But with the drastic lowering of material culture following the Mycenaean collapse, many of the old references would have become at first irrelevant, then anachronistic, and finally incomprehensible. As this loss of memory progressed, more and more Mycenaean references, current in the thirteenth and twelfth centuries, would by the eleventh and tenth have been edited out, with perhaps new cultural references more understandable to Dark Age audiences taking their place. By the time of Homer, we have a situation in which the late Dark Age and early Archaic cultural references greatly outnumber those that may reasonably be traced to the Late Bronze Age.

The few relics that make up the final Mycenaean residue may have been allowed to survive for any number of reasons, including the very archaic nature of the relics. In presenting their tales, storytellers must strike a fine balance between the strange and the familiar. Part of the appeal of tales in any age, whether epic adventures or fairy tales, lies in the measured use of exotic or archaic material within a familiar context. Odysseus' boars' tusk helmet might fall into this category. Another reason for retaining certain artifacts might be that they are so closely associated with certain heroes or events that they could not easily be edited out. Such artifacts as Ajax's shield or the use of chariots would be retained for such reasons. Finally, one must never underestimate the force of memory and nostalgia in evaluating such quasihistorical tales as are told in the *Iliad*. If, as many scholars believe, the Homeric Epic Tradition dates back to the Bronze Age, then such tales would have continued to be sung even after the Mycenaean collapse.[6]

Some of the earliest auditors of the Trojan War Cycle may have heard these tales amid the ruins of post-collapse Mycenae or perhaps in some remote haven such as Cyprus or Achaea where a Mycenaean remnant lingered. They would have remembered Mycenae and Pylos in the height of their glory, and listening to the tales of their great war against the might of Troy would have answered the very human need to be reminded that poverty and darkness were not always the lot of men.

Surely such memories, even though embroidered by nostalgia, must have some basis in reality. But memory, particularly in hard times, may play us false, and the imaginations of ancient poets were doubtless no less active than our own. Although we may safely say that Homer was neither novelist nor historian, as to the truth of the tale he was telling we can only say that his audience, and many succeeding generations of audiences, did believe the tale of the Trojan War to be a true tale.

## ADDITIONS TO THE HOMERIC TRADITION

Later audiences of the Homeric epics did not question the reality of Homer himself: he was the poet who had recounted one of the most important events of their earliest history. One of Homer's more recent admirers stated boldly, "What the Greeks might have been, if there had been no Homer, we cannot guess, but what they were at their best was largely because of him."[7]

The *Iliad* and *Odyssey* did not contain the full story, however; it was buttressed by other later poems that collectively are termed the Epic Cycle. Only fragments remain of these lost works, but later descriptions of them indicate their general themes. The *Kypria* recounted events before the Trojan War. Credited to one Arctinos is the *Aethiopis*, which dealt with Achilles' slaying of the queen of the Amazons, Penthesileia, and the Ethiopian warrior Memnon. A poem known as the *Little Iliad* began with the struggle for the armor of Achilles by Odysseus and Ajax, and finished with the drawing of the Trojan horse into the walls of Troy while the *Destruction of Ilios*, also credited to Arctinos, recounts the debate of the Trojans over the wooden horse through the departure of the Greeks for home. The *Nostoi*, or the "Returns," describes the events of the Greeks' homeward travels, while the latest poem, the *Telegonia*, was an appendix to the *Odyssey*.

The Homeric epics as well as the poems in the now lost Epic Cycle were major sources for the Classical tragedians; many of the tragedies were centered on heroes of the Trojan War. Aeschylus described his dramas as "slices from the banquet of Homer." A trilogy by Aeschylus describes, first, the return of Agamemnon to Mycenae where he was slain by his wife Clytemnestra and her lover, Aegisthus. The second play of the trilogy recounts the revenge by Orestes for the murder of his father through his slaying of his mother, Clytemnestra, and Aegisthus. Resolution of the cycle of vengeance is the subject of the third tragedy, the *Eumenides*, through the intervention of the goddess Athena. Both tragedians Sophocles and Euripides recounted the plight of the warrior Philoctetes: while sailing with the other Greeks to Troy, he was bitten by a snake. When the wound became infected, he was left on an island. Ten years later, the Greeks at Troy learned that Philoctetes must be present for the Greeks to prevail against the Trojans. Euripides presented the consequences of that success in his *Trojan Women*, now captives of the Greeks.

Historians, too, appreciated the importance of Homer and his tale of the Trojan War. Herodotus, known as the father of history, believed that the Achaean attack on Troy in order to recover Helen was the cause of the perpetual hostility between the Greeks and the Asians that culminated in the Persian Wars against the Greeks in the late sixth and early fifth centuries B.C.E. His successor, Thucydides whose history recounts the Greek civil war known as the Peloponnesian War from 431 to 404 demarcates early history as the situation before the Trojan War and after it. Agamemnon's host surpassed every force before its time although it was less than the armies of Thucydides' own time, "if," as Thucydides wrote "we can accept the testimony of Homer's poems."

The tradition was regarded as remembering a major event of the Heroic Age of Greece not only by the Greeks but by other Mediterranean peoples. Rule over the glorious Tyrsenians or Etruscans was ascribed to the sons of Odysseus and Circe by the poet Hesiod who is dated to c. 700 B.C.E. (*Theogony* 1011–1015). One of the few Trojan heroes to escape from Troy was Aeneas whose fate it was to lead his companions to Italy, thereby becoming the ancestors of the Romans. In the second book of his *Aeneid*, the Roman poet Virgil portrays the fall of Troy through the eyes of the Trojan Aeneas. Two works dated to the first century C.E. pose as a journal of the Trojan War by Dictys of Crete and a history of the fall of Troy by Dares of Phrygia. Thus, not only the war itself but its consequences directed the ongoing history of the ancient Mediterranean world.

Not even with the collapse of the classical civilizations of Greece and Rome did serious doubts arise about the Trojan War as a historical event. Latin translations of the *Iliad* and *Odyssey*, Virgil's *Aeneid*, and the poems attributed to Dictys and Dares were important authorities in the medieval period. The events that they described served especially as sources for *Le Roman de Troie* by Benoit de Sainte-Maure, a French minstrel of the twelfth century C.E.

In the next two chapters we will explore not only how Homer's poems gained universal currency throughout the Hellenistic and Roman worlds, but also how the poems continue to affect western and, indeed world wide culture to this day. Among the questions we will attempt to answer are what sort of impact the unmatched popularity of the epic tales, particularly among the educated elite, had on political behavior during the last millennium of antiquity and how their continued popularity affects us today.

## NOTES

1. Thersites is the ordinary soldier "of no account in battle or counsel" who dares to speak at an assembly controlled by the leaders. When he is beaten for his audacity by Odysseus, the other ordinary soldiers laugh, though they feel sorrow for the man.

2. R.L.N. Barber, *The Cyclades in the Bronze Age* (Iowa City: University of Iowa Press, 1987), p. 224.

3. M. L. West, "The Rise of the Greek Epic," *JHS* 108 (1988): 151–172.

4. E. S. Sherratt, "'Reading the Texts': Archaeology and the Homeric Question," *Antiquity* 64 (1990): 807–824.

5. Sarah P. Morris, "A Tale of Two Cities: The Miniature Frescoes from Thera and the Origins of Greek Poetry," *AJA* 93 (1989): 511–535.

6. John Chadwick, who assisted in deciphering Linear B, the script used during the Mycenaean Age, investigated the connection between the form of Greek preserved in the tablets and that of Homeric Greek preserved by the traditional dialect in "Mycenaean Elements in the Homeric Dialect," *Minoka* 12 (1958): 116–122. "If more than a few such words can be shown to occur on the Mycenaean tablets," he wrote, "the existence of a direct link can then be inferred" (p. 118). His findings of 1958 were impressive, and the evidence has grown over the succeeding decades.

7. John A. Scott, *Homer and His Influence* (New York: Longmans Green and Co., 1925), p. 101.

# CHAPTER 4

# THE FORCE OF LEGEND

Homer almost certainly believed in the essential events of the tale he was telling. Although he likely left out many details that other bards included, it is equally likely that he added a few things. For instance, the names of local heroes might be added, the better to gain the favor of their would-be descendants among his audience. It is in the nature of oral epic to take a story thought to be true and heighten the impact of its telling through poetic embroidery. So powerful was the poetic tradition concerning the Trojan War and so ingenious was Homer's retelling of it that for centuries afterward not only the Greeks, but the Romans as well, regarded the *Iliad* and *Odyssey* as a true account of the heroic deeds of their progenitors.

So the question we will examine in this chapter does not ask whether a Trojan War actually happened, but rather what effect did the almost universal belief that it did happen have on the behavior of Greeks and Romans in their later histories? That this material did have an almost incalculable effect can be seen in the subject matter of Athens' three great tragedians, Aeschylus, Sophocles, and Euripides, and in that of Rome's great epic poet Virgil. More concretely, the career of Alexander the Great was inspired in no small measure by the deeds of Achilles as told by Homer.

## THE EPIC TRADITION AFTER THE BRONZE AGE COLLAPSE

If at some time during the Late Bronze Age a Mycenaean sea-borne coalition in actual fact raided or laid siege to the city on and around

Hissarlik, we cannot on the basis of present evidence be sure when it occurred. Herodotus calculated that the Sack of Troy happened about 800 years from the time he was writing, or about 1250 B.C.E., and most scholars, ourselves included, are content to follow Herodotus, although their arguments are now buttressed by the archaeology of the thirteenth-century destruction of Troy VI as well as Hittite documents such as the Alaksandu Treaty. Meanwhile, E. S. Sherratt, based on evidence internal to the epics has argued for a date closer to 1400. As we have seen, some aspects of his argument are strengthened by S. P. Morris' discussion of the frescoes preserved on the Aegean island of Thera, but Morris does not arrive at Sherratt's conclusion that the Trojan War, if it happened, must have taken place much earlier than has hitherto been thought. Morris may be included among a growing number of scholars who suggest that the events of a real Trojan War may have become attached to an already existing narrative or narratives that featured a sea-borne attack on an island or coastal city. Such an explanation would go far toward reconciling such Homeric inconsistencies as the use of long pikelike spears, more at home in the sixteenth century, and horned helmets which properly belong to the thirteenth.

Whatever the case may be, 1250 is about the latest date at which a Trojan War could take place, for as we have described above (p. 17ff.) within a few decades from this time both the Mycenaeans and Hittites came under attack. Although we do not know the nature of these disruptions, we do know that they proved fatal to both civilizations. Almost all the great citadel states in Greece were destroyed or abandoned, and there are signs of catastrophic population loss, with many people fleeing overseas to Cyprus or Rhodes or moving inland away from the coasts to rugged, out-of-the-way places like Arcadia in the central Peloponnese or to the mountainous interior of Crete. The argument for a thirteenth-century date for the Trojan War is reinforced by the faint glimmerings of these violent events detected in many of our ancient sources. Both Herodotus and Thucydides writing in the fifth century B.C.E. speak of the sack of cities, rebellion, and the movements of peoples following the Trojan War. A favorite theme of the epic poets, including Homer, and later of such playwrights as Aeschylus, was the returns, or *Nostoi*, of the Greek heroes from Troy. Several of the *nostos* heroes, such as Diomedes of Argos or Idomeneus of Knossos, were the victims of coups that forced them into exile. In the case of Agamemnon, the coup plotted by his wife Clytemnes-

tra and his cousin Aegisthus proved fatal. As for Odysseus, the most famous of the *nostos* heroes, his return sparked a short, bloody civil war between the hero and his allies and the suitors and their families. Such a
disturbance, known to later Greeks as *stasis*, faction fighting or civil conflict, may dimly reflect actual events of the late thirteenth or early twelfth
century. Thus, the tales of the *Nostoi* and the related stories of widespread
conflict and disruption may be one of those rare instances when myth and
history agree.

Whether we see in these tales actual memories or simply fictions that
happened to coincide with historical reality, we cannot now tell. The
Greeks of antiquity at least believed that these stories were historically
true. So certain were they of these events that for later Greeks the Trojan War and its aftermath became an indispensable marker on either side
of which they pegged other events that they knew, or thought they knew,
had taken place. This proved to be the beginning of an historical sensi-
bility among the Greeks who now attempted to construct a history in
which events happened either before or after the Trojan War.

The Trojan War, real or not, gave depth to Greek notions of their own
past. Thus, the Aeolian and Ionian Migrations to the Anatolian coast
were thought to have occurred several generations after the Trojan War,
while the voyage of the Argo and the first assault on Thebes recounted
in *Seven Against Thebes* occurred in the generation preceding the Trojan
War. The Aeolian and Ionian Migrations, whether one views them as
the flight of refugees or as precocious colonizing efforts, were real enough
as archaeological evidence has shown. It is very likely that the migrants
brought with them various accounts of the Trojan War, some of which
would later be amalgamated into the *Iliad* and *Odyssey*. Homer, whose
birthplace has since antiquity been claimed by Chios close to the Anatolian shore, might have been inspired by different versions of these same
tales.

## EUBOEAN TRADERS AND COLONIZERS AND THE SPREAD OF HOMERIC EPIC

The spread of these stories, however, owes much to the wide-ranging
activities of the Euboeans. The island of Euboea is ideally situated to have
taken in some of the earliest refugees fleeing the Mycenaean collapse.
Very long and narrow, Euboea lies close to Thessaly in the north and At-

tica in the south. Archaeological finds from a site near the modern village of Lefkandi show that several waves of migrants settled there during the twelfth century. By the mid-eleventh century there were signs of trading contacts with the islands of the eastern and southern Aegean. This trading activity increased during the tenth and ninth centuries when the town went into a sudden decline in about 825. By 700 the site was permanently abandoned, but by then the neighboring towns of Chalcis and Eretria had continued and expanded Lefkandi's trading activities. Throughout this period, Euboeans were in a position to acquire and disperse tales of the Trojan War and the *Nostoi*. Indeed, so lively were Euboean commercial, and later, colonizing activities from the mid-tenth to the late eighth centuries, a period in which most of Greece still lay mired in the social and economic recession of the Dark Age, that some scholars have suggested that not only the Homeric epics but the alphabet itself were Euboean products.

### The Cave of Polis

A striking example of the connection between Euboean trade and the spread of the Trojan epic comes from the Cave of Polis on the western shore of Odysseus' own island of Ithaca just west of the Gulf of Corinth. First, however, the story begins at Euboean Lefkandi in a rubbish pit. In this pit containing material dated to the tenth century were found several molds used for the casting of bronze tripod legs. Such bronze tripods were enormous affairs with three massive legs supporting a large bronze cauldron. These tripod cauldrons have been found at Olympia and Delphi and were offered as aristocratic dedications to the gods. The finds of molds in so early a context is startling enough, but this is nothing compared to the discovery of thirteen such tripod cauldrons on Ithaca in the Cave of Polis with ornamentation on the legs closely matching that of the Lefkandi molds. The earliest of the Ithacan tripods date to the late tenth or early ninth century—close enough to the date of the Lefkandi molds to make a match at least possible, perhaps likely. Even without the close match between molds and tripod legs, it is probable that at least some of the Ithacan tripods were left there by Euboean traders and perhaps manufactured by them as well.

The significance of the Ithacan tripods becomes apparent when we recall the gifts bestowed on Odysseus by the Phaeacian king Alcinous. At

*Odyssey* xiii.13 Alcinous instructs each of his chief men to give a great tripod and cauldron to Odysseus as parting gifts. Later in the same book (xiii.345–371) after the Phaeacians have put Odysseus and all his gifts ashore on Ithaca, Athena instructs Odysseus to hide the gifts including the tripods in a nearby cave sacred to the Nymphs.

It is exceedingly risky to attempt the identification of geographic features based on ancient poetic descriptions. For one thing a number of such caves are scattered about the shores of modern Ithaki, but the essential point is that it matters little whether the Cave of Polis is the one Homer was describing or even the one that an historical Odysseus might have visited. Clearly, the Ithacans themselves at some point in antiquity made an identification between the Cave of Polis and Homer's cave in the *Odyssey*. Nor were Ithacans the only, or even the primary, visitors to the cave. During the late Dark Age, Ithaca was part of a northwest Greek trading network, and by the ninth century the island had become one of the last Greek ports of call for traders voyaging north into the Adriatic and west to Italy and Sicily. These traders, mostly Euboean at first but later Corinthian, seem already to have been familiar with tales of Odysseus some decades before Homer. Otherwise why would tripod cauldrons have been placed as dedications in the Cave of Polis?

Other finds from the cave indicate that it, like the one described in the *Odyssey*, was originally sacred to the Nymphs. It should be noted here that the usual dedications at such shrines include small figurines and masks. The dedication of such expensive items as tripod cauldrons in a cave sacred to the Nymphs is perhaps unique even where, as is often the case, the Nymphs share a sanctuary with other gods or heroes. Indeed, the Cave of Polis also received dedications to the great Olympian goddesses Athena, Hera, and Artemis, but these dedications appear to be sporadic and late. In any case, large dedications to deities were rarely made in caves, but rather belonged to major cult centers such as Delphi, Olympia, or the Argive Heraion. It is mainly from these centers, and the relatively obscure Cave of Polis, that tripod dedications have been found.

In summary, we find at a very early date, a full century or more before Homer, Greek traders and adventurers, Euboean and Corinthian, visiting the Cave of Polis on Ithaca where, in imitation of Odysseus, they dedicate tripod cauldrons. Here it is important to examine what the hero Odysseus must have meant to these early voyagers. Odysseus, like them, had sailed into uncharted seas and visited strange, unknown islands and coasts inhabited by equally strange people. Tales of the Phaeacians who knew the law and were generous to strangers and Cyclopes and Laestrygonians who knew no law and were savage must have had special meaning to the early voyagers. The trepidation that they no doubt felt at the possibility of encountering monsters and savage tribes must have been eased somewhat by the equal possibility of coming across more enlightened folk anxious to trade. The business of sailing even well-known waters was risky enough, as the poet Hesiod testifies in his *Works and Days* (618–694), but how much more risky it was to sail into the little known Adriatic or the waters off the south and west coasts of Italy. Odysseus had made just such a voyage, and although it cost him all his companions and ships, still he was allowed to return laden with gifts, among which were probably thirteen tripod cauldrons.[1] In the *Odyssey*, Odysseus stows the gifts of the Phaeacians in a cave sacred to the Nymphs just up from the beach on Ithaca. He promises the Nymphs that if they keep his trove safe, he will make them gifts if ever he is allowed to dwell on Ithaca again in peace (*Od.* xiii.356–359). The epic ends before Odysseus fulfills his promise. The dedication of the tripod cauldrons can thus be seen not merely as a dedication to Odysseus as an exemplar of the early Euboean and Corinthian traders, but also as a fulfillment of Odysseus' promise.

### The Cup of Nestor

The stories of Odysseus and other Homeric heroes accompanied the early Greek voyagers up and down the Adriatic and across to south Italy and Sicily. In the Kingdom of Epirus in northwest Greece, tales of Odysseus vied with those of Achilles' son Neoptolemus for popularity. Odysseus was said to have married the queen of Thesprotia, a part of Epirus, thus founding their royal house, while Neoptolemus seems to have founded the royal house of Molossia, another Epirote region. In some tales, Neoptolemus' queen was the Trojan Andromache, the widow of Hector. Likewise in Italy and Sicily, Odysseus is not the only hero to have been imported along with the Euboean and Corinthian trade goods. The names of Diomedes and Philoctetes and the stories associated with them were made known, with tales centering on Diomedes prevailing along the Adriatic coast and those of Philoctetes in the extreme south of Italy and Sicily.

Euboean traders had been visiting these coasts since the ninth century, and by the later eighth century they had established colonies at Kyme (Cumae to Latin authors) just north of the Bay of Naples, and on the island of Pithecoussae (modern Ischia) just across from the bay. In 1954 while excavating a cremation burial, the sherds of a small cup, or *skyphos*, were found scattered among the ashes. The burial was that of a twelve-year old boy, the son of an upper-middle-class or perhaps aristocratic family judging from the large number of other vessels included among the grave goods. With so many other items in the burial, the cup might easily have been overlooked were it not for the three lines of writing scratched on the cup's surface. It was estimated that both the burial and the cup dated to the second half of the eighth century, or c. 735–720. The cup appears to have been of Rhodian manufacture, but the writing has been characterized as "standard Euboean script" in retrograde.[2] The term *retrograde* refers to the practice, common in many early Greek inscriptions, of writing right to left in the manner of the Phoenician and other West Semitic scripts from which the Greek alphabet was ultimately derived.

These three lines of writing on a humble *skyphos* were of major importance for a number of reasons. First, this short inscription is quite an early example of Greek writing, which is generally thought to have been introduced to Greece by Phoenician traders in the early or middle eighth century. It is also, after the Dipylon *oinochoe* (wine cup) inscription of c. 740–730, the oldest alphabetic inscription of any length in Greek, and almost certainly the oldest literary parody, or indeed allusion, in Europe. Furthermore, the second and third lines of the inscription are hexameter verses that, together with the prose first line, were applied to the cup during a *symposion*, or *symposium* (a drinking together, or a drinking party) as we would call it today. The *symposion* was an aristocratic institution of long standing, the most famous of which was Plato's *Symposium* attended by Socrates, Aristophanes, and Alcibiades, and at which the table talk involved a philosophical discussion of the nature of love. Earlier *symposia* were no doubt more rambunctious and less elevated than the late fifth-century example recounted by Plato. The Pithecoussae cup is among the earliest evidence for this venerable institution.

Let us now look at the inscription on the cup[3]:

I am the delicious cup of Nestor.
Whoever drinks of this cup, straightway that man
the desire of beautiful-crowned Aphrodite will seize.

It is possible, but unlikely, that the cup really did belong to Nestor—that is, that the cup's owner, the boy in the burial, was named Nestor. It was in fact uncommon for children to be named after characters from Greek myth and legend until the third or second century. Almost certainly this cup was dedicated in playful parody to Homer's Nestor, the wise, though long-winded, king of Pylos who was ever willing to give sage advice to Agamemnon and Achilles or anyone else who might listen.

We have characterized these verses as a literary parody, but the joke is many-layered. The simple *skyphos* from Pithecoussae is nothing like the gigantic gold object depicted in the *Iliad*. "Another man with great effort could lift it full from the table" is how Homer describes it (xi.635). The Cup of Nestor from Pithecoussae simply does not compare with the wine cauldron of Nestor from the epic. The parody goes further in making fun of Nestor himself. The "Gerenian horseman" as he is often called in the *Iliad* and *Odyssey* was an old man, and, we must suppose, well beyond succumbing to the wiles of the love goddess Aphrodite. The verses are also parodying inscriptions found on other bowls and cups. Such inscriptions often follow the formula: "I am the cup of X," followed by a curse. Another cup from Kyme, across the bay from Pithecoussae and dating to c. 675–650, bears the inscription:

> I am the oil flask of Tataie.
> Whoever steals me shall be struck blind.

The inscription shows a community of colonists, far from their home on Euboea, whose knowledge of the Epic Tradition was secure enough that they could make fun of it. So early is the cup and burial, however, that the question arises as to just whose version of the Epic Tradition the colonists were parodying. The *Iliad* is often dated to the middle eighth century and the *Odyssey* to the period 730–710. Those who placed the "Cup of Nestor" in the boy's burial on Pithecoussae are likely to have been Homer's contemporaries, and thus it is possible that the version that was being parodied was one earlier than Homer.

## The Epic Tradition in Italy and Sicily

The tales of the various heroes were not simply stories that the Greek traders and colonists told to each other, but were taken up and spread abroad by the non-Greek populations encountered by the Greeks. The Greeks often used the heroes to help mediate the strangeness they felt in the presence of non-Greeks. It was assumed, for instance, that Odysseus or Neoptolemus founded the various tribal divisions in non-Greek Epirus mentioned above. Philoctetes seems to have been particularly favored in southern Italy and Sicily as a mediator between Greek and non-Greek. At the start of the Trojan War, he had been bitten by a poisonous snake while sacrificing to Apollo on the non-Greek island of Lemnos. His wound proved incurable, and his companions left him in the care of the Lemnians while they continued on to Troy. Only in the final year of the war, when it was discovered that Troy would not fall unless the Greeks recovered the bow and arrows of Heracles, then in Philoctetes' possession, did Agamemnon relent, sending Odysseus and Diomedes to Lemnos to fetch Philoctetes. Thus, this hero, who had spent ten years in the company of strangers, seemed admirably suited to intercede between Greek and non-Greek in colonization efforts.

Although it seems eminently reasonable for Greeks in alien circumstances to tell stories of Greek foundations of non-Greek tribes, towns, and even royal dynasties, it is less clear why the objects of these tales—the Epirotes, Macedonians, Italians, and Sicilians—should not only accept these stories but take pride in them. One might argue that such borrowing was a predictable response of a less developed culture in admiration of the superior military and social organization of the Greek traders and colonists, or that the native peoples were simply engaging in a sort of *quid pro quo*, as if to say, "Let these Greeks say what they want of our origins, so long as they continue to visit us with trade goods!" But the first argument, particularly as it relates to the earliest contacts of the tenth to eighth centuries, is untenable since it is not clear that Greek military or social organization was much in advance of the native communities. Although the second argument might carry some weight by itself, it does not explain why native peoples should take pride in or broadcast these stories. Perhaps Irad Malkin, who has made a fine study of the spread of the *nostos* legends, has provided the best explanation.[4] Throughout antiquity the Greeks tended to pay little heed to what non-Greek peoples had to say about their own origins and were more than happy to supply them with stories out of their already abundant storehouse of tales. So sure were the Greeks of the accuracy of their stories that non-Greeks, who may have had no clear notion of their origins, tended to bow to the Greeks' superior certainty. Add to this certainty the beauty of the Greek medium for imparting these tales. The power of Homeric epic has been unmatched for nearly three thousand years, and it is safe to say that it had no peer in eighth-century Epirus or Italy. The Italians, Sicilians, and Epirote peoples were therefore entranced into accepting as true the tales the Greeks told of them.

One surprising element of these *nostos* stories is the number of Trojans who accompany the Greek heroes on their journeys. We have already seen that Neoptolemus and the Trojan Andromache were said to have founded the royal house of Molossia. She was Neoptolemus' captive and came to him as his share of the spoils of war. However, another of Neoptolemus' Trojan companions was Helenus, a son of Priam and a seer. One story has it that Neoptolemus and Helenus were allies who joined forces in overthrowing the Molossian king, after which Neoptolemus founded a new dynasty. Philoctetes is said to have been joined by the Trojan Aegesthes in south Italy where they founded several cities. This Aegesthes is supposed to have gone on to Sicily where he founded Segesta. The Trojan Antenor accompanied Menelaus to Africa following the destruction of Troy and later journeyed to northeast Italy where he founded New Troy, later to be known as Venice. Odysseus himself is said to have gone to Italy accompanied by Aeneas where they founded a number of Etruscan towns in Italy north of the Tiber. Rome, itself heavily influenced by both Etruscans and Greeks, and for a time in the sixth century ruled by an Etruscan dynasty, was thought to have been founded by Odysseus and Aeneas.[5]

The various non-Greek peoples who were the subjects of these foundation myths by and large accepted and took pride in them. For those who had no clear idea, or perhaps many conflicting ideas, of their origins, such tales provided a welcome means of self-identification. It was an ironic result of the popularization of these stories that non-Greek communities in the Italian and Epirote hinterland were able to point to a more ancient and illustrious origin than the Greek colonial communities that were then springing up along the coasts. Sometimes, however, non-Greek communities would make variations of these tales, not so much to distinguish themselves from the Greeks as from their non-Greek neighbors whose foundation story was the same or similar. Thus, although the Molossians told of a joint foundation by Neoptolemus and Helenus, their neighbors, the Epirote Chaones, insisted that Helenus alone was their founder. This variation apparently arose to avoid being confused with the Molossians.

## ROME AND THE EPIC TRADITION

A similar phenomenon, one with greater implications for the future, occurred at Rome. As we have seen, the story current at Rome and in Etruria in the seventh and sixth centuries featured a joint foundation by Odysseus and Aeneas. This tale appears to have been popular alongside the canonical myth of Rome's founding by the twins Romulus and Remus, and in some versions seems to have been connected to it. Odysseus is said to have fathered two sons with the powerful, divine sorceress Circe, Latinus and Agrius, with Latinus being the ancestor of Romulus and Remus. Circe who could transform men into beasts appears to have been a popular figure in early Rome; in some accounts, the wolf who suckled the twins was herself Circe transformed. After the foundation of the Roman Republic at the end of the sixth century, Odysseus' popularity as co-founder began to decline in favor of Aeneas as sole founder. For the Roman elite, newly independent and self-governing, there was a strong inclination to distinguish the Roman identity from their Greek and Etruscan neighbors. The adoption of a new identity became particularly critical with the recent expulsion of the highly Hellenized Etruscan dynasty of the Tarquins from Rome. For some years the survivors of this dynasty remained nearby, trying to win support from the Etruscan towns for a restoration. A foundation story favoring Aeneas over Odysseus, though remaining an essentially Greek tale, would be distinctive enough to act as a rallying point against either Greeks or Etruscans.

Having chosen Aeneas over Odysseus, the Romans from the fifth century on found themselves on the opposing side of a new Greek dialectic. Early in this century, in response to the threat of Persian expansion, the idea of Greco-Trojan collaboration previously popular among Greek colonists, began to give way to a more truculent attitude in which the Asiatic Trojans became identical with Persians who were conceived of as barbarians. Herodotus alludes to this idea in the first book of his *Histories* when he mentions the idea that the Persian invasion was an act of revenge for the destruction of Troy. Although he ultimately rejects this notion, Herodotus later (vii.40–47) lends some credence to it in reporting that the Persian king Xerxes, when he had reached the site of Troy on the eve of his invasion of Greece, made sacrifice to Trojan Athena and the spirits of the Trojan dead. In any case, the Greeks' changed attitude toward the Trojans tended to reinforce Roman adherence to Aeneas. Their allegiance to Aeneas became solidified when in the third century King Pyrrhus of Epirus, preparing for his invasion of Italy, asked for Greek support against the "Trojan colonists" at Rome.

Finally, the Roman successes in the east Mediterranean against Alexander's successor states during the second and first centuries seemed to the Roman nationalists of the Late Republic and the Augustan Age to be a fitting revenge for the Greek destruction of Troy, the home of Rome's progenitor. By this time Aeneas, as glorified in the first-century poet Virgil's great epic had become the subject of Julio-Claudian and ultimately Roman state propaganda. It is interesting that the *Aeneid* combines and reverses the order of the two large themes of the Homeric epics: first the wanderings and then the confrontation between foes. The *Aeneid* is not, like the *Iliad*, a story of revenge. It is rather a story of colonial conquest, and one with which the Roman imperialists of the time must have identified.

Rome was not the only power to use Homeric legend to suit the purpose of military and political expansion. Nor was Pyrrhus the first Epirote king to cast a covetous eye on Italy. In the fourth century, Alexander of Epirus, Alexander of Macedon's maternal uncle, led a force to Italy intent on "recovering" the city of Brindisium (Brindisi). This town, according to late sources, had been founded by Aetolians led by Diomedes. These Aetolians were driven out by the Apulians, and when an embassy was sent from Aetolia to Brindisium demanding perpetual possession of the land, the Apulians buried them alive within the city walls, thereby giving the ambassadors everything for which they had asked. Alexander of Epirus laid claim to the town based on this story. When the Lucanians, who then held Brindisium, refused Alexander's demands, he attacked the city but was killed in battle in 330.

## ALEXANDER THE GREAT

More famous by far is the case of Alexander of Epirus' nephew and namesake, Alexander of Macedon. Alexander the Great could claim an illustrious heritage on both sides of his family. His mother Olympias was a Molossian princess and sister of Alexander of Epirus, and as such could claim descent both from the Greek hero Neoptolemus and the Trojan Andromache. His father Philip II of Macedon claimed descent from the hero and demigod Heracles. But it was his mother's ancestry in which Alexander took most pride. Neoptolemus was the son of Achilles, Homer's foremost hero in the *Iliad*, and Alexander seems to have taken him as a model from an early age.

A number of factors in Alexander's upbringing appear to have accounted for, or at least to have reinforced, his fixation on the *Iliad* and specifically on the hero Achilles. First, there was the example of Macedonia itself. At a time when most Greek communities were either oligarchies or democracies, Macedonia, like Sparta, was a conservative society that maintained its attachment to kingship. Unlike the Spartan kings whose actions were severely limited, the Macedonian king was closer to a true monarch who exercised much more freedom of action. In fact, in Sparta kingship was vested in two men of two different royal lineages, a situation that further tended to weaken the power of individual kings. Still the power of the Macedonian king was not unlimited but was closer to the model of a medieval king whose powers were theoretically balanced by his feudal barons. The king of Macedon's power and freedom of action were, in fact, not unlike these of Agamemnon, balanced and checked as he was by his chief warriors at Troy. The Macedonian king, like Agamemnon, was commander-in-chief but could not govern in total independence from his baronial council. So Macedonia at the time of Alexander could perhaps best be characterized as an aristocracy featuring a strong, though somewhat limited, monarchy.

A number of other conservative features of Macedonian society were reminiscent both of the aristocratic warrior ethos found in the *Iliad* and in the aristocratic societies of ninth- and eighth-century Greece. One was the institution of the king's *hetairoi* or Companions, aristocratic warriors who followed the king into battle and in times of peace feasted at his table. Both Philip and Alexander maintained a picked force of Companions throughout their reigns. Another factor was adherence to the aristocratic ideal of *arête*, a complex quality roughly equivalent to Roman *virtu* and comprising the qualities of excellence, manliness, and prowess. Only through the achievement of *arête* could the Macedonian kingship as an institution be justified. It was a common opinion among earlier Greeks and certainly shared by Alexander that Achilles was the greatest exemplar of *arête*.

One might argue that any young Macedonian nobleman growing up in such a society would be predisposed to act as Alexander did. If so, this predisposition was greatly strengthened by the examples of his mother who reveled in her Homeric lineage, making sure that her son was aware of his heritage, and of Philip whose dominance of the Greek states following the Battle of Chaeronea in 338 seemed an imitation of the conquest of the Peloponnese by the Sons of Heracles after the Trojan War. The pairing of Philip and Achilles as influences on the young Alexander brings us to another ancient quality seen often in aristocratic societies—the *agon*, or *agonisma*. *Agon* is any struggle or contest, and it may be argued that Alexander had adopted the quality of *agonisma*—seeing life as a contest by which one gains distinction. Thus, Alexander not only modeled himself after his father and Achilles, but also viewed himself as competing against them. Philip had made Macedonia the strongest state in the Greek world, and Achilles had proven himself to be the most formidable warrior in the Trojan War. But Achilles had been killed before Troy fell, so while there was little for Alexander to do in Greece save maintain his father's hegemony, his great aim came to be the completion and surpassing of Achilles' exploits.

Alexander's desire to be a second Achilles was explicitly sanctioned by his tutor, one Lysimachus. This man continually referred to himself as Phoenix (Achilles' guardian), to Philip as Peleus, the father of Achilles, and of course to Alexander as Achilles himself. But if Lysimachus was Phoenix, then Aristotle was the centaur Cheiron, to whom the boy Achilles was apprenticed. Aristotle, one of the greatest minds of antiquity, had been hired by the Macedonian court to instruct the young Alexander in science, mathematics, and philosophy, and it was a misfortune certainly for the Persians and perhaps for future East-West relations that Alexander seems not to have been much interested in any of these disciplines. Although Alexander, while in Asia, was assiduous in sending exotic plants and animals back to Macedonia for the furtherance of Aristotle's studies, it was plain that philosophy could not compete with Homeric poetry, nor Aristotle with Achilles for Alexander's affections. One thing Aristotle conveyed to Alexander seems to have left a mark: that was the prejudice among Greeks beginning as early as the late sixth century that all Asiatics were inferior and were addicted to tyranny and sensuality. Thus, the Persians and other Asiatic peoples came to be seen as lacking in the very quality of *arête* that Alexander saw as the finest trait of the Greek heroes at Troy, most particularly Achilles.

Given the tendencies at work in Greek and Macedonian society, the young prince's education and influences, and his obsession with Homer and Achilles, the subsequent conquests of Asia and Egypt seem almost inevitable, particularly when these forces were coupled with Alexander's undoubted genius as a field commander and a charismatic leader of men. But Alexander's motives were not simply to equal and outstrip Philip or even Achilles. In some respects, Alexander's conquest of the Persian Empire is the mirror image of Rome's conquest of Greece and the Hellenistic kingdoms two centuries later. Both, to a greater or lesser degree, used the Trojan War as a rallying point. By the first century if not earlier, Rome saw itself as the avenger of the Trojan Aeneas. Alexander, whose first destination within the Persian Empire was the site of Troy, saw himself doubly as an avenger: first for the Persian invasions of Greece, and second as the avenger of Achilles against that model of corrupt, Asiatic sensuality, the Trojan Paris.

## Summary

In this chapter we have traced the development of the story of the Trojan War from the collapse of the world of Bronze Age citadels and palaces to the world of the newly thriving city-states of the eighth century. From there we have followed the spread of these tales during the first millennium from their home in Greece and the Aegean east to Asia Minor and west to Italy and Sicily. By the third century, these tales would have been known as far east as the Indus Valley and as far south as the cataracts of the Nile. By the first century c.e., owing to Roman expansion into northwestern Europe, the Matter of Troy—the Homeric poems and Virgil's *Aeneid*—would have been known as far north as Scotland and as far west as the Atlantic coast of Portugal and Morocco.

The *Aeneid* of Virgil which initially served as a sort of counterargument to Homer's glorification of the Greek heroes, acted in the long run to preserve an awareness of the story of the Trojan War during the succeeding centuries of the Roman imperium and the following Medieval Age. Meanwhile, Alexander's conquests made the numerous peoples of the Middle East familiar with the poems of Homer. By the early medieval period when the former provinces of the Western Roman Empire had fragmented into a number of petty, warring kingdoms, the new, cosmopolitan Islamic centers of Baghdad in the east, Alexandria in Egypt, and the cities of Moorish Spain in the west preserved and popularized the poems of Homer as well as the writings of many other Classical and Hellenistic Greek authors. Between the semibarbarian states of transalpine Europe and Islam there was the Eastern Roman Empire, known to us as the Byzantine Empire, which remained intact for a thousand years after the collapse of the Western Empire. Here, too, Greek writings of all sorts were preserved and commented on. The preservation, transmission, and commentary on ancient Greek literature by Islamic and Byzantine scholars were crucial for the cultural development of the West. The Italian Renaissance and the awakening of rational and critical thought in Western Europe would have been greatly impeded were it not for the transmission of Classical Greek writing by Syrian and Moorish traders or Byzantine refugees from the destruction of the East Roman Empire during the fourteenth and fifteenth centuries. The West owes a large debt to Islam and Byzantium—a debt that has been forgotten and remains unpaid.

We mentioned the possibility that the traditions surrounding an historical Trojan War may have become attached to a preexisting Bronze Age epic cycle featuring the capture of an island or coastal city by a seaborne army. Such a situation would be an example of an historical event influencing the development of a poetic tradition. From the eighth century B.C.E. on, however, we find the opposite situation. The spread and popularization of Homeric poetry throughout the Mediterranean Basin and large portions of Europe, Asia, and North Africa was to some degree the result of social, political, and military behaviors being influenced by epic poetry. This is not necessarily a good thing. From the late nineteenth to the mid-twentieth century C.E., Germans and Austrians abused and corrupted the Arthurian romances and medieval German epics in the creation of the dystopia known as the Third Reich. Similarly, Alexander's corrupt use of Homeric epic in a misguided, and ultimately unsuccessful, attempt to create a Greco-Asiatic Empire on the ruins of Persia was motivated by similar base impulses.

A healthy admiration of Homeric epic or Arthurian romance does not have to result in such evil. The Greeks were fond of the motto "All things in moderation," and they had a word for actions that violated that dictum—*hubris*. Achilles, not as he was imagined by Alexander but as he was represented in the *Iliad*, is indeed guilty of violating this fundamental ethic of right behavior. Although his anger against Agamemnon is understandable, his reaction in absenting himself and his Myrmidons from the fighting at a crucial time of the war is immoderate. Achilles himself pays dearly for this unwise fit of anger with the loss of his best friend Patroclus. At the close of the poem, Achilles has come to understand that such behavior does not go unpunished. A proper reading of Homer and the tragedians who followed him is that the favor of the gods does not give men license to do anything they desire, but rather to know that he who is favored today may be destroyed tomorrow. The Greeks then were realistic in their approach to life and in their relations with the gods. They were also hopeful, for while the hero who gets above himself and acts arrogantly will be punished, he may also, like Achilles, learn from his mistakes.

## NOTES

1. The total of thirteen tripod cauldrons is arrived at by adding Alcinous' twelve chief men (*Od.* viii.390) to Alcinous himself. The fact that thirteen tripod cauldrons were found in the Cave of Polis appears to be a happy coincidence since the evidence seems to indicate their placement in the cave one or two at a time between 900 and 700.

2. Barry Powell, "Why Was the Greek Alphabet Invented? The Epigraphical Evidence," *Classical Antiquity* 8:2 (1989): 321–350.

3. The translation is that of Barry Powell, Ibid, who follows the reconstruction of P. A. Hansen, "Pithecusan Humour: The Interpretation of 'Nestor's Cup' Reconsidered," *Glotta* 59 (1976): 25–43.

4. Irad Malkin, *The Returns of Odysseus: Colonization and Ethnicity* (Berkeley and Los Angeles: University of California Press, 1998).

5. Aeneas, Antenor, Helenus, and Aegesthes share a common trait in that stories are told of each of them which cast doubt on their loyalty to Troy. Antenor had at times advised Priam to return Helen to the Greeks, and the tyrannical behavior of Deiphobus, upon whom Priam relied after the deaths of Hector and Paris, drove both Antenor and Helenus to desert the Greeks. Aeneas was rarely on good terms with Priam, who seems to have had little respect for him or his father Anchises. Aeneas, who did not join the Trojan side until after Achilles had sacked his city of Lyrnessos, had little reason to continue fighting

after Achilles' death. In the last year of the war, he was implicated in Antenor's plot to betray the city. Aegesthes is the exception that proves the rule. This little known hero was born in Sicily, the son of Aegesta and the river god Crimissus. Aegesta was the daughter of a Trojan noble named Phoenodamas. He had been slain in a dispute with King Laomedon of Troy, the father of Priam. Afterward Laomedon sold Aegesta to Sicilian slave traders who carried her off to Sicily where she was freed by Aphrodite. So although her son Aegesthes was a Trojan by blood, he had no cause to love Troy.

# CHAPTER 5

# TROY AND THE TWENTY-FIRST CENTURY

When we were invited to contribute a volume to the Greenwood Guides to Historic Events of the Ancient World, we were pleased but at the same time somewhat puzzled: why does the Trojan War stand beside the rise of the Han or Roman empires as an event that defines a milestone in the long human story? The Han and Roman empires established in general outline the future political and cultural demarcations of China and Western Europe, respectively. Can similar claims be made for the Trojan War as both the fulfillment of previous, and the harbinger of future, political tendencies? We hope that you have been persuaded of the Trojan War's centrality in the world of the Late Bronze Age, not only as a likely occurrence but also illustrative of the international character of the civilizations of the eastern Mediterranean at that time. In addition, we have argued for its significance for later Greeks and, even more extensively in time and place, for peoples of a great many times and places. But additional questions need to be addressed: why should Troy be the window to understanding the Greek Age of Heroes in the twenty-first century? Why should we, in 2004 C.E., worry about people and events so seemingly remote? What is the value of staying familiar with this "legend?" A good beginning is to follow the view of Greeks of the Classical Age regarding the power of the poetry.

## HOMER AND THE WORD "POET" ARE SYNONYMOUS

Early in the eighteenth century, John Sheffield, duke of Buckinghamshire, declared in his *Essay on Poetry*:

Read Homer once, and you can read no more
For all books else appear so dull and poor,
Verse will seem prose, yet often on him look
And you will hardly need another Book.

This opinion is in agreement with that of the philosopher Xenophanes, the first writer to mention the name of Homer, in the sixth century B.C.E. Some two centuries later, Plato described Homer as the best and the most divine of poets. Cicero expressed the general view of the Romans in stating that Homer made the word "poet" his own proper name through his excellence. Since antiquity, Homer has been the subject of accolades that have become universal as knowledge of the epics has spread. Another form of praise is imitation, and, as early as the third century B.C.E., the *Odyssey* was translated into Latin so that the Romans could read it. The great epic of the Latin poet Virgil combined the tales of war sung in the *Iliad* with the long journey remembered in the *Odyssey* in his *Aeneid*. More recently, James Joyce and Nikos Kazantzakis were inspired by Homer in producing their respective epics, *Ulysses* and *The Odyssey: A Modern Sequel*. To sample the number and nature of the influence of Homer's epics, one can now turn to the Internet: Amazon furnished 5,658 results to a search for the *Iliad* and 16,072 for the *Odyssey*.[1] To be sure, there are some duplications in these lists: different editions of the same text or translation or study. Still the quantity is staggering.

The range of titles is equally mind-boggling. A search for *Iliad* produces such results as *A Byzantine Iliad*; *Realms of Gold: An Iliad of Our Time*; *The Mourner's Song: War and Remembrance from the Iliad to Vietnam*; *An American Iliad: The Story of the Civil War*. *Odyssey* called up even greater diversity and a greater number of titles as *The African-American Odyssey*; *2001: A Space Odyssey*; *The Journey of Man: A Genetic Odyssey*; *Left Illusions: An Intellectual Odyssey*; *Earth Odyssey: Around the World in Search of Our Environmental Future*; *Mathematics with Infotrac: A Practical Odyssey*. These examples are a tiny tip of the iceberg.

To define the primary reason for this praise, we need go no further than the power of the poetry and the force of the tales. They are classics. Expanding on the basic definition that a classic is something of recognized value that serves as a standard of excellence, we can identify three qualities that raise an object or work to this level. First it is rooted in elemental human concerns. Thus, it is timeless and can reach across great expanses of time and speak to widely different people. As a dear friend was passing her last days in hospice, she asked to hear particular parts of the *Iliad*, one of which was the passage where the divine horses of Achilles wept over the death of Patroclus:

> They were unwilling to go aboard ship onto the wide Hellespont
> Nor into battle together with the Achaeans
> But stood as immovable as a stele, one that is fixed upon
> The tomb of a dead man or woman.
> Just so they stood firm holding the splendid chariot.
> Their heads drooping toward the ground, as warm tears
> Ran down from their eyes they poured upon the ground
> In grief for their charioteer. The tears stained
> Their thick manes as they flowed under the yoke cushion
> On both sides of the yoke.
>     (xvii.432–440, translated by Carol Thomas and Tristan Goldman)

Surely this is death's ache, timelessly evoked.

Second, it is brilliantly demonstrated within its own time frame. The power of the epics was openly admitted by the Greeks of antiquity to be notable in their own right. The tragedian Aeschylus described his own extraordinary plays as "slices from the banquet of Homer," while the philosopher Plato spoke of Homer as "THE" poet even though Plato's own style is often powerfully poetic. Consequently, a classic is admirable in its own right.

These two features combine for a third: a classic provokes a desire to know more about it and to use this knowledge to understand and inform one's own world. An interesting example of this quality is associated with studies like that of J. Shay's *Achilles in Vietnam: Combat Trauma and the Undoing of Character* whose premise is that the experiences of Vietnam combat veterans and those of the warriors in Homer's *Iliad* illuminate each other in demonstrating and furthering an understanding of the re-actions of humans caught up in warfare.[2] Symptoms of post-traumatic stress that arise from witnessing and experiencing the horrors of battle are similar in widely separated times in human history. As Shay summa-rizes them, the major symptoms of post-traumatic stress disorder include the loss of control of mental functions; a persistent readiness of body and mind for lethal danger which has a potential for explosive violence and chronic health problems stemming from this condition; carryover and use of combat survival skills in civilian life; an ongoing expectation of betrayal; loss of the capacity for social trust; preoccupation with the veteran's own military/governmental authorities as well as feelings of despair, isolation, meaninglessness, thoughts of suicide, and the abuse of alcohol and drugs.

The opening lines of the *Iliad* announce its binding theme:

> Sing goddess, the wrath of Achilles, son of Peleus,
> That cursed wrath that hurled myriad woes to the Achaeans.

And rage Achilles does, first against Agamemnon who has dishonored him, causing Achilles and his men to withdraw from battle and, finally, returning to battle, against any and every Trojan, like fire sweeping in fury setting all ablaze, so did Achilles sweep everywhere until the black earth ran with blood. He strained to win glory with invincible hands covered with gore (*Iliad* xx.490–503). In its striking encapsulation of the raw emotions of war, Achilles' rage not only adds another dimension to Homer's epic poems but casts light on the behavior of veterans in all cultures. Thus, through a close reading of Achilles' wrath we may come to understand such events as the Mylai massacre. Nicholas D. Kristof, who seems more than commonly attuned to the explanatory power of Homer, wrote in the *New York Times* (October 22, 2003) using Troy for another purpose in a column entitled "Swift-Footed W."

> On the eve of our invasion of Iraq, I went to ancient Troy in Turkey. It's a haunting spot, quiet and deserted, though if you scrunch up your eyes you may still catch a glimpse of Helen on the walls. Those walls include a gate that shows signs of having been widened—or so my guide claimed, probably fancifully—as if to accommodate a giant wooden horse. "The Iliad" is the greatest war story ever told, but it's not fundamentally about war . . . but rather about how great men confront tragedy, learn moderation and become wise.

In similar memorable fashion, the *Odyssey* reaches across centuries through its powerful, timeless theme of journeying and homecoming. The bard again calls on the Muses, this time to sing of the much traveled, wily man who wandered ever so far after he had taken the holy citadel of Troy. He saw the cities of countless men and learned their ways of thinking but suffered many woes upon the sea. He faced unbelievable dangers such as the Cyclops Polyphemus who made a meal of a good many of Odysseus' men. The nymph Calypso held him captive with her love and magical spells for years. And he was washed ashore on the island of the Phaeacians whose ships outpace even a hawk, the quickest thing on wings. Odysseus finally returned to Ithaca but encountered other woes there, having to establish his identity—after an absence of twenty years—to those closest to him and to those he had once led as their respected king. Although the specific figures in this tale of journeying are not those a modern traveler would fear or hope to find, the tale itself is "eerily modern" in its ability to speak to any adventurer, modern or ancient. Both epics include a full sweep of being—mortals, immortals, animals, both familiar and alien to normal experience, and the natural world. Their range of emotions is equally broad, and to repeat our point of departure, their poetic form has a power of its own.

## THE SUBSTANCE OF LEGENDS

The tales of Troy are just that, stories that have epic proportions, so grand that they are often classified as legends or myths. Memory of a long, drawn-out battle at Troy reaches back to a time far earlier than the lifetime of the singer who admits that it would take many men to lift a boulder that a single hero could raise aloft without the assistance of another. Much of the action in both the *Iliad* and *Odyssey* rests with the gods who insert themselves regularly and easily into the affairs of mortals. Why should historians living in the twenty-first century concern themselves with this kind of "evidence" of the past?

The short answer is that we have come to a new understanding of the nature of legend that has been found to be grounded in reality. Recent examination of the different nature of remembrance in oral and literate cultures offers another tool for penetrating life in societies without the skill of writing. Accounts of their pasts seem to be an integral part of all societies, even those without the knowledge of writing. For nonliterate societies, the means of preserving such knowledge will be different from the precise, durable accounts produced with the aid of writing. Remembered from generation to generation by word of mouth, they must take on a form and content that is memorable.

One aid to memory is the patterning of language: poetic patterns of speech are easier to recall than prose composition since they fit into a convenient metrical rhythm. And those who recount traditions often employ the additional aid of instrumental accompaniment just as performers in literate societies rely on guitars to stimulate their memory of the words of their songs. One modern performer admitted that he could sing for four or five hours without written words as long as he was playing his guitar. Without that stimulus, he might remember the words of two or three songs at most.[3] Other attributes of accounts passed on through speech alone concern the nature of the account. In the first place, there is a group recognition that a particular kind of information should be remembered and, thus, cast into memorable form. Although gifted bards craft the form, the substance of the tradition is communal knowledge. Occasions of offerings to the gods, ancestry of kings, momentous occasions, rules of the community—all of these kinds of information are likely to promote the crafting of memorable accounts to pass the knowledge to future generations for it would be foolish to ignore matters such as these. To increase memorability, certain features are important: a "plot" that is easy to follow, characters that are larger than ordinary folk, situations that hold the attention of the audience as well as the singer, and verbal "pictures" that can be seen in the mind's eye are regular traits of tales that originate in nonliterate societies. Moreover, such tales are human-centered. Other forms of life—animals, plants, divinities—relate closely to humans: plants talk, horses weep, gods give advice to mortals. The interaction is intense, and, as a consequence, the tale is filled with activity.

Historians are reluctant to admit oral traditions into the categories of evidence to reconstruct the past. For many, they belong elsewhere than in the list of proper evidence due to their nature and intent. Myth is a term derived from the Greek word *mythos* meaning word or speech and, by extension, a tale, story, or narrative in which the real world interacts easily with an imaginary world. In mixing the two realms, myth is often defined as fictitious. Legend is an account of a wonderful event, handed down for generations among a group of people and generally believed to have an historical basis, although that basis is not verifiable. A common differentiation between myth and legend is that myth turns on cosmic and divine subjects while mortals play a larger, though not exclusive, role in legend. Certain tales relating to the Trojan War can be classified as mythical. An example of a Trojan War myth is the Judgment of Paris in which the hero awards the Golden Apple to Aphrodite, thereby gaining the promise of possession of the most beautiful of women, Helen. Most of the characters in this tale—Aphrodite, Athena, Hera, and Hermes— are immortal. Only Paris is mortal.

On all counts, however, the Homeric poems seem to fit into the category of legend. While the gods are ever present, even to the extent of taking part in battle, it is the mortals who demand our attention. In addition, there are grounds for seriously examining the view that the poems do have an historical basis. One of the outstanding scholars of early Greek history in the first half of the twentieth century, Martin Paul Nilsson, observed that stories of Troy had been valuable guides to the archaeological discoveries at places like Hissarlik and Mycenae. What is more, he pointed out the connection between the sites to which the legendary cycles are attached and those where finds from the Bronze Age had been made. The leader of the Achaean force at Troy was Agamemnon, king of Mycenae; the great hero Heracles is linked with Tiryns; doomed King Oedipus ruled over Thebes; Theseus who defeated the Minotaur is from Athens, while the Minotaur itself was the creature of King Minos whose capital was Knossos on Crete; and the talkative elder Nestor ruled from Pylos. Each of these locations has revealed an impressive citadel dating to the late Bronze Age or the Age of Heroes, and, at present, excavations are underway at the site identified as ancient Iolchos near modern Volos that may well be the kingdom from which the Argonauts set sail. Although some of these places were important in later periods, many were either insignificant or absent in the Classical Age of Greek history. Nilsson concluded that the legends go back into the Mycenaean age, at least in their main outlines.

Other efforts to understand the true function of myth and legend concur with the conclusion of Nilsson. Investigating the nature of the earliest written evidence of Classical Greece, Geoffrey Kirk noted that Greek has few words to denote differences between myth and legend and, we may add, from other types of accounts that we might, from today's perspective, identify by specific terms. The poems of Hesiod, who lived in the early seventh century B.C.E. when alphabetic writing was just entering Greek culture, contain "that mixture of personification, allegory, speculative myth, fable, literal statement, loose association, intermittent logic, and native shrewdness—[that] was probably around in Greece for a very long time before him; and the stage when virtually all theorizing unconsciously took narrative and purely mythical form may have lain thousands of years in the past."[4] It is important to keep in mind the continued reliance on oral transmission even when literacy provided another tool. Only toward the end of the fifth century B.C.E.—that is, the time described as the Golden Age of Greek culture—did writing become the means of preserving the communal store of knowledge, and even then some Greek states—notably Sparta—persisted in relying on oral tradition. Surely the Spartans had need of some sort of systematic preservation of the rules of their society that had been established in the distant centuries of Spartan history.

Tales passed on from generation to generation by word of mouth lack the specificity of historical records: precise dates are one missing ingredient. Yet, as we have seen, physical remains from the past may provide at least part of that missing ingredient. In the belief that such tales embody remembrance of the actual past, we may test that hypothesis by means of physical remains from the past. One such believer was Heinrich Schliemann who began the endeavor of validating the tale of Troy. He was convinced that Homer's epics recounted actual events of the early past of Greek history. His evidence was the epics, but he realized the need to demonstrate that Greece had a history earlier than the usual date of 776 B.C.E. believed to define its beginnings. To fill that need, he determined to find physical proof by digging into the ground at likely locations.

## THE ROLE OF ARCHAEOLOGY

As we have seen in Chapter 2, archaeology is a relatively recent term used to designate the evidence that emerges from archaeological investigation. The work of archaeologists has become increasingly essential in understanding the human story since by far the largest portion of that story is not accompanied by written evidence. It reaches back a million or more years, while the invention of written symbols to express language occurred little more than 5,000 years ago. Even then, literacy did not come to be a distinguishing characteristic of most societies until the modern age.

People have always been interested in remains from the past. The father of history, Herodotus, traveled to see wondrous memorials of civilizations far more ancient than his own Greece. Pausanias, the Roman writer who produced the ancient equivalent of a travel guide to Greece, walked throughout the land of his subject recounting such details as the account of the Sanctuary of the Graces near Sparta where there is a stone tablet naming a champion of the pentathlon, a portrait of him, and a number of bronze tripods. In his description of the place, Pausanias mentions a richly detailed throne, and although he states, "It would weary my readers if I went through all its workmanship in detail," he proceeds to do just that before turning to an account of the construction and size of the throne (iii.18.6–19.5).

Despite the interest in artifacts, the formal study of them emerged only in the eighteenth century C.E. when an antiquarian attraction was joined by a quasiscientific scholarship. Discovery of more and more varied objects prompted a curiosity about their creation, use, and dating. It was no longer enough to merely possess an old papyrus, or something that might have been a tool rather than a strangely shaped piece of stone. By the early nineteenth century, serious investigators were coming to appreciate the great depth of the human past, and they turned their efforts to determining a relative chronology of finds. A basic framework that is still followed today divided the earliest human development into three Ages: the Stone Age with its three divisions of Old, Middle, and New (or Paleolithic, Mesolithic, and Neolithic); the Bronze Age; and the Iron Age. Absolute dating continues to shift as new evidence and techniques have become available and the pace of change varies according to regions under examination. Since much of the early evidence derived from the Ancient Near East and Egypt, the scheme emerging from that region dates Paleolithic from a million or more years ago to approximately 10,000 B.C.E.; Mesolithic, from c. 10,000 to 7000; Neolithic, 7000 to 3000; the Bronze Age endured from c. 3000 to 1200 B.C.E. when the Iron Age began.

This broad chronology, though advanced in the first half of the nineteenth century, was based on earlier discoveries that exploded the view that the history of humankind on Earth began in 4004 B.C.E. However, providing details of the three periods was largely the result of efforts in the second half of that century: the age of the great discoverers, particularly those whose interests were in the Ancient Near East and Egypt— men like Austen Henry Layard who started digging at Nimrud in ancient Assyria just before the middle of the century, discovering the palaces of the Assyrian kings; Flinders Petrie who began his investigations in Egypt in 1881 and over the next thirty-seven years carried on study at every major site; Henry Rawlinson who spent much of the four years from 1835 to 1839 perched precariously on a ladder standing on an 18- to 24-inch wide ledge about 75 feet up a sheer face of mountain rock east of Mesopotamia in order to copy an inscription written in three versions of cuneiform. He went on to decipher one form of the cuneiform as Old Persian dating to the realm of the great Persian king Darius I (522–486 B.C.E.).

Such pioneering work laid the foundation for a systematic study of the past through its physical remains, that is, archaeology, which in the twentieth century developed new field techniques and discovered new scientific aids that we have discussed earlier in order to produce syntheses of the wealth of factual information already at hand and still being uncovered. Yet, it is important to notice the areas that attracted the earliest attention: namely, civilizations attested in ancient, especially biblical, sources. Other regions of the Mediterranean were initially unknown regions, *terra incognita*. Current conditions were often a factor, particularly in the case of the Aegean with the uncertain political and economic health of the newly independent state of Greece and the mounting problems within the Ottoman Empire centered in Anatolia. Lack of evidence of early complex society also inhibited physical exploration: what fool would rely on the Homeric epics as a reliable starting point of investigation? Sensible people knew that Homer described a time and place that never existed. The poems were rousing epics, to be sure, but they were accounts of fictitious worlds of monumental struggles located at unknown places and sea voyages through realms of imaginary monsters as well as impossibly blissful kingdoms.

A few people, however, believed that the *Iliad* and *Odyssey* were memories of an actual past far earlier than the Classical Age of Greece. One of those people, as we have seen, was Heinrich Schliemann who, in spite of attacks on his findings, demonstrated his main point: there was a material reality to life in the Aegean sphere prior to the Classical Age of Greek history. It was the power of the Trojan epic that propelled the monumental task of producing a new view of ancient Greek history. Moreover, this demonstration helped to construct the foundations of a new scholarly field—prehistoric archaeology in the Aegean sphere. Its nature has changed dramatically since Schliemann's time. Now excavation is carefully controlled, and new scientific techniques have been developed to facilitate initial excavation. In addition to excavation, survey archaeology has become a recognized approach to understanding the larger context of individual sites by shifting attention from single major centers to examination of the interconnection of entire regions. Evidence from individual sites and regions has increased to the point that it is possible to learn connections between contemporary cultures throughout the Aegean and even in further reaches of the Mediterranean.

Schliemann's own work offered the fundamental base on which the changes were built. He believed that the larger region of a site must be investigated in order to appreciate its full nature. This is the premise of survey archaeology today. Moreover, knowing that comparative examples are valuable, he compared Trojan pottery finds with Egyptian finds. Again, Schliemann anticipated the extended panorama of present-day archaeologists. Even more basically, results of his excavations at Troy between 1870 and 1890, though controversial, encouraged ongoing study at the site. More recent finds have, in turn, had an effect on the portraits painted of Schliemann himself. From a man who could not differentiate between Byzantine and prehistoric remains, he has become a pioneer in experimental archaeology. An answer to the charge that he fabricated the "treasure" that he "discovered" at Troy came in the form of the rediscovery of that treasure missing from World War II to the end of the twentieth century. When the actual objects had been rediscovered, it was possible to learn that the objects are contemporary with one another, NOT pieces assembled from a variety of times and places.

In this expansion of the discipline of archaeology Troy has been central. In new investigations of the site, more recent teams of archaeologists have revealed Troy's role in what became, by the mid-second millennium B.C.E., an interactive eastern Mediterranean culture. And if the findings of the most recent investigation are correct, it was a major *emporion* (market center) in trade activity that stretched along the northern and southern Mediterranean coasts into the western basin of that great sea and, it now seems likely, into the Black Sea as well. Consequently, Troy is more than a fortified hill once defended by its residents from foreign attackers. It is a microcosm of the varied, far-reaching activities of the Bronze Age peoples, subjects as well as rulers.

## ENHANCED HISTORICAL UNDERSTANDING

In sum, by joining the embedded background of legend with the results of excavation, we can enhance or even alter our understanding of the past. In a sense, the epics become "documents." They were instrumental in forming the ancient Greeks' own memory of the past as Anthony Raubitschek, a scholar with a deep understanding of the ancient Greek world, understood. In an article entitled "What the Greeks Thought of Their Early History" (1989), Professor Raubitschek inquires, first, whether the Greek historians distinguished between a mythical and a historical period and, second, whether they and their contemporaries had a "reasonably comprehensive view of the mythical period."

Herodotus resolved to understand how the Greeks and the eastern barbarians fell into the conflict that was the subject of his account, namely, the Persian Wars of the early fifth century. He found an answer in the ongoing theft of women by both parties: the capture of the king of Argos' daughter by the Phoenicians; then the carrying off of the daughter of the king of Tyre by Cretans; next the Argonauts' abduction of Medea from her home at the eastern edge of the Black Sea; and finally, the seduction of Helen, wife of the king of Sparta, by Paris, one of the sons of King Priam of Troy.[5]

Herodotus provides us with a rough chronology for these legendary events when he says that under the three consecutive generations of the Persian kings Darius, Xerxes, and Artaxerxes more disasters happened to Greece than under the twenty other generations before the time of Darius (vi.98). Professor Raubitschek links "this extraordinary statement" with "an equally extraordinary statement by Thucydides," who somewhat later than Herodotus recorded the origin and nature of the Peloponnesian War. Thucydides' statement is very similar in content to that of Herodotus. Reckoning that three generations span a century, twenty generations would result in a date some 700 years before the event to which Herodotus is referring—the Battle of Marathon of 490 B.C.E.—in other words, the end of the Age of Heroes, or c. 1200 B.C.E. Moreover, not only did the ancient historians calculate the number of generations between themselves and their heroic past, but they also provided names of people and accounts of events of those earlier years.

Thucydides' account begins with a summary of events that had occurred before the outbreak of the Peloponnesian War in 431 B.C.E. "What is remarkable," Professor Raubitschek observes, "is not so much that the age of heroes is treated as historical but that the Persian Wars and the Trojan War are considered equally as events of earlier history." Later historians continued to begin their histories in the deep past. The Hellenistic writer Eratosthenes grounded his efforts to fix precise dating of the Trojan War to 1184 B.C.E. For Diodorus Siculus writing in the first century B.C.E., the Trojan War acted as a great chronological divide, with the first six books of his universal history treating events before the Trojan War while subsequent books dealt with events between that conflict and the Sicilian Expedition toward the end of the Peloponnesian War.

Professor Raubitschek's inquiry concludes with the observation that "we have come up with two startling answers: the story is continuous and uniform. This means the Greeks felt that there had not been any radical change in population, and they also felt that they basically agreed on the main events. These were the heroic stories recorded in the epics." Awareness of these events "gave the Greeks the knowledge and the understanding of their own past and enabled them to approach the problems of their own day more intelligently" (p. 45).

Our understanding of the ability of legends to preserve knowledge of the past—albeit far less precise concerning dates and specific events than modern historians hope to know—buttresses the conclusion that the ancient historians had a memory of their past extending into the second millennium. Adding the results of archaeological efforts to uncover physical evidence of an "Age of Heroes" provides the third leg of a tripod of verification that the Trojan War did not belong to a world that never existed on land or sea as many scholars believed even into the twentieth century.

And so we can return to our point of departure that examined "Troy and the World of the Late Bronze Age." Greece was part of the youthful revolutions in human history that led to the first complex civilizations of the Mediterranean sphere. As early as 7000 B.C.E., settled villages rooted in farming and herding were established in Greece. And with increasing control of their environment, inhabitants of the Aegean lands gained the same skills that produced the civilizations of Egypt and Mesopotamia: metal technology, diversification of crops, specialization by skills and responsibilities, and increasing population. To this list, dwellers on the islands and on the mainland of Greece added seafaring that allowed them to participate in the growing interaction between civilizations ringing the Mediterranean that brought diverse peoples together through trade, warfare, diplomacy, and cultural borrowing. Thus, in what is often classed as one of Odysseus' "lying" tales, he could recount that he was a Cretan who recalled the time when:

> My heart urged me to make sail for Egypt
> On ships well equipped, with god-like comrades.
> I made ready nine ships, a crew gathered quickly.
> For six days my trusty comrades feasted with me.
> I supplied many sacrifices to be offered to the gods
> And to be prepared for their own feasting.
> But on the seventh day, setting out from wide-stretching Crete
> We sailed on the sharp-blowing wind of Boreas
> Effortlessly as if moving downstream on a river.
> No harm touched the ships, but unharmed and without sickness
> We sped, the wind and steersmen moving the ships straight for-
>     ward.
> On the fifth day we reached fair-flowing Egypt.
>     (xiv.245–257, translated by Carol Thomas and Tristan Goldman)

Odysseus may have invented the tale to hide his true identity, but Minoan Cretans certainly could have undertaken the voyage often.

Legends, physical evidence recovered in recent times, and written accounts from literate peoples of the Bronze Age have enlarged our picture not only of Greece but the larger world in which pre-Classical Greeks were situated. Part of that picture has become an abiding theme in subsequent history: the ongoing contest between East and West, with which Herodotus began his account and which he regularly points out in describing the vast differences between the culture of Egypt and the Near East, on the one hand, and Greece on the other. Such variations have continued: the rapid spread of Islam from the seventh century c.e. produced a demarcation that was military and religious as well as cultural that spread throughout the Mediterranean. The division lies at the heart of contemporary global politics. Can the distinct cultures of the Near East coexist with the cultures of the Western World or must one pattern prevail?

Thus, the tale of Troy—which we have argued seems to be built on a factual base—may serve to describe much more than the wrath of Achilles and the difficult homecoming of Odysseus. It embodies and may illuminate the condition of a people who are situated between the seemingly antithetical spheres of East and West.

## NOTES

1. One reason for this imbalance is the entrance into the English language of the word "odyssey" as a term meaning a long, eventful journey or, more metaphorically, any lengthy development resulting in the transformation of a person or group. Of course, the very fact that *Odyssey* has entered the language as a noun is tribute to the continuing influence of Homer.

2. New York and Toronto: Athenaeum and Maxwell Macmillan, 1994.

3. Another benefit of musical accompaniment is its ability to heighten the dramatic effect of the poetry. Music has been used effectively not only with poetry, but with plays and movies as well. Did you ever wonder why movies have "sound tracks?" Music acts to dramatize, in the case of plays and movies, both words and actions. The meaning of words is intensified when they are ordered into poetic patterns. The effect of music on poetry is the same as poetry's effect on simple words. It serves to intensify and dramatize meaning.

4. Geoffrey Kirk, *Myth: Its Meaning and Functions in Ancient and Other Cultures* (Berkeley: University of California Press, 1970), p. 247.

5. To this list, we could add the tale of the abduction of Priam's own sister, Hesione, by Telamon the king of Salamis and father of Great Ajax. Priam tried in vain to win her back, a failure that makes his unwillingness to give up Helen more understandable.

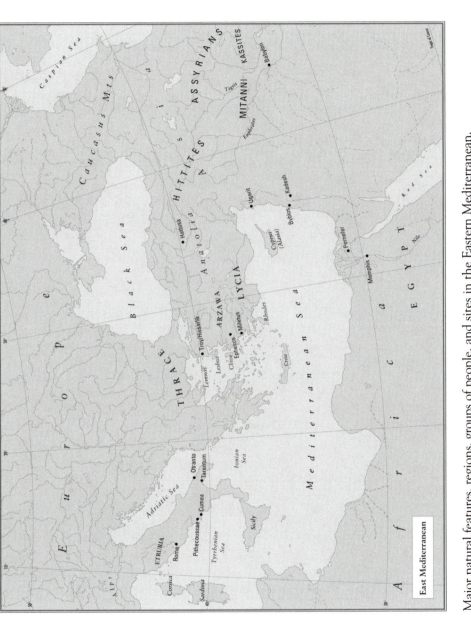

Major natural features, regions, groups of people, and sites in the Eastern Mediterranean.

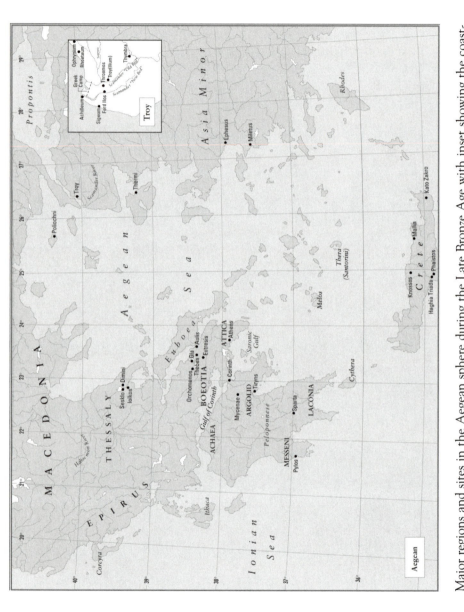

Major regions and sites in the Aegean sphere during the Late Bronze Age with inset showing the coastline and interior of the Troad.

Heinrich Schliemann: a portrait of determination? *From Carl Schuchhardt*, Schliemann's Evacuations: An Archaeological and Historical Study *(London and New York: Macmillan, 1891)*.

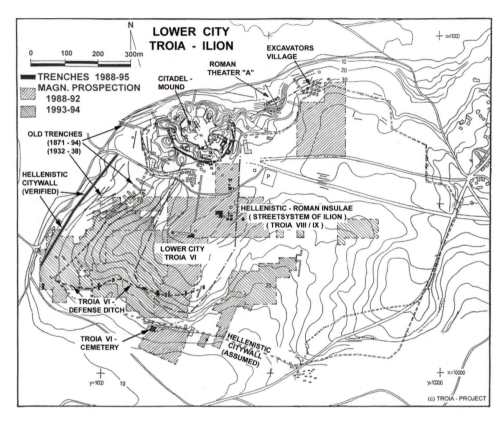

Below the citadel of Hissarlik excavated first by Schliemann extends a lower settlement, ten times larger than the citadel site. It has been revealed in the most recent study of the site through magnetic detection that reads what lies below the earth's surface. *By courtesy of the Troia-Project of the University of Tübingen.*

Aerial photo of Mycenae. *By courtesy of the Hellenic Military Geographical Service, Athens.*

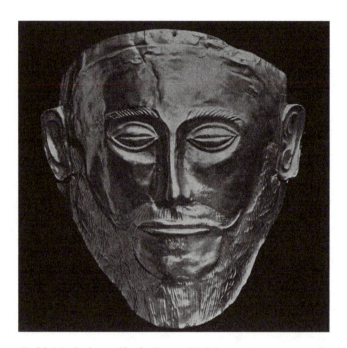

Gold Mask from Shaft Grave V, Mycenae, c. sixteenth
century B.C.E. Heinrich Schliemann, upon discovering
this object while excavating Grave circle A, referred to
it as the death mask of Agamemnon. In reality the mask
predates the Trojan War by nearly four hundred years.
*From* Cambridge Ancient History, *Volume of Plates I (New
York: Macmillan and Cambridge: Cambridge University
Press, 1927), p. 165a.*

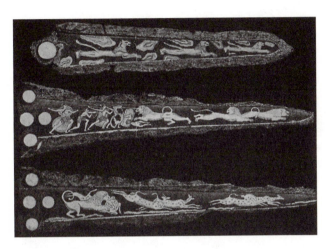

Mycenaean dagger inlaid with silver and gold from shaft Grave VI (sixteenth/fifteenth centures B.C.E.). In the scene of a lion hunt, notice the large figure-eight and rectangular body shields employed by the hunters. The Homeric hero Ajax might have carried just such a shield. *From* Cambridge Ancient History, *Volume of Plates I (New York: Macmillan and Cambridge: Cambridge University Press, 1927), p. 165b.*

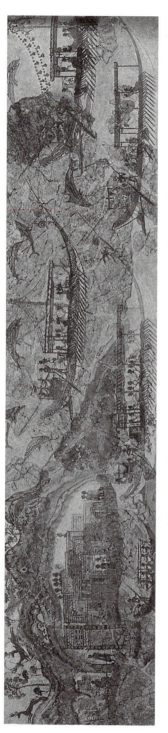

The Ship Procession Fresco from the West House, Akrotiri. By permission of the Hellenic Republic Ministry of Culture.

The Battle Scene Fresco from the West House, Akrotiri. By *permission of the Hellenic Republic Ministry of Culture*.

Achilles slaying Penthesileia. Attic black figured vase of Exekias, c. 540–530 B.C.E.
Many episodes of the Trojan War cycle not mentioned in the *Iliad* can be found pictured on the vases of the Archaic and later periods. This scene is described in Quintus of Smyrna's *The Fall of Troy, Book I*. © *Copyright The British Museum*.

A relief from the Gandharan region of India depicting what is likely to be the story of the Trojan horse. Greek warriors, hidden inside the horse, were transported into the citadel when the Trojans were convinced that the horse was a peace offering from the Greeks who abandoned the siege of Troy. The Indian source is testimony to the wide circulation of the Trojan tale. *From John Allen, "A Tabula Iliaca from Gandhara," Journal of Hellenic Studies 66 (1946): 22.*

# Biographies:
# The Personalities
# of the War

Because the Trojan War stands between legend and history, biographies of those connected with the tradition fall into those same categories. The first group is known through legends that may have a footing in history but are not supported by documentary evidence. The people in this group are divided among Greeks and Trojans. Those in the second group are attested by evidence that provides specific dating and evidence of their lives.

## GREEKS IN LEGEND

### The Line of Atreus

The mystery of myth and legend surrounds the lineage of Agamemnon, the leader of the Greeks at Troy, and his brother Menelaus, whose honor was the cause of the war. Their ancestry reaches back to a time when mortals invited gods to banquets and when the gods could repair seemingly fatal harm to earthly men and women. The founder of the line was named Tantalus, and it was he who provided a banquet for the gods. Discovering that he was short on provisions, he had his own son Pelops cut up and put in a stew. When the dinner was served, all the gods but one discovered the ruse. Demeter, however, ate one of Pelops' shoulders. Zeus condemned Tantalus to eternal punishment in the underworld but knit Pelops back together.

Whole again, Pelops succeeded to his father's throne in northern Anatolia. Learning that a king of a realm in Greece had a widely praised daughter, Pelops became intent upon winning her hand. He was successful by means of foul play that brought a curse on Pelops and all his progeny. Pelops and his wife became rulers of her father's kingdom and had many children; chief among them were Atreus, father of Agamemnon and Menelaus, and Thyestes, the father of Aegisthus. So important was Pelops in tradition that his name served to identify the part of Greece in which he ruled: the Peloponnese or the "island" of Pelops.

Archaeologists and ancient historians find interesting associations between these accounts and their own evidence for the "Age of Heroes." The spread of agriculture, for example, seems to have moved from Anatolia westward, first to Greece and onward from there. Archaeology confirms tradition in suggesting the change of control of major sites from one dynasty to another. So, a "Pelops" may have migrated from Anatolia to Greece and by marriage into a ruling family may have become king of a realm in Greece in the distant past of Greek memory.

The curse that was put on Pelops played out in succeeding generations, with the result that cannibalism and child sacrifice became a feature of the tales surrounding both Pelops' sons, Atreus and Thyestes, and his grandson Agamemnon. Atreus and Thyestes were implicated in foul play early on, for they were suspected of murdering their half-brother. The two fled their father's realm and made their way to Mycenae. When the Mycenaean throne became vacant at the death of the last king of the Perseid line, Atreus and Thyestes fell to quarreling over who should be king. Their feud culminated in Atreus' invitation to Thyestes to attend a banquet, ostensibly with the purpose of making peace. But peace was far from Atreus' mind, for Thyestes was served a stew in which Atreus had placed the dismembered flesh of Thyestes' infant sons. After discovering the nature of the dish he had just consumed, Thyestes laid a heavy curse on Atreus and fled the country.

Eventually Thyestes had his revenge upon Atreus. This was accomplished by fathering a son on his one surviving daughter. This child of incest was Aegisthus, later to be the bane of his cousin Agamemnon. Aegisthus while yet a boy slew Atreus, whereupon Thyestes gained the Mycenaean throne and drove Atreus' sons, Agamemnon and Menelaus, into exile.

The two brothers took refuge with King Thestius of Aetolia. Thestius was a friend of King Tyndareus of Sparta who, as a favor to the Aetolian king, led an army against Thyestes, forcing him to abdicate in favor of Agamemnon. In Tyndareus, both Agamemnon and Menelaus gained a stalwart ally, and this alliance was strengthened by the marriage of

Agamemnon to Tyndareus' daughter Clytemnestra and of Menelaus' marriage to his other daughter, the beautiful Helen.

Recent study of Bronze Age Greece has demonstrated the existence of several major kingdoms located in the Peloponnese, Attica, and central and northeastern Greece. In the Peloponnese, one of the most important centers was at Mycenae, while a subsidiary center was at Sparta. Each center had its own ruler, and while names of these rulers have not been preserved from the second millennium, the roles of an "Agamemnon" at Mycenae and a "Menelaus" at Sparta accord with the archaeological and written evidence. That these kingdoms were politically and militarily independent from one another is attested both by traditional stories and archaeological evidence. At the site of Pylos in the southwestern Peloponnese, for example, tradition has it that this center was taken by Neleus who had quarreled with his brother over rule in northeastern Greece.

## Agamemnon

With the Spartan alliance, Mycenae became the most powerful state, and Agamemnon the most powerful king, in the Peloponnese, and when the Trojan prince Paris abducted Helen, it was Agamemnon who led the Greek forces against Troy. But powerful though he was, he could not escape the curse laid on his grandfather Pelops, nor the one laid on his father Atreus. When the Greek fleet was kept from sailing to Troy because of contrary winds, Agamemnon was forced to sacrifice his most beautiful daughter, Iphigeneia, to the goddess Artemis. Only then was the fleet allowed to set sail for Troy.

Once at Troy, it took ten years to capture the city, and then it was only accomplished by the ruse of the Trojan Horse. During the siege, Agamemnon had to deal with many proud warriors; many were kings of their own cities and were not used to taking orders, not even from so august a person as the lord of Mycenae. Inevitably, he got into conflicts, the most famous of which was the nearly disastrous quarrel with Achilles, the son of King Peleus of Phthia and the most formidable warrior in the Greek army.

Meanwhile back in Mycenae, events were transpiring which would bring ruin to Agamemnon and nearly to Mycenae itself. Clytemnestra could never forgive her husband for sacrificing their daughter, and her anger was inflamed by Aegisthus who had returned to the city in Agamemnon's absence. He soon became Clytemnestra's lover and assuaged her guilty conscience by telling her that Agamemnon planned to return with a Trojan concubine whom he intended to be his queen. The only way for her to maintain her position would be to join Aegisthus in a plot to assassinate Agamemnon if ever he should return from Troy.

When Agamemnon did return after the sack of Troy, he was indeed accompanied by a Trojan concubine: none other than Priam's daughter Cassandra who was a seer. She refused to enter the palace, saying it smelled of blood, so Agamemnon left her standing in the courtyard while he entered, greeting Clytemnestra who showed every evidence of delight at his return. She led him to a bath and after bathing he stood up, at which point Aegisthus crept up from behind and smote him with an ax. Then after assuring herself that Agamemnon was dead, Clytemnestra took the ax and walked out into the courtyard where she dispatched Cassandra.

## Menelaus

The old myths tell us that although Agamemnon may have been the most powerful of the Greek kings, his brother Menelaus was the wealthiest, and some say that it was his great wealth that enabled him to seek and win the hand of Helen. Helen's father, King Tyndareus of Sparta, had great difficulty in choosing a husband for his daughter, for no matter who among Helen's innumerable suitors was chosen, the others would feel slighted and the result would be war. However, Tyndareus' quandary was resolved when Odysseus, the king of far-off Ithaca, broached the idea of having all the suitors swear an oath to defend whomever was chosen as Helen's husband from anyone who would attack him out of envy. After the suitors had sworn the oath, Menelaus was chosen, and the wedding took place without mishap.

While the swearing of the oath insured that peace would be maintained among the Greek princes, it also made inevitable the formation of a grand coalition against the envious attacks of anyone who had not sworn the oath. Thus, when the Trojan prince Paris abducted Helen, what might have otherwise remained a local conflict between Sparta and Troy was turned into a great war between Troy and its numerous allies and most of the Greek cities. While Menelaus called on all the suitors to fulfill the terms of their oath, he also went about mustering a substantial force that consisted of sixty ships and many warriors levied from nine Laconian towns, including Sparta and Amyclae.

Although not the equal of Achilles, Great Ajax, or Diomedes, Menelaus was still a formidable warrior, and had it not been for the intervention of Aphrodite, he almost certainly would have slain Paris in the single combat described in Book III of Homer's *Iliad*. Menelaus was one of the warriors chosen to hide in the belly of the Trojan Horse which King Priam, disregarding the dire prophecies of his daughter Cassandra, insisted on dragging into Troy. When night fell, Menelaus, Odysseus, and the other warriors crept out of the Trojan Horse, opened the gates to Agamemnon's forces, and attacked the sleeping city. Menelaus raced toward Helen's apartments intent on slaying her for the dishonor she had brought on him. But upon seeing her for the first time in ten years, he was overcome by her beauty and, throwing his sword aside, he escorted her to the safety of the Greek ships.

Anxious to return home, Menelaus failed to heed Agamemnon's advice to give thanks to Athena for the fortunate conclusion to the war. As a result of this transgression, the angry goddess sent a destructive storm that caught Menelaus' fleet in the mid-Aegean. He lost all but five of his sixty ships and was blown off course into the eastern Mediterranean. He and Helen spent the next eight years sailing between Egypt, Phoenicia, and Crete and back again to Egypt, and never were they allowed to come near the Greek mainland. Menelaus finally discovered the means by which he could return home only by catching and forcing this information from the shape-shifter Proteus, the king of the island of Pharos. Following his advice, Menelaus returned to Egypt where he made a great sacrifice to all the gods, after which Athena relented and he and Helen were allowed to sail home. We last meet Menelaus and Helen two years later in semiretirement in their palace at Sparta and entertaining young Telemachus who has come seeking news of his father Odysseus.

## Clytemnestra and Helen

It is said that before Clytemnestra and Helen were born, their father the king of Sparta, while sacrificing to all the gods, foolishly overlooked Aphrodite, who as punishment decreed that neither of his daughters would be happy in their marriages. It is certainly true that neither Clytemnestra nor Helen enjoyed a tranquil domestic life.

We have already seen that Agamemnon gave Clytemnestra plenty of cause for unhappiness, but her life with Aegisthus, whom she married after Agamemnon was dead, was no less unhappy. Aegisthus, who was plagued by a guilty conscience for having murdered Agamemnon, and fearing the vengeance of his son Orestes, was incapable of ruling the vast Mycenaean realm. Thus, it fell to Clytemnestra to make the day-to-day decisions by which the kingdom was ordered.

But in the end all her effort was of no avail, for Orestes was still very much alive and intent on revenge. After eight years in exile, he returned to Mycenae and, gaining entrance to the palace disguised as a wandering suppliant, he slew Aegisthus at the first opportunity, and though Clytemnestra begged for her life, reminding Orestes that she was "his own mother, she also he slew with the same sword."

So great was the hatred of the Mycenaeans for the odious regime of Aegisthus and Clytemnestra that they would not allow Orestes to bury them within the city walls, and so great tombs were built for them by the road leading away from the Lion Gate where they can be seen to this day.

These tombs, and seven others scattered about the plain outside Mycenae are known as *tholos* tombs (tholos is the Greek word meaning dome or circular vault), and there are many such tombs found throughout southern and central Greece. The ones found at Mycenae, however, are larger and grander than any found elsewhere. Dating from the late sixteenth or early fifteenth to the mid-thirteenth centuries B.C.E., they are great circular chamber tombs usually cut into the sides of hills. The most magnificent examples, of which the so-called tomb of Clytemnestra is one, features an interior vault and walls of dressed stone and a long entryway, or *dromos* (Greek word for race course), also walled in dressed stone. Although no one knows actually who is buried in these tombs, the tomb of Clytemnestra might well date from the period of the Trojan War. The less imposing tomb of Aegisthus is probably considerably earlier.

Though sisters, Clytemnestra and Helen were quite different in their natures, a difference that is made plain by the tales surrounding Helen's birth. Once while Helen's mother, the queen of Sparta, was walking on the banks of the river Eurotas, Zeus appeared to her in the form of a swan and ravished her. Nine months later, the queen produced an egg from which Helen was hatched. As an infant Helen possessed a beauty such as only the children of gods are likely to possess, and as she grew older she became ever more beautiful. By the time she was twelve, her beauty had become renowned throughout Greece. But what others would consider a blessing was for Helen a curse. News of Helen's beauty reached the ears of King Theseus of Athens who promptly led an army against Sparta, took Helen captive, and carried her off. It was four years before the Spartans discovered where she was hidden and recovered her.

Intent on getting her safely married before more harm could befall her, Helen's father arranged for her to marry Menelaus, King Agamemnon's brother. But this marriage also ended in disaster when the Trojan prince Paris, who was Menelaus' guest, violated his host's hospitality and abducted Helen. Again Helen was eventually returned but this time at the cost of many lives and the ruin of a great city.

In his rush to return home, Menelaus failed to make a thank-offering to Athena, with the result that he and Helen were stranded in Egypt and Phoenicia for eight years. In another tale, Helen was not carried off to Troy by Paris, but only a likeness, or phantom, of her accompanied him to Troy. Helen herself was taken to Egypt by Hermes, and there she lived under the protection of King Proteus through all the years of the Trojan War and Menelaus' wanderings. Finally, after he was shipwrecked in Egypt, Menelaus discovered that Helen had been there all along, that she had never deserted him for Paris, and that the whole Trojan War had been no more than a trick played by the gods on poor mortals with the aim of decreasing the world's population.

Some scholars believe that Helen's miraculous hatching from an egg, her multiple abductions or disappearances, and her association with the south, represented as Egypt to the early Greek mind, are signs that Helen was originally a fertility or vegetation deity. Eggs have always symbolized fertility and rebirth, and just as the sun each winter departs, or is abducted, to the south, it is not to be wondered at that a goddess who represents in some fashion the waning and waxing of the sun's intensity and the growth and dying away of vegetation would be conceived of as periodically being spirited away by hostile forces. Finally, in support of the idea of a goddess Helen, there is the very real hero cult of Menelaus and Helen at the Menelaion near Sparta. Some scholars believe that Helen was more important to this cult than Menelaus and that her worship pre-dates his.

## Achilles

Achilles was the greatest fighter in the Greek army. Indeed, he was nearly invulnerable, for his mother, the sea goddess Thetis, tried to burn away the part of him that was mortal, inherited from his father, by placing him in the hearth fire. Before she could complete this operation, her husband discovered what she was attempting and so Achilles' ankle remained mortal and vulnerable.

It had been prophesied that Troy could not be taken without the aid of Achilles, and the young warrior soon displayed his powers by capturing a number of towns allied to Troy. In one such town he took captive the daughter of the priest of Apollo who, after the division of the spoils, became Agamemnon's concubine. When Apollo forced Agamemnon to return the girl to her father, he comforted himself at Achilles' expense by taking Achilles' concubine. Enraged at this insult, Achilles said he would fight no more and would sail home the next day.

With Achilles out of the fight, the Trojans forced the Greeks back to their camp and even set one of the ships alight. At this Achilles' great friend Patroclus persuaded Achilles to let him borrow his armor and attack the Trojans. Thinking Achilles had returned to battle, the Trojans fled before Patroclus who slew the Lycian chieftain Sarpedon before he himself was slain with the aid of Apollo.

Nearly mad with grief at the loss of Patroclus, Achilles, newly armed by the smith-god Hephaestus, rejoined the fight the next day. To the dismay of the Trojans, Achilles slew Hector, their best warrior, and tying the Trojan's body to his chariot, dragged him back to the Greek camp. With the aid of Hermes, Priam stole into Achilles' encampment where he was able to persuade the hero to relinquish his son's body.

But the time of Achilles' own death was now fast approaching, for it had been foretold that he would either live long and ingloriously, or go off to Troy, cover himself in glory, and die young. In fulfillment of this prophecy, he was slain when an arrow struck his vulnerable ankle. Some say it was Paris who launched the fatal shaft, but others say it was the Archer God Apollo, ever a friend to Troy, who slew him.

Later stories concerning the death of Achilles say that the hero was granted immortality in the Elysian Fields, but in the *Odyssey* of Homer he, like all the dead, is consigned to a wretched, shadowy existence as a ghost in Hades. "I would rather follow the plow as thrall to another man . . . than be king of all the perished dead," is Achilles' grim assessment of his present situation in the Underworld (*Odyssey* xi.489–491, R. Lattimore translation).

Like many characters in the Homeric poems, Achilles is a multifaceted personality. Certain of his characteristics appear to be Mycenaean, and indeed the name Achilleus (in the form *a-ki-re-we*) appears in the Linear B tablets from both Knossos and Pylos. His boast in *Iliad* ix.328 of having sacked twelve cities by sea and eleven by land sounds like the sort of raiding forays that might well have led up to a general assault on Troy.

Other of the hero's traits, however, are less easy to place. Like Hector, Achilles is a paramount champion whose sense of worth is gained through his unmatched exercise of arms and in wise and eloquent utterance in council. For one such as Achilles, displaying virtuosity in both endeavors not only advances the war effort but gains imperishable glory and honor for the warrior. For the Homeric warrior such honor serves the same purpose as humility for the Christian, for in the absence of a meaningful afterlife, immortality can be attained only through the achievement of glorious and honorable deeds. It is for this reason that Achilles takes such offense when Agamemnon deprives him of his concubine. Since he could easily get another, it is the principle of the thing, the slight to Achilles' honor, which he cannot tolerate.

Although it is impossible to date this warrior ethic, it seems to be more characteristic of an aristocratic society with little centralized authority than of a society in which royal power is paramount. While the great palace centers of the Mycenaean world appear to have been highly centralized, particularly at the time a Trojan War would have been fought, that is, in the thirteenth century B.C.E., nearly the opposite seems to be the case in the period between 900 and 700 B.C.E. At this time, the time in which Homer was singing his tales, kingships were rapidly being supplanted by aristocracies in most of the Greek world. Thus, while Homer has perhaps borrowed a character named Achilles from Bronze Age epic or saga history, he has provided him with the personality and motivations of an eighth-century warrior who might be recognizable to the poet's largely aristocratic audiences.

## Idomeneus and Meriones

Idomeneus was leader of all the warriors who came to Troy from Crete in their eighty ships. In numbers of men and vessels, the Cretans were only slightly inferior to the contingents from Mycenae (100 ships) and Pylos (90). Idomeneus was a redoubtable force at Troy. Meriones, special companion of Idomeneus, was one of the most outstanding younger warriors, a skilled archer and charioteer as well as wielder of the spear.

Although the presence of the Cretans at Troy is important, their somewhat inferior role masks the great significance of the island of Crete in Bronze Age history. In the *Odyssey*, the island is remembered as a rich and lovely land in the middle of the dark blue sea, densely populated with people living in ninety cities. One of them is a great city, Knossos, where King Minos ruled for nine years, enjoying the friendship of Zeus (xix.172–179). Minos' son Deucalion was held to be the father of Idomeneus. In uncovering the reality of the early, flourishing civilization on Crete, Sir Arthur Evans named it after the legendary king—the Minoan civilization.

These lineages as well as the prestige of cities like Knossos reflect the remembered grandeur of Crete. Archaeology has shown that the island was inhabited in the Neolithic Age by peoples who made their way by sea from Anatolia. They found a land suitable for agriculture and herding; on these two foundations a sophisticated culture based on several palatial centers emerged in the second millennium B.C.E. Knowledge of seafaring coupled with specialized use of products such as grapes, olives, the wool of sheep and goats, as well as elaborate metal goods drew Crete into an international trade with civilizations of the eastern Mediterranean extending from Egypt to the Levant. The importance of Minoan activity is embodied in the term *thalassocracy*, or strength by sea.

Minoan influence was as strong, if not stronger, in the Aegean: colonies and trading centers have been identified on the Aegean islands, the coast of Anatolia, and on islands close to the Greek mainland. The influence on the mainland of Greece was potent in impelling the Greeks in a similar direction.

Although the cultural interaction is clear, the relationship between Crete and the mainland is uncertain. Evidence from surviving written records indicates that the Minoans were non-Greek speakers. Mainlanders may have taken advantage of the effects of a massive volcanic eruption that brought devastation to Crete in the late seventeenth century to establish their control of parts of the island, notably Knossos. Idomeneus and Meriones, then, may represent the transplanted Greeks rather than the non-Greek Eteocretans—or "true" Cretans—who survived the merging of peoples and culture. In the *Odyssey*, Odysseus, in his "false" tales, pointedly traces his lineage to Crete.

## Jason

Jason of Iolkos is best known as the legendary hero who led a band of companions from Greece to the eastern edge of the Black Sea in search of the Golden Fleece. The ship that carried them there and back was named the *Argo*; they are therefore known as the Argonauts or sailors on the *Argo*. The full account is that of one Apollonius of Rhodes who lived in the third century B.C.E., but the story itself possesses all the ingredients of myth: heroes interact with gods in facing daunting obstacles in lands so distant that they appear to be never-never-land.

Iolkos had a troubled history. When its king seized the throne from the rightful heir, his half-brother, an oracle was received that the wicked king would be killed by a relative. As a result, the king put to death any person related to him, so that when his half-brother (surprisingly allowed to live) and wife gave birth to a child, Jason, the baby was smuggled out of the palace to be raised by a kindly Centaur in the remote mountains. On coming of age, Jason returned to Iolkos. He was wearing only one sandal, having lost the other one carrying across a river an aged woman who was the goddess Hera in disguise. Since the wicked king had received another oracle to beware a man wearing only one sandal, he immediately was suspicious of the newcomer and asked, "If an oracle announced to you that one of your fellow-citizens were destined to kill you, what would you do?" Jason answered, "I would send him to fetch the golden ram's fleece from Colchis." And this is what Jason was ordered to do; if successful, the throne would be his. So Jason gathered a crew, ordered a ship constructed, and sailed with heroes like Heracles to the edge of the world. With the help of the daughter of the king of Colchis, he snatched the fleece even though it was guarded by an unsleeping dragon. That helpmate, Medea, became his wife; their lives together continued to be as tumultuous as they had been at the start.

So unlike normal human experience is the entire tale that it is regularly included in collections of myths. Surprisingly, however, recent archaeological work has identified a place known as Iolkos, where remains suggest that it was the northernmost kingdom in the Late Bronze Age configuration of Greek society. The land in the region is excellent for farming and animal husbandry, and the site overlooks a bay with a good harbor. The adventures of Jason were mentioned in the Homeric epics whose roots reach back to the "Age of Heroes." Written references from the Bronze Age itself include names like I-wa-so (an early form of Jason) and Ko-ki-da (perhaps Colchis). Suitable vessels and sufficient navigational skills existed in the second millennium to allow passage from the Aegean into the Black Sea, and ongoing study in the Black Sea is revealing objects of Aegean type.

Consequently, although cast in a new form much later, the adventures of Jason may well reflect memory of actual travel during what was once thought to be a "world that never existed on land or sea."

## Nestor and Pylos

Nestor, the king of sandy Pylos in the western Peloponnese, was the elder Achaean leader at Troy, for "In his time two generations of mortal men had perished . . . and he was king in the third age" (*Il.* i.250, 252). He continued to marshall his troops and urge them to battle, although his great age prevented him from fighting among the forefront (*Il.* iv.294). But age had brought much wisdom for which Nestor was greatly honored. At the funeral games that Achilles held for his slain comrade Patroclus, Achilles presented Nestor with a prize even though he had not contended for it, saying "This, aged sir, is yours to lay away as a treasure in memory of the burial of Patroclus . . . I give you this prize for the giving" (*Il.* xxiii.618–621).

According to legend, Nestor's family hailed from northern Greece, the kingdom of Iolkos. As we have seen (see entry on Jason), Iolkos was a contentious place. The usurper king who sent Jason on his search for the golden fleece had a brother, Neleus, whom the king exiled from the kingdom. With others Neleus made his way southward, marrying the daughter of the king of Orchomenos, and then he traveled to Pylos where he defeated the ruling king and established his own control. Neleus and his wife had twelve children, eleven of whom were slain by Heracles when he took revenge for the Pylians' aid to one of his enemies. Nestor alone survived to succeed his father.

Archaeological excavation has uncovered what is identified as Bronze Age Pylos, and evidence shows that the settlement was burned in about 1300, to be rebuilt with larger, palatial structures. This new settlement would be the candidate for Nestor's Pylos. Archaeological evidence in conjunction with written information preserved on clay tablets indicates that this settlement was the administrative hub of a kingdom in which some 40,000 to 50,000 people lived in villages under the control of a central authority. According to tradition, Nestor was one of the few Achaean leaders at Troy to return unscathed from the ten-year struggle. It is to Nestor that Odysseus' son, Telemachus, appeals for news of his father, still missing ten years after the war's end. Telemachus is advised to:

> Go straightway to horse-taming Nestor,
> So we may know the counsel hidden in his breast.
> Beseech him to speak the truth.
> He will tell no lie for he is exceedingly wise.
> (*Odyssey* iii.17–20, translated by Carol Thomas and Tristan Goldman)

To return to the physical tale of archaeological evidence, Pylos itself was destroyed before the end of the thirteenth century B.C.E., not to be rediscovered until the twentieth century C.E. Stories tell of Nestor's descendants taking flight to Athens, one of the few Mycenaean centers to avoid destruction in the late thirteenth and twelfth centuries.

## Odysseus and Penelope

When Odysseus joined the other Achaean Greeks in their war on Troy, he hoped to return to his wife, Penelope, far sooner than twenty years later. It took ten years to take Troy and another ten years of wanderings and suffering to return to his Ithaca. In the *Iliad*, he is among the major heroes knowing that to win honor in battle, "one must stand his ground whether he be struck or strike down another" (xi.409–410). At the same time, Odysseus is especially beloved by Athena for his cleverness. He is one of three Greek leaders sent to Achilles in an effort to persuade him to return to battle. And a quick mind is a quality he must employ constantly in dealings with creatures like the cannabilistic Cyclops or the sorceress Circe in the *Odyssey*.

Odysseus is recognized as the king of the realm of the Ionian Islands to the west of the Corinthian Gulf. His own estate is on Ithaca, but his flocks graze even on the mainland. His father, Laertes, was king before him, and his own son, Telemachus, is a likely successor should Odysseus be dead. However, his claim is contested by other men of the realm. In the twenty years that Odysseus has been away, conditions have grown more and more hectic to the degree that a number of would-be kings are courting Odysseus' wife while regularly encamped in the residence of their missing king.

Penelope is desirable as a bride not simply because she has been the wife of Odysseus. As one of the suitors tells her, "in beauty, stature and sense there is not a woman to touch you" (*Od.* xviii.248–249). Her birth has provided some of these endowments: her cousin is the lovely Helen sired by Zeus whose brothers are Castor and Polydeuces. The family holds a special place in the eyes of the gods and, consequently, in the eyes of mortals. Penelope's great wealth is symbolized through her skill at weaving; she is an expert at the loom in creating both physical and intellectual products, for she uses weaving as a ruse to forestall the suitors. Every night she pulls out the progress of that day in weaving a shroud.

Unraveling wool is not likely to be a permanent solution to the suitors' courting. With the help of the goddess Athena, young Telemachus—born a few months after Odysseus' departure—must learn to take charge. The first step is to learn whether his father is dead or alive, which takes him to the realms of Nestor at Pylos and Menelaus at Sparta. On his return he goes to the remote cottage of the loyal swineherd Eumaeus where Odysseus himself seeks refuge on his final return to Ithaca. Together they plot and carry out the execution of the suitors and their accomplices.

Odysseus' wanderings were remembered when Greeks again took to the sea in the eighth century. A cave on Ithaca was the site of dedications by those about to undertake the same fearful voyages that the hero had experienced. Today the word "Odyssey" is a common way of describing important travels.

---

# TROJANS IN LEGEND

## Aeneas

Aeneas was the son of the goddess Aphrodite and the mortal Anchises, a cousin of King Priam. Once, when he was drunk, Anchises
boasted that he had lain with the Goddess of Love herself, and for this
impiety Zeus struck him with a thunderbolt that left him lame.

Although clearly related to the Trojan royal house, it had been several generations since Anchises and Priam had shared a common ancestor. As a result, Anchises and Aeneas were slighted by Priam and his
sons. For this reason Aeneas stayed out of the fighting during the first
years of the Trojan War. He might well have stayed out permanently had
it not been for Achilles, who foolishly attacked Aeneas' lands around
Mount Ida and captured his city of Lyrnessos. These events forced Aeneas to take up arms in the Trojan cause.

Even so, Aeneas saw that there would be no peace until Helen was
returned, and he often supported Antenor and his sons in their periodic
attempts to formulate a settlement agreeable to Priam. All of this was to
no avail, for Priam was obsessed with Helen, and by the tenth year of the
war Aeneas became a more active member of what can only be described
as a peace party led by Antenor.

Some accused Aeneas of betraying Troy to the Greeks, but most believed, as the Romans did, that he defended the city to the end, and only
when the situation was truly hopeless did he make his escape. He left the
burning city with his son Ascanius and his aged father perched on his
shoulders holding the images of the Trojan hearth gods. In his wanderings, Aeneas eventually made his way to Carthage where for a time he
became the lover of Queen Dido who had fallen in love with him. But
he was not allowed to stay: the Fates had decreed that he must go to Italy,
there to found a new nation that would assure the Trojans' survival.

## Hector and Andromache

If Achilles is the greatest Greek warrior at Troy, Hector is that citadel's
most vigorous defender and "with him stood the greatest number and
bravest fighting men" (*Il.* ii.817). Even the resolute Greek hero Diomedes
shivered as Hector drove on the Trojans shouting to his companions:

> We marvel at god-like Hektor, the spearman and courageous warrior
> But with him always is one of the gods, who wards off destruction.
>                                                                   (v.601–2–3)

Under his leadership, the Trojans break through the protection of the Greek camp near their ships. Only the intervention of the god Poseidon spared the Greeks and their vessels. It is Hector, too, who slays Patroclus, who has begged Achilles to allow him to rejoin the battle to aid the hard-pressed Greeks. Wearing his friend's armor, Patroclus deceives the Trojans into believing that the invincible Achilles has returned. Action by another god, this time Apollo, prevented Patroclus from surmounting the Trojan fortress, then stripped him of his protective armor and helmet so that Hector could strip away his life. Patroclus' death brought an even more resolute Achilles back into the fray. One of his key targets was, of course, Hector.

Hector is a singular figure not only in his dedication to Troy, but in his tender treatment of others—even Helen—and especially his parents Priam and Hecuba and his wife, Andromache, and their son Astyanax. When he encounters his wife while making his way through the great city, she begs him to keep out of battle, for he is father, mother, and brother to her as well as her husband. Holding his son, he prays that the boy one day will rule strongly over Ilion, as the son of the eldest of Priam and Hecuba's nineteen sons, and he pities Andromache "smiling in her tears."

Well might he pity both of them. Hector is fated to be slain by Achilles who, with the help of the gods and an ash spear heavy with bronze, ends Hector's life and then fastens his body to a chariot to be dragged, defiled, back to his tent. Priam will bravely make his way by night to the Greek camp to ransom Hector's body. Although he cries out to the shade of Patroclus that the ransom was not worthy of Patroclus' life, Achilles' rage has abated, and he says simply "Your son is released, aged sir, as you asked" (xxiv.599). Andromache will survive the sack of Troy to become the prize of Achilles' son, Neoptolemos, but her son will be thrown from the walls of the citadel lest he one day avenge the destruction of Troy. Priam will also be slain in the sack, while Hecuba is the prize of Odysseus. To Agamemnon goes Cassandra, the prophetic daughter of Priam and Hecuba who can correctly foresee the future but is doomed to never be believed.

## Paris (also known as Alexander)

Paris, the son of King Priam of Troy and his wife Hecuba, provoked the Trojan War. As guest friend of King Menelaus of Sparta, he fell madly in love with Menelaus' wife Helen. Called by Homer "the shining among women," her beauty was such that even the Trojans hard-pressed by the Achaean Greek avengers of the outrage to Menelaus could say:

> Surely there is no blame on Trojans and strong-greaved Achaians
> if for long time they suffer hardship for a woman like this one.
> (iii.156–157, translated by R. Lattimore)

The gods had a hand in the affair, according to legend. Paris was appointed to decide who was most beautiful of the goddesses Hera, Athena, and Aphrodite, each of whom offered a bribe. Aphrodite promised that Helen would be his wife if Paris voted Aphrodite the fairest of the three. That promise swayed the decision and provoked the dreadful anger of both Hera and Athena, who determined that Troy would be destroyed.

The Athenian tragedians Sophocles and Euripides both composed plays on *Alexandros* which give other details of Paris' life. When Hecuba was about to give birth, she dreamed that she had delivered not an infant but a firebrand. Learning her dream, Priam, consulted a seer who revealed that the child must be destroyed for, if he were allowed to live, he would be the ruin of Troy. Though exposed, Paris was rescued by a kind-hearted herdsman and raised to adolescence. Learning of games to be celebrated at Troy, Paris impetuously determined to participate. His success after success angered the acknowledged sons of Priam to the point that they attacked this ignoble son of a herdsman with their swords. In the nick of time, the seer cried out to Priam, "This is your long-lost son!" and Paris' life was saved, only to become the ruin of Troy.

As presented in the *Iliad*, Paris is not a redoubtable warrior. In fact, while fighting rages beyond the walls of Troy, Paris says to Helen, "Come, then rather let us go to bed and turn to love-making" (iii.441). Later, his brother Hector, who is the bastion of Troy's defense, accosts Paris in his chamber:

> The people are dying around the city and around the steep wall
> as they fight hard; and it is for you that this war with its clamour

has flared up about our city. . . .
Up then, to keep our town from burning at once in the hot fire.
                                                      (vi.327–329; 331)

Later accounts report that Paris was killed by the Achaean warrior
Philoctetes in the final destruction of the city.

## Priam and Hecuba

Priam had the mixed fortune of being king of Troy. He was fortunate
because his kingdom was wealthy but unfortunate in that his wealth produced enemies. He was its last king.

Heroic lineage made Priam a son of Laomedon, who gained the favor
of Zeus: the father of men and gods sent Poseidon and Apollo to build
the great walls of Troy. When Laomedon failed to pay the two divinities
their due reward, Apollo sent a plague on the land and Poseidon un-
leashed a sea-monster on its coast. In seeking recourse against the monster, Laomedon learned from an oracle that he must chain a daughter to
a rock on the coast for the monster to devour. Heracles in his incessant
wanderings happened to see the maiden in this sad condition, freed her,
and offered to slay the sea-monster in return for a gift of the glorious
white, immortal horses that Zeus had given to Laomedon. With the bar-
gain sealed, Heracles slew the monster, claimed the horses, and took the
maid as his bride. Apparently very duplicitous, Laomedon substituted ordinary white horses for the immortal creatures. Heracles' response was to
besiege and destroy Troy, killing Laomedon and all but one of his sons,
Priam, whom he established as king over the ruined city.

Archaeological excavation of the site identified as Troy has revealed
seven major phases. Settlement VI was destroyed c. 1275 B.C.E.; it was
replaced with the less imposing Troy VII. While we are reluctant to pro-
pose sea-monsters or heroes as the destroying agent, it is likely that the
trading center that Troy had become brought enemies as well as peace-
able traders to its harbor in the thirteenth century.

Priam's wife Hecuba—whose mother may have been a nymph—bore
nineteen sons. The other thirty-one sons of Priam were the offspring of
other wives or concubines. Among the sons of Priam and Hecuba were
Hector and Paris; one of their daughters was the prophetic Cassandra
who could foresee the future. In the fall of Troy, all of the sons perished,

Cassandra was awarded to Agamemnon, and her mother, Hecuba, to Odysseus. Priam was slain by Achilles' son. According to tradition, only one noble Trojan escaped—Aeneas who managed to rescue his son and elderly father from the blazing citadel. His destiny was to transplant Troy to Italy.

## Sarpedon and Glaucus

Sarpedon was lord of the Lycians, some of the most distant allies of the Trojans coming from the southwestern corner of Anatolia. Glaucus was his companion and second in command. These two men were honored as if they were immortals and were granted a large estate of excellent land along the banks of the Xanthos River. They therefore knew that it was their duty to stand and fight in the forefront of their Lycian contingent. Neither would live to return to their lovely estates: even his father, Zeus, was unable to save Sarpedon from the spear of Patroclus, though Zeus wept bloody tears knowing his son's fate (xvi.459). Later tradition shows that Glaucus was killed by Ajax.

Beyond their valiant efforts at Troy, the lives of both men suggest the larger interactions of the Late Bronze Age. In fact, the centuries from 1600 to 1200 are correctly understood only through the internationalism in the eastern Mediterranean sphere in which the Aegean peoples played an important role. Studies at the site of Troy in the last decade of the twentieth century discovered the city at the base of the citadel first excavated by Schliemann. The dimensions of the lower settlement are ten times the size of the citadel, and the population of the city is estimated at between 5,000 and 10,000. In addition, geologists have shown that the bay stretching inland from the waters of the Hellespont was far more extensive in antiquity than it is now; thus a safe harbor lay at the front door of Troy. In a word, it may well have been the northernmost trade center in a vast interlocked system. And as a major emporium it is likely to have had allies and enemies.

Tablets from the Hittite archive—a major power in Anatolia during the second half of the second millennium—seem to describe one such alliance between a place named Assuwa and twenty-two other locations. If it is correct that the names are listed from south to north, Assuwa would be situated in southern Anatolia. Second to last in the list is Wilusa, which may be the Hittite name for Ilium, another designation for Troy. Another tablet details difficulties between the Hittites and the Ahhiyawans—perhaps the Hittite name for Achaeans—over Millawanda, almost certainly the settlement of Miletus founded by Minoan Cretans and during this period under Mycenaean control.

A picture of vigorous trade emerges from archaeological evidence such as the ship wrecked off the southern coast of Anatolia at Ulu Burun in the fourteenth century. Objects recovered represent products from Egypt, Cyprus, the coast of the Levant, the Aegean, and even more distant places such as the Baltic lands and Mesopotamia. Diplomacy, cultural influence, intermarriage, and the travel of craftsmen accompanied the trade but so too did nonpeaceful activities of expansion and struggle for control of important sites. Troy was such a site, and war over Troy fits nicely into this picture. Men akin to Sarpedon and Glaucus may well have been drawn, through alliance, into the fray.

## HISTORICAL PERSONAGES

### Homer

For the ancient Greeks, Homer was THE poet. That reputation caused Alexander the Great to make Troy his initial destination in the campaign against Persia; the first epic in Latin was a translation of the *Odyssey*; the emperor Caracalla, claiming to be a descendant of Achilles, planned to defeat the Parthians who were thought to be descendants of the Trojans. Homer's influence has lasted to the present. The two epic poems attributed to Homer—the *Iliad* and the *Odyssey*—continue to inspire writers, filmmakers, archaeologists searching for concrete clues of Homer's age of heroes, historians, classicists as well as readers who simply want to experience the power of these tales of the Trojan War and the difficult return of one of the survivors of the war.

The grandeur of the poems is certain; far less certain is knowledge about the poet. Although one ancient author produced a "life" of Homer that dated him to around 1100 B.C.E., Herodotus places him closer to 850 B.C.E. Other scholars, ancient and modern, deny that such a man ever existed. Rather, they maintain, the poems were sung by a long line of bards through the nonliterate centuries from c. 1200 to 750 B.C.E., each of whom would recite from memory portions of the Trojan War saga. In this view, Homer was a title for such bards. A reconciliation of both views

seems sensible. Following on the hundreds of years of varying oral per-
formances, an especially gifted singer cast the tales in something like
their present compelling form. Fortunately, the skill of writing had recently returned to Greece so that this form could be permanently captured.

Many places claim to be the birthplace of Homer; most of them are
in Asia Minor along the eastern coast of the Aegean Sea. This location
would help to explain the form of Greek in the poems. What is more,
mainland Greeks in some numbers moved eastward following the destructions of the late twelfth and early eleventh centuries to establish settlements that eventually stretched from the region around Troy to the
southern coast of Anatolia. A tale of a great war at Troy might well be
nourished in this area.

Putting these clues together would date the monumental singer to the
mid-eighth century, a period that is reflected in the epics. To be sure,
their frame of reference is the "Age of Heroes" or the late second millennium B.C.E. Over the intervening centuries, however, the framework
of the stories was gradually changed, both inadvertently and by design to
make them intelligible to the current audience since many of the institutions of Bronze Age society had disappeared. Thus, while the heroes of
the *Iliad* and *Odyssey* are described as mighty kings, they resemble local
chieftains rather than kings of the earlier palace-citadels at places like
Mycenae and Pylos.

Both poems, however, are set in the past when a single man could lift
a stone, "an enormous thing which two men could not bear as men now
are" (*Iliad* xx.286–287). The *Iliad* describes the battle of such men at Troy
where Greeks, known as Achaeans, have been besieging the citadel for
nine years in an effort to retaliate against Paris' theft of Helen from her
husband Menelaus. Events leading to, but not including, the defeat of
the Trojans center on the quarrel between Agamemnon, leader of the
Achaean force, and Achilles, the mightiest warrior at Troy, resulting in
Achilles' withdrawal from fighting and his return when his closest friend
is slain by Hector. Odysseus plays an important role at Troy, but he is the
central figure of the *Odyssey*. The epic opens with the plight of his wife,
Penelope, and son, Telemachus, in Ithaca, over which Odysseus is king.
Affairs are in a state of chaos because Odysseus has not returned from
Troy for ten years following the Greek victory. Telemachus' search for
knowledge of his father and Odysseus' years of wanderings are recounted

in the first half of the poem. The second half brings a disguised Odysseus home to confront the massive problems plaguing his family, position, and the welfare of his realm.

## Heinrich Schliemann (1822–1890)

Heinrich Schliemann told a story explaining his early conviction that the epic tale of the Trojan War described a real event. As a Christmas gift when he was less than eight years old, his father gave him a *Universal History* by Ludwig Jerrer with an illustration showing Troy in flames. The young boy cried out "Father . . . Jerrer must have seen Troy, otherwise he could not have represented it here." After father and son argued about the reality of Troy, Schliemann continues, "at last we both agreed that I should one day excavate Troy." And against all odds that is precisely what he did.

Schliemann's first quarter century of life was not promising. When his mother died in 1830, he was sent to live with an uncle in a small German village where he was an eager student. Six years later, however, he was forced to leave school to work as an apprentice in a small grocer's shop. When bad health forced him to leave that job in 1841, he decided to make a fresh start in the New World. But the ship bound for Venezuela was wrecked off the coast of Holland. His life spared, Schliemann took a job as an officeboy in an Amsterdam warehouse using his time in running errands about the city in learning languages. Eventually he mastered twelve ancient and modern languages, an ability that took him far in space and success. Ventures in Russia and America produced sufficient wealth for him to retire in 1863, when he began worldwide travels. The year 1868 found him in Greece and in northwest Anatolia, more precisely at the site of Hissarlik where he would seek to uncover the remains of Troy.

That search, conducted with his Greek wife Sophia, consumed much of the remainder of his life, 1870–1890. Promising finds in the first probe were rewarded by discovery of a treasure horde in 1873. Altogether, excavations under Schliemann's direction produced seven levels of prehistoric occupation at the site ranging in date from c. 2800 to 1100 B.C.E. Realizing that one site was not sufficient to prove the reality of an entire civilization, Schliemann also excavated on the Greek mainland. He was especially keen to learn whether there were signs of prehistoric occupation at Mycenae, the legendary home of Agamemnon, leader of the expedition to Troy. Success at Mycenae and other locations demonstrated a civilization contemporary with that at Troy.

When much of the scholarly world refused to accept the accuracy of Schliemann's claims, confrontations between Schliemann and his critics became bitter and numerous. Although most scholars now accept the identification of Hissarlik as ancient Troy, debates about his finds continue. One explanation for the ongoing controversy lies in the newness of the discipline of archaeology at the time of Schliemann's life: it was only just emerging from undisciplined hunts for treasure. Schliemann's own work was pivotal in laying the foundations of archaeology as a new scholarly field. He understood the importance of intrinsically worthless finds and of topography; he appreciated the need to preserve his finds and to share them through publication; and he used comparative examples to interpret the evidence. As one scholar assessed his importance, he was "epoch-making." Indeed, he opened a new era of Greek history.

## Hattušili III and Tudhaliya IV

As we saw in Chapter 1, there are strong, though by no means conclusive, arguments for accepting the identification of the Ahhiyawans mentioned in Hittite texts with Mycenaeans—the *Achaioi* of Homer. Of the several Hittite kings who had dealings with Ahhiyawa, those nearest in time to a possible Trojan War are Hattušili III (1267–1237) and his son Tudhaliya IV (1237–1209).

We have already noted the difficulty with which the Hittites maintained their dominance in the western Anatolian vassal states. As long as Ahhiyawa maintained its beachhead, so to speak, at Millawanda, the likelihood remained that they would take advantage of disaffection among the Hittite's clients.

But Ahhiyawa was not the only, nor the most serious, problem facing Hattušili and his son. Even before Hattušili attained the throne, he and his brother King Muwatalli II were forced to concentrate much of the Hittite Kingdom's armed force in Syria to meet the rising challenge of the Egyptian pharaoh Ramses II. After the Battle of Kadesh (1276), which was a Hittite victory despite Ramses' propaganda to the contrary, it was some years before the Egyptian threat subsided.

In addition to Egypt, the increasing power and pugnacity of Assyria was a worry, and although this threat would not become critical until the reign of Tudhaliya, Assyrian activities among the Hittite's southeastern client states had a direct impact on the fortunes of Hattušili. Muwatalli's immediate successor was his son Urhi-Tešub, and it was in part Urhi-Tešub's failure to deal effectively with Assyrian encroachments that led to Hattušili's successful rebellion against him.

Having set aside his nephew, Hattušili made the mistake of giving Urhi-Tešub an important position as overlord of a number of border towns on the southeast frontier far from the capital of Hattusa. Hattušili's trust was misplaced, for within a few years Urhi-Tešub had fled the country and made his way to Babylon and thence to Egypt. In both places, Urhi-Tešub made continuing efforts to raise forces with which he might win back the Hittite throne. Although he was unsuccessful in these endeavors, he continued to be an embarrassment and a worry to Hattušili, many of whose diplomatic initiatives abroad and acts at home were designed both to establish his own legitimacy and to regain custody of his troublesome nephew.

These efforts met with some success. Another of Muwatalli's sons, Kurunta, was bought off with a large province in southern Anatolia and, while Ramses refused even to admit the presence of Urhi-Tešub in Egypt much less hand the rebel over to the Hittites, Hattušili did manage to arrange a marriage between his daughter and the Egyptian pharaoh and establish a treaty of peace (1259). Hattušili also made a marriage alliance and treaty with the king of Babylon. Meanwhile, the Assyrians, recognized by now as the chief threat to Hittite power, were mollified with soothing letters and public acceptance of Assyrian dominance east of the Euphrates.

Hattušili's son Tudhaliya also came to the throne in less than ideal circumstances. His older brother Nerikkaili could have expected to succeed his father to the throne but, for reasons unknown to us, was set aside by Hattušili in favor of Tudhaliya. Although Nerikkaili does not seem to have contested this decision, Tudhaliya's long and troubled reign presents the image of a regime less and less able to contend with a growing host of threats faced not only by the Hittites, but as we have seen, by the Mycenaeans as well during the latter half of the thirteenth century.

Early in Tudhaliya's reign there was a widespread rebellion among the central and southern provinces in Anatolia. While these uprisings were dealt with in a summary fashion, Tudhaliya expressed alarm in a letter to his mother that such disaffection should be possible in a region that for many years had been peaceful and stable.

Further afield, the new king of Assyria, Tukulti-Ninurta, launched an invasion of the territory between the upper reaches of the Tigris and Euphrates. Obviously, Hattušili's policy of appeasement was no longer working, and since the affected area had long been a Hittite sphere of influence, Tudhaliya felt compelled to meet force with force. It was as these events were unfolding that Tudhaliya established his treaty with Šaušgamuwa, king of Amurru, which among other things called for an embargo of Ahhiyawan trade with Assyria. The culmination of this emergency was a severe defeat for Tudhaliya in the mountains of eastern Anatolia. The situation would have been dire indeed had Tukulti-Ninurta followed up his victory with an invasion of the Hittites' Syrian dependencies or even of the home provinces of central Anatolia. But instead the Assyrian king spent his force on a conquest of Babylonia after which he seems to have concerned himself with internal matters for the rest of his reign. Even so, the Hittite defeat encouraged Tudhaliya's cousin Kurunta to rebel against his overlord. The rebellion was initially successful and Kurunta even managed to capture the capital, but within a year or two at the most Tudhaliya was restored to his throne and we hear nothing further from Kurunta.

Against this bleak record of defeat abroad and rebellion at home we must set Tudhaliya's seemingly successful efforts to pacify the western vassal states, including Millawanda and Wilusa, and a victorious invasion of Cyprus. But even Tudhaliya's successes can be seen as signs of the fragility of his regime. In the west Tudhaliya installed none other than the grandson of the notorious renegade Piyamaradu as king of Millawanda, and in addition granted him what was tantamount to vice-regal powers over other western clients including Wilusa and the Šeha River Land. Whereas before the Hittite king had dealt directly with each client state, now there would be a larger, nearly imperial power centered at Millawanda that would henceforth be responsible for western affairs.

As for the invasion of Cyprus, this event is peculiar, for while earlier Hittite kings had often claimed overlordship of the island, they had never felt the need to personally intervene in Cypriot affairs, leaving such tasks to other clients such as the king of Ugarit. The reasons for this attack are not known, but it has been suggested that Tudhaliya wanted a secure source of copper to replace the one lost to the Assyrians after Tukulti-Ninurta's victory.[1] It has also been suggested that Cyprus, often a haven for pirates and sitting astride the trade routes from Syria–Palestine and Egypt, was interfering with Egyptian grain shipments, which seem to have assumed ever greater importance during the reigns of Hattušili III and his successors.[2] Whatever the reasons for this invasion—which may have included operations against Ahhiyawans/Mycenaeans who were then immigrating to the island in large numbers—the conquest was short-lived. Tudhaliya's son Suppiluliuma II was forced, in a last act of Hittite military expansion, to reconquer it sometime between 1209 and the turn of the twelfth century.

## Ramses II and the Battle of Kadesh

In this book, we have of necessity limited ourselves to a study of Greece, the Aegean, and Anatolia in the Late Bronze Age, particularly the thirteenth century. This region was on the northwest fringe of what was then considered the civilized world stretching from the Iranian Plateau on the east to the central Mediterranean in the west. East and south of the Mycenaeans and the Hittites were powerful states that were already ancient when Troy VI was destroyed. Chief among these states was Egypt with a nearly continuous history of 2,000 years by the time of the Trojan War. Although Egypt has no direct bearing on the tale of the Trojan War, it was a major player in the international culture of the Bronze Age. Therefore, any account of the thirteenth century would be incomplete without some mention of Nineteenth Dynasty Egypt and the pharaoh who reigned for most of that century, Ramses II.[3]

The Egyptians were well aware of their own antiquity, as is attested by their periodic refurbishing of the tombs and monuments of previous dynasties. This attachment to the past was also expressed in the conservative nature of Egyptian society. Viewed from the outside, little change is apparent in terms of dress, social habits, religious practice, artistic conventions, and architecture from the First to the Nineteenth Dynasty and beyond. Certainly for ordinary folk whose lives were dependent on the annual flooding of the Nile, bringing with it rich deposits of silt to fertilize their farms, the idea of change was both foreign and repugnant.

This impression of Egyptian immutability, present even today among visitors to the country, is inaccurate particularly with regard to the Late

Bronze Age. Egypt and Egyptian society during the second millennium underwent several profound changes. In the eighteenth century, Egypt's Middle Kingdom collapsed into chaos following a number of reigns by weak monarchs. In its weakened state, the Nile Delta and northern Egypt became prey to invaders known in later times as the Hyksos. These people controlled much of Egypt for 200 years before being driven out by a Theban prince, Ahmose I, the founder of the Eighteenth Dynasty and the Egyptian Empire. Prior to the Hyksos' incursions, Egypt had been something of an isolationist state, seemingly secure within its own borders and with little interest in the doings of peoples outside the Nile Valley. The Hyksos' invasion and subsequent domination taught the Egyptians that such incuriosity was potentially fatal.

Not content to simply chase the Hyksos from Egyptian soil, Ahmose and his successors pursued them northeastward beyond Sinai, eventually conquering an Asiatic empire that comprised Palestine, Canaan, and most of Syria. However, by the time Ramses II began his long reign, the empire had fallen into decay and its restoration became a matter of great urgency for the new pharaoh.

The groundwork for this project had already been laid by Ramses' father Seti I (c. 1293–1279). Ramses, who had accompanied his father on campaign, was determined to complete Seti's great task. In the third year of his reign, Ramses led an expedition into Syria–Palestine, securing the loyalty of the cities and towns under Egyptian control. In addition, Ramses "persuaded" Bentešina, the king of Amurru in north Syria and sometime vassal of the Hittite king, to allow the pharaoh to station a division of elite troops in his city. This turned out to be one of the pharaoh's more fortunate decisions.

Ramses' expedition was in preparation for an invasion in earnest of north Syria, with the city of Kadesh as the immediate target. Lying in a bend of the north-flowing Orontes River, Kadesh controlled a major north-south route connecting Canaan and south Syria with the major east-west route from the Euphrates to the Mediterranean Coast. Conquered in the fifteenth century, it had since fallen out of the Egyptian orbit and had become tributary to the Hittites. Thus, any move against Kadesh was likely to initiate war with the formidable power of Hatti.

As we have seen, the Hittite king Muwatalli II had been concerned for some time about the Egyptian buildup in Syria, and in the spring of 1276, just as Ramses was leading a large force north toward Kadesh,

Muwatalli and his brother, the future Hattušili III, headed south leading perhaps 30,000 men. Bypassing the Egyptian division at Amurru, Muwatalli went inland following the Orontes Valley and established a base on the east side of the river just north of Kadesh. There he awaited Ramses.

The pharaoh's force consisted of four divisions of about 5,000 men each, which were named after the Egyptian gods Amon (Ramses' own), Re, Ptah, and Set. Ramses foolishly allowed this force to advance in a long, straggling line so that by the early afternoon of the day of the battle the Amon Division was separated from the rearmost Set Division by many miles. To make matters worse, Ramses intended to set up camp to the west of Kadesh, a maneuver that required his infantry and chariots to ford both the Orontes and a tributary stream. As Ramses was establishing his camp, both Ptah and Set were still miles from the Orontes ford.

The Re Division had just crossed the ford and was heading toward the tributary when Muwatalli struck, sending a division of chariotry west over the Orontes taking the Re Division in the rear, putting them to flight. Crossing the tributary, the Hittite force launched a second attack on the Amon Division.

Although Ramses showed a lack of wisdom in the positioning of his divisions, he also demonstrated marked qualities of a successful field commander in the ensuing emergency. Rallying the shaken Amon Division and haranguing the fleeing remnants of the Re Division into obedience, the pharaoh personally led charge after charge against the Hittite division threatening to encircle him. There was also luck on Ramses' side. When the pharaoh found it necessary to abandon his camp, part of the Hittite force became preoccupied in plundering it. Meanwhile, Muwatalli had inexplicably kept his other divisions on the east side of the Orontes and failed to commit them when the battle began turning in Ramses' favor. Finally as the pharaoh began pushing the Hittite force back across the river, the Ptah Division and, quite unexpectedly, Ramses' crack troops from Amurru arrived, forcing a general retreat of the Hittites over the river.

The next day neither the Hittites nor the Egyptians had much stomach for fighting. Ramses had suffered the heaviest losses, with both the Amon and Re Divisions badly mauled. As for the Hittites, they had lost much of their chariotry that had led the assault of the previous day. In short, neither side felt up to the challenge presented by the other. In avoiding further action, both Muwatalli and Ramses displayed hard-won wisdom and a new respect for each other. It must be remembered that neither power, great as it was, was accustomed to picking on anyone its own size. Like the Hittites in their dealings with fractious western vassals, the Egyptians were used to dispatching rebellious cities in piecemeal fashion. If it could be avoided, empires did not fight empires.

Ramses never did take the stronghold of Kadesh, nor did he make any subsequent attempts to do so. Kadesh would remain tributary to Hatti until the end of the century. The failure at Kadesh and the subsequent Egyptian retreat left Ramses' Asiatic empire in tatters as one Syrian and Canaanite city after another, sensing a change in fortune, threw off the Egyptian yoke. A lesser pharaoh might have accepted this as a permanent state of affairs and concentrated his energies in building a Fortress Egypt. Instead Ramses returned to the field and over the next twenty years restored the Canaanite and Syrian tributaries left to him by his father Seti.

Although there was never again a major clash between Egypt and Hatti, both empires felt it necessary during these years to maintain troops in Syria and Phoenicia to keep an eye on each other. As it turned out, the Hittites blinked first. When Muwatalli's son, Urhi-Tešub, assumed the throne in 1272, he was confronted almost immediately by a crisis arising from incursions west of the Euphrates launched by Assyria in which an erstwhile Hittite tributary state was captured. Instead of sending a force against the Assyrians, as his uncle Hattušili urged, Urhi-Tešub settled for making known his displeasure with the Assyrian king in a series of letters. Hattušili put up with what he considered to be the weakness of his nephew for five years before deposing him and sending him into internal exile at Carchemish in northeast Syria. This was a mistake, for Urhi-Tešub promptly escaped, first to Babylonia and then to Egypt.

Thus, Hattušili was anxious to conclude a treaty with Ramses. The Hittite king had much to gain from such a treaty, indeed much more than did his Egyptian counterpart. First, he craved recognition from Ramses as the legitimate ruler of Hatti; next, he wanted an end to the continued low-level hostilities with the Egyptians in Syria; third, he desired a mutual defense pact against an unnamed third foe (here he had Assyria in mind); and lastly, he wanted Ramses to deliver Urhi-Tešub into his hands. In the treaty that was eventually agreed upon (1259), Hattušili got everything he wanted except his wayward nephew. Ramses claimed to the end of Hattušili's reign that the royal refugee was not in Egypt, but in Babylonia, or perhaps Cyprus. Despite the pharaoh's protestations, Urhi-Tešub probably spent the rest of his days in Egypt fulminating against his sorry fate and futilely trying to win support for an invasion of Hatti which would restore him to his throne.

After the bloodshed at Kadesh and nearly twenty years of tensions, the treaty produced one other notable effect. It was that rarest event in the history of great power rivalry: the emergence of a genuine, if long-distance, friendship between the royal houses of the two empires. Hattušili and his queen Pudukhepa sent letter after letter to Ramses and his family, and the pharaoh and his queens, sons and daughters responded in kind. As is usual with royalty, the two families cemented their relationship with an exchange of princesses sent to marry a prince of the opposite house. In the end, Ramses lost some of his impetuosity, becoming more of a realist in the process. In one of his letters, Hattušili begged Ramses to send a good Egyptian physician to cure his sister's infertility. Ramses replied with blunt realism and a little humor:

> As for . . . my brother's sister, the king your brother knows her. Fifty years old, you say? She is certainly sixty! . . . I will send a good magician and an able physician and they will prepare some fertility drugs for her anyway.[4]

---

## NOTES

1. J. G. MacQueen, *The Hittites and Their Contemporaries in Asia Minor* (Boulder, CO: Westview, 1975).

2. Trevor Bryce, *The Kingdom of the Hittites* (Oxford: Clarendon Press, 1998).

3. The dating of Ramses' reign, and that of many other Egyptian pharaohs, is a matter of debate. We have opted for the currently preferred low dating of 1279–1213.

4. K. A. Kitchen, *Pharaoh Triumphant: The Life and Times of Ramesses II* (Warminster, UK: Aris and Phillips, 1982), p. 92.

# PRIMARY DOCUMENTS

## THE CLASSICAL GREEK VIEW

### DOCUMENT 1
### The History of Herodotus

*Herodotus, who lived between 484 and c. 430, is credited with the title the father of history for his account of the confrontation between the Greeks and the Persians. He recognized the importance of the event beginning in the middle of the sixth century with the expansion of the Persians into the west coast of Anatolia where Greek communities had existed since approximately 1000. Herodotus was born in one of these communities, Halicarnassus, and had heard of the Greeks' response to their loss of independence. When he left his home, he spent much of his time in Athens, one of the main targets of the Persian invasion of Greece in 490, and, a decade later, in 480–479. While residing in Athens, he could have heard reminiscences from people who had been alive at the time.*

*Appreciating the significance of the wars, Herodotus took advantage of new tools for recording the history of the confrontation. He traveled to witness for himself the places he was describing; he wrote in prose rather than the earlier poetic form; and he attempted to isolate causes and their effects. At the same time, he retained the Homeric quality of powerful storytelling which would entertain as well as inform his readers.*

*For our purpose, it is interesting to note the beginning of his account of events of the "Age of Heroes."*

These are the researches of Herodotus of Halicarnassus, which he pub-
lishes, in the hope of thereby preserving from decay the remembrance of
what men have done, and of preventing the great and wonderful actions
of the Greeks and the Barbarians from losing their due meed of glory;
and withal to put on record what were their grounds of feud.

1. According to the Persians best informed in history, the Phoenicians
began the quarrel. This people, who had formerly dwelt on the shores of
the Erythraean Sea, having migrated to the Mediterranean and settled
in the parts which they now inhabit, began at once, they say, to adventure on long voyages, freighting their vessels with the wares of Egypt and
Assyria. They landed at many places on the coast, and among the rest at
Argos, which was then pre-eminent above all the states included now
under the common name of Hellas. Here they exposed their merchan-
dise, and traded with the natives for five or six days; at the end of which
time, when almost everything was sold, there came down to the beach a
number of women, and among them the daughter of the king, who was,
they say, agreeing in this with the Greeks, Io, the child of Inachus. The
women were standing by the stern of the ship intent upon their pur-
chases, when the Phoenicians, with a general shout, rushed upon them.
The greater part made their escape, but some were seized and carried off.
Io herself was among the captives. The Phoenicians put the women on
board their vessel, and set sail for Egypt. Thus did Io pass into Egypt, according to the Persian story, which differs widely from the Phoenician:
and thus commenced, according to their authors, the series of outrages.

2. At a later period, certain Greeks, with whose name they are unac-
quainted, but who would probably be Cretans, made a landing at Tyre,
on the Phoenician coast, and bore off the king's daughter, Europé. In this
they only retaliated; but afterwards the Greeks, they say, were guilty of a
second violence. They manned a ship of war, and sailed to Aea, a city of
Colchis, on the river Phasis; from whence, after dispatching the rest of
the business on which they had come, they carried off Medea, the daughter of the king of the land. The monarch sent a herald into Greece to
demand reparation of the wrong, and the restitution of his child; but the
Greeks made answer, that having received no reparation of the wrong
done them in the seizure of Io the Argive, they should give none in this
instance.

3. In the next generation afterwards, according to the same authorities, Alexander the son of Priam, bearing these events in mind, resolved

to procure himself a wife out of Greece by violence, fully persuaded, that as the Greeks had not given satisfaction for their outrages, so neither would he be forced to make any for his. Accordingly he made prize of Helen; upon which the Greeks decided that, before resorting to other measures, they would send envoys to reclaim the princess and require reparation of the wrong. Their demands were met by a reference to the violence which had been offered to Medea, and they were asked with what face they could now require satisfaction, when they had formerly rejected all demands for either reparation or restitution addressed to them.

4. Hitherto the injuries on either side had been mere acts of common violence; but in what followed the Persians consider that the Greeks were greatly to blame, since before any attack had been made on Europe, they led an army to Asia. Now as for the carrying off of women, it is the deed, they say, of a rogue; but to make a stir about such as are carried off, argues a man a fool. Men of sense care nothing for such women, since it is plain that without their own consent they would never be forced away. The Asiatics, when the Greeks ran off with their women, never troubled themselves about the matter; but the Greeks, for the sake of a single Lacedaemonian girl, collected a vast armament, invaded Asia, and destroyed the kingdom of Priam. Henceforth they ever look upon the Greeks as their open enemies. For Asia, with all the various tribes of barbarians that inhabit it, is regarded by the Persians as their own; but Europe and the Greek race they look on as distinct and separate.

*Source*: George Rawlinson, *The History of Herodotus*, 4 vols. (New York: D. Appleton and Company, 1875), I.1–4.

---

## THE ARCHAEOLOGICAL EVIDENCE

## DOCUMENT 2
### Discovery of the Great Trojan Treasure

*A contemporary of Heinrich Schliemann, the classical scholar Walter Leaf, described Schliemann's contribution to the Homeric question realistically. "Dr. Schliemann was essentially 'epoch-making' in this branch of study, and it is not for epoch-making men to see the rounding off and com-*

*pletion of their task. That must be the labour of a generation at least. A man who can state to the world a completely new problem may be content to let the final solution of it wait for those that come after him"* (Introduction to Carl Schuchhardt, Schliemann's Excavations *[London: Macmillan, 1891] xxi).*

Schliemann was a pioneer in a discipline that only gained maturity in the twentieth century. His methods were crude and inexact by today's standards, but as more recent archaeologists have acknowledged, he set some remarkably high standards in appreciating the value of intrinsically worthless finds; in learning the nature of the region in which his sites were located; and in publishing his finds as quickly as possible. It must be admitted that he was also thrilled to find marks of wealth and power in his excavations. Certainly, a ten-year battle over Troy suggests that there was something worth taking in addition to the runaway wife of Menelaus.

This excerpt from Schliemann's book describing his work at Ilium is a good demonstration of both his method and his delight at special finds.

While following up this circuit-wall, and bringing more and more of it to light, close to the ancient building and north-west of the Gate, I struck upon a large copper article of the most remarkable form, which attracted my attention all the more, as I thought I saw gold behind it. On the top of it was a layer of red and calcined ruins, from 4¾ to 5¼ ft. thick, as hard as stone, and above this again the above mentioned wall of fortification (5 ft. broad and 20 ft. high), built of large stones and earth, which must have been erected shortly after the destruction of Troy. In order to secure the treasure from my workmen and save it for archaeology, it was necessary to lose no time; so, although it was not yet the hour for breakfast, I immediately had *païdos* called. This is a word of uncertain derivation, which has passed over into Turkish, and is here employed in place of ανάπαυτις, or time for rest. While the men were eating and resting, I cut out the Treasure with a large knife. This required great exertion and involved great risk, since the wall of fortification, beneath which I had to dig, threatened every moment to fall down upon me. But the sight of so many objects, every one of which is of inestimable value to archaeology, made me reckless, and I never thought of any danger. It would, however, have been impossible for me to have removed the treasure without the help of my dear wife, who stood at my side, ready to pack the things I cut out in her shawl, and to carry them away. All the different articles of which this Treasure was composed will be described at the proper place in the precise order in which they were taken out of the ruins. . . .

As I found all these articles together, in the form of a rectangular mass, or packed into one another, it seems certain that they were placed on the city wall in a wooden chest. This supposition seems to be corroborated by the fact that close by the side of these articles I found a copper key. It is therefore possible that some one had packed the treasure in the chest, and carried it off, without having had time to pull out the key; when he reached the wall, however, the hand of an enemy, or the fire, overtook him, and he was obliged to abandon the chest, which was immediately covered, to a height of 5 ft., with the ashes and stones of the adjoining house.

Perhaps the articles found a few days previously in a room of the chief's house, close to the place where the Treasure was discovered, belonged to this unfortunate person. These articles consisted of a helmet and a silver vase, with a cup of electrum [a mixture of silver and gold], which will be described in the chapter on this Third City.

On the thick layer of *débris* which covered the Treasure, the builders of the new city erected a fortification-wall already mentioned, composed of large hewn and unhewn stones and earth. This wall extended to within 3¼ ft. of the surface of the hill.

That the Treasure was packed together at a moment of supreme peril appears to be proved, among other things, by the contents of the largest silver vase, consisting of nearly 9000 objects of gold, which will be described in the subsequent pages. The person who endeavoured to save the Treasure had, fortunately, the presence of mind to place the silver vase, with the valuable articles inside it, upright in the chest, so that nothing could fall out, and everything has been preserved uninjured.

Hoping to find more treasures here, I pulled down the upper wall, and I also broke away the enormous block of *débris* which separated my western and north-western trenches from the great massive walls which I used to call the "Tower." But to do this I had to pull down the larger of my wooden houses, and to bridge over the Gates, so as to facilitate the removal of the *débris*. I found there many interesting antiquities; more especially three silver dishes . . . , 1 ft. 9 in. below the place where the Treasure was discovered; two of them were broken in pieces by the labourer's pickaxe; the third is entire. That the Treasure itself escaped injury from the pickaxes, was due to the large copper vessel, which projected in such a way that I could cut everything out of the hard *débris* with a knife."

Source: Heinrich Schliemann, *Ilios: The City and Country of the Trojans* (New York: Harper & Brothers, 1881), pp. 41–43.

# DOCUMENT 3
## Recent Exploration: The Ulu Burun Shipwreck

*In the early decades of archaeological efforts to discover the roots of the human story, it was sufficiently challenging to excavate—or even attempt to excavate—a single site or to understand the significance of a few pieces of evidence. Thus, the results of initial investigations produced isolated snapshots of specific locations at particular moments in time. Egypt was one focus of study, Anatolia another, Greece yet a third. The relationship between them—and other—areas was little explored.*

*A panoramic view of the connection of these snapshots has only begun to appear. For example, the deeper understanding of Egyptian and Ancient Near Eastern civilization influenced the view of the Aegean cultures, uncovered later than those of the eastern Mediterranean. They were initially viewed as somewhat pale duplicates of the earlier civilizations. The addition of new tools has greatly enlarged the possibility of understanding interactions between contemporary cultures. For example, pottery can now be analyzed to reveal the source of the clay, and the results allow an understanding of the movement of that pottery by trade or other means. Or the diffusion of techniques can be traced to the original source, also demonstrating the spread of ideas and, most likely, people.*

*Archaeology has undergone considerable change, particularly aided by the incorporation of new scientific technologies. Some of those techniques permit exploration under water as well as under ground. The fruits of one find buried deep within the sea have demonstrated how tightly connected the cultures of the late Bronze Age were. Excerpts from one of the outstanding examples are from the account of the director of the excavation, marine archaeologist George Bass.*

The first hint of a wreck at Ulu Burun came in the summer of 1982. A young diver named Mehmet Çakir told his captain that he had seen strange "metal biscuits with ears" on the seabed while working at a depth of 150 feet off the point.

The captain recognized the description as that of a Bronze Age copper ingot from a drawing Don [Frey, an American colleague] had circulated among the sponge boats. Çakir's discovery was reported to Turkey's Museum of Underwater Archaeology in the town of Bodrum, where INA [the International Nautical Association] has its Turkish base. Divers from the museum and from INA quickly visited the site. They confirmed the existence of a wreck and estimated its date as the 14th or 13th century B.C.

The following summer my assistant Cemal [Pulak] led a preliminary survey of the Ulu Burun site along with Don Frey and Jack Kelley [another American colleague]. They returned to Texas in September with sketches and photographs to show me, and they were literally breathtaking.

Beginning at a depth of 140 feet and stretching another 30 feet down a steep slope lay a total of 84 copper ingots, many of them still in neat rows as they had been stowed nearly 34 centuries ago. Many more ingots lay partly obscured beneath the upper rows.

Other exposed items included six enormous storage jars, each as large as the one that hid the thieves in *Ali Baba and the Forty Thieves*. There were also dozens of terra-cotta amphorae . . .

Examining all the sketches and photographs, I could only agree with Don Frey: "We're looking at an archaeologists' dream."

. . . .

Almost at once [during the 1984 season] the wreck fulfilled our expectations. The first dives yielded disk-shaped copper ingots as well as the familiar four-handled style, a mace head of stone, a Canaanite amphora full of glass beads, and a second amphora filled with orpiment, a yellow sulfide of arsenic once used as pigment.

We also brought up samples of a grayish, brittle material that later proved to be 99.5 percent pure tin—the very substance that spurred on the Bronze Age but is seldom found from that period in raw form. . . .

Soon afterward we did find tin ingots. A day or two later, Tufan brought up what appeared to be a bronze dagger, though the concretion surrounding it disguised all but the general shape.

. . . .

The great number of copper ingots at Ulu Burun could support a theory I had held for more than a quarter of a century: that the Canaanites, or Bronze Age Phoenicians, played a major role in the maritime commerce of the eastern Mediterranean.

Even from underwater we recognized the importance of our next discovery—a pair of opaque, cobalt blue glass disks, each six inches in diameter and two and a half inches thick. They were slightly rounded on their bottom edges. During the weeks that followed, we were to find many more such disks, some still stowed as neatly as they had originally been loaded aboard.

The secrets of the Bronze Age glass trade apparently were well kept.
. . . .
We turned our attention next to the huge storage jars, known as *pithoi*, that Cemal had seen during his 1983 survey. [The first to be investigated was found to contain large quantities of small pottery types.] I quickly dived with Aşkin and Yaşar to look at the pithos, and we removed more pottery from inside it. In the end we found nearly every major type of pottery made on Cyprus during the Late Bronze Age.
. . . .
And now the gold cup . . . shaped like a chalice, formed of two gold cones riveted together at their apexes. Almost touching the chalice was a common Mycenaean terra-cotta stemmed cup known as a *kylix*, which has since proved of greater historical value than the chalice. The date and origin of the chalice remain unknown, but the humble kylix is of a distinctive shape in vogue only at the end of, and shortly after, the reign of Egyptian Pharaoh Amenhotep III, who ruled from 1417 to 1379 B.C. So our ship probably sank during the early 14th century, or shortly after. . . .
. . . .
On one of my dives . . . I had noticed a pointed object—a stick of wood, I thought—protruding from the sand nearby. After a single glance at the object Cemal surfaced and announced happily: "We have a hippopotamus tooth on the wreck!" Once again he was correct.

From the area of the hippopotamus tooth we brought up an eight-inch length of elephant tusk neatly sawed at both ends. . . . Near the elephant tusk we uncovered several silver bracelets that I later identified as probably Canaanite, followed by a gold pendant. . . .

The raw materials on board the Ulu Burun ship, together with the Cypriot pottery and Canaanite amphorae, weapons, and jewelry, all had eastern Mediterranean connections, establishing that our ship was sailing from east to west when it sank.

But the discovery of several carved amber beads presented a problem . . . the Ulu Burun beads were later identified as Baltic amber which occurs in an arc sweeping across northern Europe from the Baltic south to the Black Sea.

. . . .

[Examination of remains of the ship itself pushed] back our knowledge of seagoing ship construction by nearly a thousand years [and thus] we now know that ships at the time of the mythical Greek heroes such as Odysseus and Achilles were built in the same manner as later Greek and Roman vessels. And we know too that Homer's description of Odysseus' constructing a boat was accurate.

. . . .

[During the next season] for the first time we had recovered Egyptian artifacts from the wreck! . . . a scarab of bone or ivory framed in gold and carved with ornamental hieroglyphs on its base; . . . a small rectangular plaque of greenish stone [on which] could be read: "Ptah, Lord of Truth;" . . . a gold ring; . . . a solid gold scarab [bearing the name] "Nefertiti."

. . . .

We try not to speculate on the exact date or nationality of the wreck. It's hard not to, but after all, we've dug only half the site so far. For the moment it's enough to savor the ship as an archaeologists' dream come true. But even I would never have imagined a site with such an abundance of new information for scholars from so many fields—Egyptologists, geographers, Homeric scholars, students of ancient metallurgy, glass, ship construction, sea trade, agriculture, art, and religion.

In short, we are salvaging the greatest of all treasures—the treasure of knowledge.

*Source*: George Bass, "Oldest Known Shipwreck Reveals Bronze Age Splendors," *National Geographic* (December 1987): 693–732. Permission of the National Geographic Society.

Final excavation at the site took place in 1994. Since then study and conservation of the finds has become a year-long operation at headquarters in Bodrum. A large building houses offices, dormitories, a library and research facilities. Objects are on display in the Bodrum Museum of Underwater Archaeology, housed in the Castle of the Hospitaller Knights of St. John. The facilities can be viewed on the web at www.dive turkey.com/inaturkey/ulub.htm.

---

# CONTEMPORARY RECORDS
## THE HITTITE RECORDS (C. 1420–1220)

*The Hittite Royal Archives, like the Linear B tablets for the Myce-naean world, are an invaluable resource for the study of the politics, so-ciety, and culture of Bronze Age Hatti. Also like the Linear B tablets, however, they are frustratingly imprecise about many things that scholars would like to know. In particular, the geographic location of regions, states, and cities mentioned in the archives is often not given, leaving the student to speculate by indirect means. This difficulty is at the heart of the debate over the identity and whereabouts of Ahhiyawa.*

*The first text is particularly thorny in regard to geographic location, for it contains a long list of states or cities, very few of which can be located on a modern map. All that may be said with certainty is that all or most of these places are in western Anatolia. The list itself comprises the mem-bers of a confederacy, called the Confederacy of Assuwa, which is hostile to the Hittites who, led by their king Tudhaliya I, have invaded their ter-ritory. For our purposes the importance of this list lies in the mention of Wilusiya and Taruisa at the end of the text. Wilusiya, or Wilusa in later texts, is thought to be (W)Ilios, whereas Taruisa may possibly be Troia, or Troy. The fact that they are listed next to each other may indicate that the Hittites considered them to be neighboring cities. Assuwa itself is very likely the earliest reference to Asia that in Roman times was a province in northwest Anatolia.*

*The context of the action is Tudhaliya's invasion of the Kingdom of Arzawa, a strong state that may have been situated between the Hermus River (modern Gediz) on the north and the Cayster River (Kücük Menderes) on the south. The capital of Arzawa, referred to in the texts as Apasa, may have been Bronze Age Ephesus. Tudhaliya had defeated Arzawa and was on his way back to Hattusa when twenty-two states formed what was called the Confederacy of Assuwa and rose against him.*

## DOCUMENT 4
## The Confederacy of Assuwa

But when I turned back to Hattusa, then against me these lands declared war: [ ]ugga,[1] Kispuwa, Unaliya, [ ], Dura, Halluwa, Huwallusiya,
Karakisa,[2] Dunda, Adadura, Parista, [ ], [ ]waa, Warsiya, Kuruppiya, [
]luissa, Alatra, Mount Pahurina, Pasuhalta, [ ], Wilusiya, Taruisa. [These
lands] with their warriors assembled themselves . . . and drew up their
army opposite me . . . I, Tudhaliya, brought up my forces at night, and
surrounded the army of the enemy. The gods handed their army over to
me, the Sun Goddess of Arinna, the Storm God of Heaven, the Protective Genius of Hatti, Zamama, Istar, Sin, Lelwani. I defeated the army of
the enemy and entered their country. And from whatever country an
army had come to battle, the gods went before me, and the countries
which I have mentioned, which declared war, the gods delivered them
to me. All these countries I carried off. The conquered population, oxen,
sheep, the possessions of the land, I brought away to Hattusa. Now when
I had destroyed the land of Assuwa, I came back home to Hattusa. And
as booty 10,000 foot-soldiers and 600 teams of horses for chariots together
with the "lords of the bridle" I brought to Hattusa, and I settled them in
Hattusa.

*Source: Annals*, obv. 13'–26', excerpts from J. Garstang and O. R. Gurney, *The
Geography of the Hittite Empire* (London: British Institute of Archaeology, 1959),
pp. 121–122. Reprinted with permission of Mrs. O. R. Gurney and The British
Institute of Archaeology at Ankara.

---

## NOTES

1. Possibly *Lukka*, that is, Lycia in southwest Anatolia.
2. Possibly a reference to Caria, also in southwest Anatolia. It is possible that
the list is naming places from south to north along the Aegean coast. Caria and
Lycia were both in the south. The list ends with Wilusiya and Taruisa, places
that are most probably in the north, as would be expected if Wilusiya is Ilios
and Taruisa is Troy.

# DOCUMENT 5
## The Indictment of Madduwatta

*This text was probably written late in the fifteenth century B.C.E. by Arnuwanda I, the son of Tudhaliya of the previous text. Madduwatta, the ruler of an unnamed western or southwestern Anatolian state and a vassal of the king of Hatti, has been driven from his land by Attarsiya (or Attarrissiya), the "Man of Ahhiya." This is the first mention of Ahhiyawa, or Ahhiyawans, in the Hittite records. Madduwatta fled to Arnuwanda's father, Tudhaliya, who at that time was still king, and he intervened, preventing Attarsiya from pursuing the refugee further. Tudhaliya gave Madduwatta the land of Mount Zippasla[1] on condition that he have no further contact with Attarsiya. But Attarsiya sought out Madduwatta, seeking to kill him, and to prevent this Tudhaliya sent out an army against Attarsiya.*

*The document is called* The Indictment of Madduwatta *because some time after these events, Madduwatta allied himself with Attarsiya and together they raided Cyprus, which was claimed by King Arnuwanda of Hatti.*

Subsequently Attarsiya, the Man of Ahhiya, came and sought to kill you, Madduwatta. But when the father (Tudhaliya) of My Sun (Arnuwanda) heard [of this], he dispatched Kišnapili, troops, and chariots to do battle against Attarsiya. And you, Madduwatta, offered no resistance to Attarsiya, and fled before him . . . Kišnapili marched in battle against Attarsiya. And on Attarsiya's side, 100 chariots and . . . infantry took the field. They engaged (each other) in battle, and they (the Hittites) killed a nobleman of Attarsiya, and on our side they (the enemy) killed a nobleman, Zitanza. And Attarsiya abandoned (his attack on?) Madduwatta and went back to his own land. And they restored Madduwatta to his vassal status.

---

## NOTE

1. This location is unidentified. Might it not be Mount Sipylus not far south of the Hermus and just northeast of Smyrna (modern Izmir)? Mount Sipylus is likely to have been in what the Hittites called Arzawa.

Source: *Keilschrifturkunden aus Boghazkoi* XIV1 + *Keilschrifttexte aus Boghazkoi* XIX 38 (*Catalogue des textes hittites* 147) sec. 12. Excerpts from T. R. Bryce, "Ahhiyawans and Mycenaeans—Anatolian viewpoint," *Oxford Journal of Archaeology* 8:3 (1989): 297–310. Blackwell Publishing. Reprinted with permission.

# DOCUMENT 6
## The Career of Piyamardu

*Western Anatolia was for the Hittites a frontier region, and their control over the states in this area was often shaky. Regions in which such conditions are prevalent are often the haven of adventurers, fortune hunters, or political opportunists. Piyamaradu, a Hittite nobleman who had apparently fallen out of favor at Hattusa, became one such adventurer. There follow two letters that focus on the activities of this freebooter. The first is from early in the reign of Muwatalli II (1295–1272), and the second is from that of his brother Hattušili III (1267–1237). Special attention should be paid to the changed condition of Millawanda, which is now a vassal of Ahhiyawa, and to the heightened status of the king of Ahhiyawa mentioned in the second letter. Hattušili refers to him as "the Great King, my brother."*

*Manapa-Tarhunda, king of the Šeha River Land near Arzawa and author of the first letter, has been defeated in an attempt to dislodge Piyamaradu from Wilusa over which he has made himself overlord. Piyamaradu has followed up his victory by deposing Manapa-Tarhunda and replacing him with his (Piyamaradu's) son-in-law Atpa, the Ahhiyawan vassal ruler of Millawanda. Muwatalli, the Hittite king to which the letter is addressed, has sent out an army to capture Piyamaradu and expects Manapa-Tarhunda to aid in this effort. Manapa, perhaps out of fear of Piyamaradu, excuses himself on account of illness.*

[To . . . ] speak! [Thus says] Manapa-Tarhunda thy servant. [With] thy [ . . . ] all is well. [ . . . ] came and brought Hittite troops. [ . . . they] went back to attack the Land of Wilusa. [ . . . But with me] it goes ill, I am grievously sick; the sickness has [ . . . ] prostrated me. How [Piyama]radu has humiliated me! He has appointed Atpa [ . . . ] over me, and he has attacked the Land of Lazpa (Lesbos?). [And the] . . . men who belonged to me all made common cause with him, and those who belonged to My Sun (Muwatalli) also made common cause with him.

*Source*: KUB XIX 5 (CTH 191), excerpts from J. Gartang and O. R. Gurney, *The Geography of the Hittite Empire* (London: British Institute of Archaeology, 1959), pp. 121–122. Reprinted with permission of Mrs. O. R. Gurney and The British Institute of Archaeology at Ankara.

# DOCUMENT 7
## The Tawagalawa Letter

*Although the Hittites apparently succeeded in driving Piyamaradu from Wilusa, he appears again in the Hittite archives many years later, taking advantage of a rebellion against Hittite rule by the Lukka Lands (Lycia) of southwest Anatolia. While the Hittites sent out a force to quell the uprising, the rebellious Lukka people appealed to Tawagalawa, a high Ahhiyawan official, for aid. Piyamaradu went east to escort the Lukka folk to Millawanda where Tawagalawa would take them by ship to safety. At the approach of the Hittite army, Piyamaradu appeared to negotiate, hinting at the exchange of the refugees in return for a vassal kingdom. But when Hattušili sent an ambassador to deal with Piyamaradu, Piyamaradu offended him by demanding a kingdom "on the spot." With the failure of negotiations, Hattušili resumed his march. Meanwhile, Piyamaradu escaped with all the fugitives presumably to Ahhiyawa or Ahhiyawan-controlled islands. Hattušili entered Millawanda, where he harangued Piyamaradu's son-in-law Atpa for allowing him to escape and subsequently sent a complaining letter to Piyamaradu's ally, the king of Ahhiyawa.*

Now when I came to Sallapa, he (Piyamaradu) sent a man to meet me (saying) "Take me into vassalage and send me the Crown Prince (Hattušili's son Nerikkaili) and he will conduct me to My Sun!" And I sent him the Crown Prince (saying) "Go, set him beside you on the chariot and bring him here!" But he—he snubbed the Crown Prince and said "no." But is not the Crown Prince the proper representative (?) of the king? He had my hand. But he answered (?) him "no" and humiliated him before the lands; and moreover he said this: "Give me a kingdom here on the spot! If not I will not come . . ."[1]

**Later in the context of his entrance into Millawanda, Hattušili writes:**

But when [my brother's messenger (the king of Ahhiyawa's ambassador)] arrived at my quarters, he brought me no [greeting] and [he brought] me no present, but he spoke [as follows]: "He (the king of Ahhiyawa) has written Atpa (saying) 'Put Piyamaradu at the disposal of the King of Hatti.' So I went [into] Millawanda. But I went [also] in [this] resolution. 'The words which I shall speak to Piyamaradu, the subjects of my Brother also shall hear them.' But Piyamaradu escaped by ship. Awayana and Atpa heard the charges which I had against him. Now since he is their father-in-law, why are they concealing the matter? I obtained an oath from them, so they ought to report the matter truthfully to you."[2]

**There follows a list of grievances against Piyamaradu and an appeal to the Ahhiyawan king to exercise some control over him.**

Now according to this rumor, during the time when he (Piyamaradu) leaves behind his wife and children and household in my Brother's land, your land is affording him protection. But he is continually raiding my land; but whenever I have prevented him in that, he comes back into your territory. Are you now, my Brother, favorably disposed to this conduct? (If not), now, my Brother, write him at least this: "Rise up, go forth into the Land of Hatti, your lord has settled his account with you! . . . From my country you shall not conduct hostilities. If your heart is in the Land of Masa (Mysia), then go there! The King of the Hatti and I—in that matter of Wilusa over which we were at enmity, he has converted me and we have made friends . . . a war would not be right for us."[3]

**The *Tawagalawa Letter* is also famous among scholars for its brief and somewhat cryptic reference to the king of Ahhiyawa as a Great King. In support of arguments in favor of the notion that Hattušili considered the king of Ahhiyawa his equal are the repeated references to the latter as "my Brother," a form of address normally reserved for the Egyptian Pharaoh and the kings of Assyria and Babylonia.**
**Having received a message from the Ahhiyawan king, Hattušili said:**

If anyone of my lords (?) had spoken to me—or one of my (other) Brothers—I would have listened even to *his* word. . . . But now, my Brother, the Great King, my equal, has written to me; shall I not listen to the word of my equal?"[4]

## NOTES

1. *Tawagalawa Letter*, 16–15, excerpts from J. Garstang and O. R. Gurney, *The Geography of the Hittite Empire* (London: British Institute of Archaeology, 1959), pp. 111–114. Reprinted with permission of Mrs. O. R. Gurney and The British Institute of Archaeology at Ankara.

2. KUB XIV 3 I 53–67, excerpts from J. Garstang and O. R. Gurney, *The Geography of the Hittite Empire* (London: British Institute of Archaeology, 1959), pp. 111–114. Reprinted with permission of Mrs. O. R. Gurney and The British Institute of Archaeology at Ankara.

3. KUB XIV 3 III 54–IV 10, excerpts from J. Garstang and O. R. Gurney, *The Geography of the Hittite Empire* (London: British Institute of Archaeology, 1959), pp. 111–114. Reprinted with permission of Mrs. O. R. Gurney and The British Institute of Archaeology at Ankara.

4. KUB XIV 3 II 9–20, H. G. Güterbock, "The Hittites and the Aegean World: Part I, The Ahhiyawa Problem Reconsidered," AJA 87 (1983): 135.

# DOCUMENT 8
## The Millawanda Letter

*In the latter half of the thirteenth century B.C.E., another revolution occurred among the Hittite vassal states of west Anatolia. The Ahhiyawan vassal king of Millawanda, possibly Atpa, was still making trouble among the neighboring states loyal to Hatti. Utima and Atriya are specifically mentioned as having suffered raids from Millawanda with many hostages taken. These states appealed to the Hittites for aid, and a force was sent out by King Tudhaliya IV (1237–1209). Meanwhile, Walmu, king of Wilusa and a loyal vassal to Tudhaliya, had been deposed and fled to the son of the Millawandan king for protection. It is unclear whether the Millawandan king had caused Walmu to be deposed, but the letter makes apparent that the former's son was in open rebellion against him, and thus it would make sense for Walmu to seek his aid. The son of the Millawandan king joined forces with the Hittites and succeeded in driving his father out. Tudhaliya then placed the son on the throne of Millawanda. The Millawanda Letter addressed from Tudhaliya to his new Millawandan ally gives instructions for the restoration of Walmu and goes on to clarify questions regarding the borders of Millawanda.*

But Kuwalanaziti kept the documents which [I/they (?) made] for Walmu. Now behold he is bringing them to you, my son (the new king of Millawanda). Examine them! Now, my son, as long as you protect the welfare of My Sun (Tudhaliya), I, My Sun, will trust your good will. Now, my son, send Walmu to me, and I will install him as king again of Wilusa. And just as previously he was king of Wilusa, now let him be so again! As Walmu was previously our kulawanis vassal, so let him (again) be a kulawanis vassal! . . .

.
.

When we, My Majesty, and you, my son, established/fixed the border of Milawata (Millawanda) for ourselves . . . I did not give you (such and such a place) within the territory of Milawata.

*Source:* KUB XIX 55 + KUB XLVIII 90 38–43, translated by H. Hoffner [1982]; KUB XLVIII 90 47, 49, translated by T. R. Bryce, "Ahhiyawans and Myce-naeans—Anatolian Viewpoint," *Oxford Journal of Archaeology* 8:3 (1989): pp. 297–310. Blackwell Publishing. Reprinted with permission.

## DOCUMENT 9
## The Šaušgamuwa Treaty

*The result of the realignment of Millawanda back to the Hittite sphere of influence was a sharp diminution of Ahhiyawan influence in Anatolia. This decline in power is shown in dramatic fashion in the passage from The Šaušgamuwa Treaty in which the king of Ahhiyawa is stricken from a list of kings who are of equal rank with the Hittite king. Šaušgamuwa was the king of Amurru in northern Syria and a Hittite vassal. The aim of this treaty, drawn up by Tudhaliya IV, was to strengthen the Hittites' southern defenses against Assyria, which was then threatening Hatti from the east. The purpose of the king list in the treaty was to inform Šaušga-muwa against whom he might be expected to supply forces in the event of war. The erasure of the king of Ahhiyawa may only be a scribal error. Still his absence from the list is strange considering how anxious Tudhaliya's father was to bestow on the Ahhiyawan king the title of Great King some years before. Even so, Ahhiyawan mercantile power was still recognized elsewhere in the treaty where Tudhaliya is at some pains to make sure Šaušgamuwa allows no Ahhiyawan ships "to sail to him" (KUB XXIII 1 IV 23, transl. by E. Cline [1991]).*

And the kings who (are) of equal rank with me, the king of Egypt, the king of Babylonia, the king of Assyria, ~~the king of Ahhiyawa~~, if the king of Egypt is a friend to My Sun, let him also be a friend to you, if he is an enemy of My Sun, let him be your enemy also . . .

*Source:* KUB XXIII 1 IV 1–7, translated by T. R. Bryce, "Ahhiyawans and Mycenaeans-Anatolian Viewpoint," *Oxford Journal of Archaeology* 8:3 (1989): 298. Blackwell publishing. Reprinted with permission. Edited by C. Kühne and H. Otten (1971).

# DOCUMENT 10
## The Battle of Kadesh

### EGYPTIAN ACCOUNTS

*The great battle of Kadesh fought in the early part of the thirteenth century pitted the Egyptian army headed by Pharaoh Ramses II against the Hittite force led by King Muwatalli. Each leader commanded at least 20,000 troops. The conflict arose out of the long-standing contest for control of the Levant in northern Syria, the Egyptians expanding northward while the Hittites pushed south from Anatolia. Kadesh, in northern Syria, was meant to decide the successful claimant to most of the Levant. Although the Hittites enjoyed an initial advantage in catching the Egyptian army unprepared for battle, the outcome was essentially a draw. A few years later, the Pharaoh and the Hittite king agreed to a treaty of peace and brotherhood that was sealed by the marriage of Ramses II to a daughter of the Hittite king. An account of the battle is pictured in reliefs and in texts carved in the walls of several Egyptian temples, so great was the pride of Ramses. However, since we do not have a Hittite version, we may imagine that the description is biased in its praise of Egyptian victory.*

Year 5, third month of the third season, day 9; under the majesty of [the great god] Horus: Mighty Bull, Beloved of Truth; King of Upper and Lower Egypt; Usermare-Setepnere; Son of [sun god] Re; Ramses Meriamon, given life forever.

Lo his majesty was in Zahi on his second victorious campaign. The goodly watch in life, prosperity and health, in the tent of his majesty, was on the highland south of Kadesh.

When his majesty appeared like the rising of Re, he assumed the adornments of his father, Montu. When the king proceeded northward,

and his majesty had arrived at a locality south of the town of Shabtuna . . . , there came two Shasu, to speak to his majesty as follows: "Our
brethren, who belong to the greatest of the families with the vanquished
chief of Kheta [the Hittites], have made us come to his majesty, to say:
"We will be subjects of Pharaoh . . . and we will flee from the vanquished
chief of Kheta. . . ." Now, these Shasu spake these words, which they
spake to his majesty, falsely, (for) the vanquished chief of Kheta made
them come to spy where his majesty was, in order to cause the army of
his majesty not to draw up for fighting him, to battle with the vanquished
chief of Kheta.

Lo, the vanquished chief of Kheta came with every chief of every
country, their infantry and their chariotry, which he had brought with
him by force, and stood, equipped, drawn up in line of battle behind
Kadesh the Deceitful, while his majesty knew it not. Then his majesty
proceeded northward and arrived on the northwest of Kadesh; and the
army of his majesty [made camp] there.

Then, as his majesty sat upon a throne of gold, there arrived a scout
who was in the following of his majesty, and he brought two scouts of
the vanquished chief of Kheta. They were conducted into the presence,
and his majesty said to them: "What are ye?" They said: "As for us, the
vanquished chief of the Kheta has caused that we should come to spy out
where his majesty is." Said his majesty to them: "He! Where is he, the
vanquished chief of Kheta? Behold, I have heard, saying: 'He is in the
land of Aleppo [some distance from Kadesh]. Said they: "See the vanquished chief of Kheta is stationed, together with many countries. . . .
they are standing, drawn up for battle, behind Kadesh the Deceitful."

Then his majesty had the princes called into the presence, and had
them hear every word which the two scouts of the vanquished chief of
Kheta . . . had spoken. Said his majesty to them: "See ye the manner
wherewith [men] have stood, daily, saying to the Pharaoh: "The vanquished chief of Kheta is in the land of Aleppo; he has fled before his
majesty. . . . But see, I have held a hearing in this very hour with the two
scouts [who report] they are stationed behind Kadesh the Deceitful. . . .

Said the princes who were in the presence of his majesty: "It is a great
fault, which the governors of the countries and the officials of
Pharaoh . . . have committed in not informing that the vanquished chief
of Kheta was near the king; and (in) that they told his report to his
majesty daily.

Then the vizier was ordered to hasten the army of his majesty, while they were marching on the south of Shabtuna in order to bring them to the place where his majesty was.

Lo, while his majesty sat talking with the princes, the vanquished chief of Kheta came, and the numerous countries, which were with him. They crossed over the channel on the south of Kadesh and charged into the army of his majesty while they were marching, and not expecting it. Then the infantry and chariotry of his majesty retreated before them, northward to the place where his majesty was. Lo, the foes of the vanquished chief of Kheta surrounded the bodyguard of his majesty, who were by his side.

When his majesty saw them, he was enraged against them, like, his father, Montu, lord of Thebes. He seized the adornments of battle, and arrayed himself in his coat of mail. He was like [the powerful god] Baal in his hour. Then he betook himself to his horses, and led quickly on, being alone by himself. He charged into the foes of the vanquished chief of Kheta, and the numerous countries which were with him. His majesty was like Sutekh, the great in strength, smiting and slaying among them; his majesty hurled them headlong, one upon another into the water of the Orontes.

[Ramses reported] "I charged all countries, while I was alone, my infantry and my chariotry having forsaken me. Not one among them stood to turn about. I swear, as Re loves me, as my father, [the god] Atum, favors me, that, as for every matter which his majesty has stated, I did it in truth, in the presence of my infantry and my chariotry."

*Source*: James H. Breasted, *Ancient Records of Egypt* (Chicago: University of Chicago Press, 1906), Vol. 3, sections 317–327.

# DOCUMENT 11
## Land and Sea Peoples

*During the reign of Pharaoh Merneptah (1213–1204 B.C.E.), Egypt was attacked by what seems to have been a temporary coalition of Libyans and other groups known collectively as the Land and Sea Peoples. Their names are recorded in an account of the invasion carved into the walls of the temple at Karnak. Precise identification is impossible in most cases, although the Lukka may well be peoples from Lycia in southern Anatolia and some scholars identify the Ekwesh with Ahhiyawans, and thus Achaeans/Mycenaeans. This record is one of a number coming from all parts of the eastern Mediterranean sphere in the late thirteenth and early twelfth centuries B.C.E. Whatever the cause of these movements and invasions may have been, they were instrumental in the collapse of the flourishing internationalism that had characterized the eastern Mediterranean since the middle of the second millennium. The inscriptional evidence reporting the invasion is incomplete in many places but even so provides a vivid account of a major event.*

[Beginning of the victory which his majesty achieved in the land of Libya] . . . Ekwesh, Teresh, Luka, Sherden, Shekelesh, Northerners coming from all lands.

. . . . Every country is in fear at the sight of him, King Merneptah . . . desolated, made a waste, commanding that the invader of his every boundary of Egypt bow himself down in his time . . .

. . . he [assumed] the throne of Horus, he was appointed to preserve the folk alive, he hath arisen as king to protect the people . . . the choicest of his bowmen were mustered, his chariotry was brought up from every side, his scouts were in. . . . His infantry marched out, the heavy armed troops arrived, beautiful in appearance, leading the bowmen against every land.

. . . the third season saying: "The wretched, fallen chief of Libya, Meryey, son of Ded has fallen upon the country of Tehenu with his bowmen . . . Sherden, Shekelesh, Ekwesh, Luka, Teresh, taking the best of every warrior and every man of war of his country. He has brought his wife and his children . . . leaders of the camp, and he has reached the western boundary. . . .

Lo, his majesty was enraged at their report, like a lion; [he assembled his court], and said to them: "Hear ye the command of your lord; I give . . . as ye shall do, saying: I am the ruler who shepherds you; I spend my time searching out . . . you, as a father, who preserves alive his children; while ye fear like birds, and ye know not the goodness of that which he does. [Shall the land] be wasted and forsaken at the invasion of every country, while the Nine Bows plunder its borders, and rebels invade it every day? . . . They have repeatedly penetrated the fields of Egypt [to] the [great] river. They have halted, they have spent whole days and months dwelling. . . . They have reached the hills of the oasis, and have cut off the district of Toyeh. . . . They spend their time going about the land, fighting, to fill their bodies daily. They come to the land of Egypt, to seek the necessities of their mouths. . . . Their chief is like a dog, a man of [boasting] without courage; . . .

. . . the leaders of the bowmen in front thereof to overthrow the land of Libya. When they went forth, the hand of the god was with them; (even) Amon was with them as their shield. . . .

Then his majesty saw in a dream as if a statue of [the god] Ptah were standing before Pharaoh. . . . He spake to him: "Take thou (it)," while he extended to him the sword, and "banish thou the fearful heart from thee.". . .

. . . infantry and chariotry in (great) number were camped before them on the shore. . . . Lo, the wretched chief of [Libya] in the night of the second day of the third month of the third season (eleventh month) when the land grew light (enough) for advancing with them. The wretched fallen chief of Libya came at the time of the third day of the third month of the third season (eleventh month) and he brought . . . until they arrived. The infantry of his majesty went forth together with his chariotry, [the god] Amon-Re being with them. . . .

. . . there was none that escape among them. Lo, the bowmen of his majesty spent six hours of destruction among them; they were delivered to the sword . . . the wretched chief of Libya halted, his heart fearing; withdrew (again), stopped, knelt, . . . [leaving] sandals, his bow, and his quiver in haste behind [him], and every [thing] that was with him . . . great terror coursed in his members. Lo, [they] slew . . . of his possessions, his [equipment], his silver, his gold, his vessels of bronze, the furniture of his wife, his throne, his bows, his arrows, all his works, which he had brought from his land, consisting of oxen, goats, and asses [and all were carried away] to the palace, to bring them in, together with the captives. Lo, the wretched chief of Libya was in speed to flee [by himself]. . . . Lo, the officers who were upon the horses of his majesty, set themselves after them . . . felled with arrows, carried off, slain. . . .

[Then returned] the captains of archers, the infantry and chariotry; every contingent of the army, whether recruits, or heavy armed troops, [carried off the plunder] . . . [driving] asses before them, laden with the uncircumcised phalli of the country of Libya, together with the hands of every country that was with them, [like fish on the grass]. . . . Lo, the whole land rejoiced to heaven; the towns and the districts acclaimed these wonders which had happened. . . .

*Source:* James H. Breasted, *Ancient Records of Egypt* (Chicago: University of Chicago Press, 1906), Vol. 3, sections 574–587.

MYCENAEAN EVIDENCE

## DOCUMENT 12
### Pylos Tablet AN657

*Another sign of crisis may be discovered in the administrative tablets of the Mycenaean kingdom of Pylos in the southwestern Peloponnese, by tradition described as the Kingdom of King Nestor who joined the other Achaeans in the struggle on the plain of Troy. The script in which the tablets were written is Linear B, an adaptation of the earlier Minoan script, Linear A. Three elements are incorporated in the script: a system of numerical notation, pictograms, and linear signs, each sign consisting of a syllable of either a consonant plus a vowel or a pure vowel. The script was deciphered by Michael Ventris with the aid of John Chadwick in the early 1950s as an early way of writing Greek. But it is a cumbersome way of expressing the Greek language, and the contents of the records are extremely abbreviated. Consequently, precise meaning is difficult to ascertain.*

*The tablet reproduced here is grouped with others that list various kinds of personnel. Some discuss rowers at or going to certain places; others list men who may be "watching" the coast. Since the Pylos tablets were baked, and thus preserved, by a fire that destroyed the palace center and collapsed the kingdom, many scholars believe that these tablets indicate the threat approaching the kingdom, probably from the sea.*

1. Linear B form

MAN

MAN

MAN

MAN

MAN

2. Transliterated into English
o-u-ru-to o-pi-a$_2$-ra e-pi-ko-wo
ma-re-wo o-ka o-wi-to-no
a-pe-ri-ta-wo o-re-ta e-te-wa-ko-ki-jo
su-we-ro-wi-jo o-wi-ti-ni-jo o-ka-ra$_3$ MAN 50
ne-da-wa-ta-o o-ka e-ke-me-de

a-pi-je-ta ma-ra-te-u ta-ni-ko
a₂–ru-wo-te ke-ki-de ku-pa-ri-si-jo MAN 20
ai-ta-re-u-si ku-pa-ri-si-jo ke-ki-de MAN 10
me-ta-qe pe-i e-qe-ta ke-ki-jo
a-e-ri-qo-ta e-ra-po ri-me-ne
o-wi-
o-ka-ra to-no MAN 30 ke-ki-de-qe a-pu₂–ka-ne
MAN 20 me-ta-qe pe-i ai-ko-ta e-qe-ta

3. Translation
Watchers [e-pi-ko-we] on guard over the coastal lands
Detachment [o-ka] of Maleus at O-wi-to-no:
Ampelitawon, Orestas, Etewas, Kokkion
50 su-we-ro-wi-jo men of o-wi-to-no at Oikhalia.
Detachment [o-ka] of Nedwatas:
Ekhemedes, Amphi-e-ta the ma-ra-te-u, Ta-ni-ko
20 ke-ki-de men from Kuparissia at A-ru-wo-te
10 ke-ki-de men from Kuparissia at Aithalewes
and with them the follower (e-qe-ta) Kerkios.
Aeriguhoitas, Elaphos, Ri-me-ne
30 men from Oikhalia to O-wi-to-no,
and 20 ke-ki-de men from A-pu-ka,
and with them the follower (e-qe-ta) Ai-ko-ta.

*Source:* Typed from drawn characters in J. T. Hooker, *Linear B: An Introduction* (Bristol, Bristol Classical Press, 1980), pp. 124–125.

# EPIC ACCOUNTS

## THE ILIAD

*The Iliad of Homer, in its present form, is over 2,500 years old, and there is growing evidence that elements at least of the Iliad story go back well into the Bronze Age. In all that time, no other epic poem, save the Odyssey, also attributed to Homer, has had so huge and lasting an impact on Western culture, habits of thought, and even politics.*

*There follow three selections from the Iliad that illuminate several key events in the story. The first of these is taken from Book I in which the acts resulting in Achilles' wrath and his retirement from the fighting are*

recounted. Agamemnon, the leader of the Achaean forces, has taken captive Chryseis, the daughter of Chryses, a priest of Apollo. Chryses has offered to ransom the girl but is rudely turned away, at which point he prays
to Apollo for vengeance. The god hears the prayers of his priest and for
nine days sends volleys of arrows into the Achaean host. On the tenth
day, Achilles convenes a council of the Achaean leaders and bids Calchas
the seer to determine what must be done to appease Apollo's anger.
Calchas reveals to the host that the god is angry over the treatment of
Chryses his priest and states that Apollo will be satisfied only with the return of Chryseis without a ransom. Agamemnon agrees to return Chryseis, but, as it would be unfitting that he alone should go without a prize,
he will take the prize of Achilles or some other of the Achaean leaders.
Now it is Achilles' turn to feel slighted, and in anger he retires from battle and threatens to return home to Phthia the next day.

# DOCUMENT 13
## The Wrath of Achilles

   *Nine days up and down the host ranged the god's arrows,*
*but on the tenth Achilleus called the people to assembly;*
*a thing put into his mind by the goddess of the white arms, Hera,*
*who had pity upon the Danaans when she saw them dying.*
*Now when they were all assembled in one place together,*
*Achilleus of the swift feet stood up among them and spoke forth:*
*'Son of Atreus, I believe now that straggling backwards*
*we must make our way home if we can even escape death,*
*if fighting now must crush the Achaians and the plague likewise.*
*No, come, let us ask some holy man, some prophet,*
*even an interpreter of dreams, since a dream also*
*comes from Zeus, who can tell why Phoibos Apollo is so angry,*
*if for the sake of some vow, some hecatomb he blames us,*
*if given the fragrant smoke of lambs, of he goats, somehow*
*he can be made willing to beat the bane aside from us.'*
   *He spoke thus and sat down again, and among them stood up*
*Kalchas, Thestor's son, far the best of the bird interpreters, . . .*
*'No, it is not for the sake of some vow or hecatomb he blames us,*
*but for the sake of his priest whom Agamemnon dishonoured*
*and would not give him back his daughter nor accept the ransom.*
*Therefore the archer sent griefs against us and will send them*

*still, nor sooner thrust back the shameful plague from the Danaans*
*until we give the glancing-eyed girl back to her father*
*without price, without ransom, and lead also a blessed hecatomb*
*to Chryse; thus we might propitiate and persuade him.'*

*He spoke thus and sat down again, and among them stood up*
*Atreus' son the hero wide-ruling Agamemnon*
*raging, the heart within filled black to the brim with anger*
*from beneath, but his two eyes showed like fire in their blazing.*
*First of all he eyed Kalchas bitterly and spoke to him:*
*'Seer of evil: never yet have you told me a good thing.*
*Always the evil things are dear to your heart to prophesy,*
*but nothing excellent have you said nor ever accomplished.*
*Now once more you make divination to the Danaans, argue*
*forth your reason why he who strikes from afar afflicts them,*
*because I for the sake of the girl Chryseis would not take*
*the shining ransom; and indeed I wish greatly to have her*
*in my own house; since I like her better than Klytaemnestra*
*my own wife, for in truth she is no way inferior,*
*neither in build nor stature nor wit, not in accomplishment . . .'*

*Then in answer again spoke brilliant swift-footed Achilleus:*
*'Son of Atreus, most lordly, greediest for gain of all men,*
*how shall the great-hearted Achaians give you a prize now?*
*There is no great store of things lying about I know of.*
*But what we took from the cities by storm has been distributed;*
*It is unbecoming for the people to call back things once given.*
*No, for the present give the girl back to the god; we Achaians*
*thrice and four times over will repay you, if ever Zeus gives*
*into our hands the strong-walled citadel of Troy to be plundered.'*

*Then in answer again spoke powerful Agamemnon:*
*'Not that way, good fighter though you be, godlike Achilleus,*
*strive to cheat, for you will not deceive, you will not persuade me.*
*What do you want? To keep your own prize and have me sit here*
*lacking one? Are you ordering me to give this girl back?*
*Either the great-hearted Achaians shall give me a new prize*
*chosen according to my desire to atone for the girl lost,*
*or else if they will not give me one I myself shall take her,*
*your own prize, or that of Aias,[1] or that of Odysseus,*
*going myself in person; and he whom I visit will be bitter.*
*Still, these are things we shall deliberate again hereafter.*
*Come, now, we must haul a black ship down to the bright sea,*

*And assemble rowers enough for it, and put on board it*
*the hecatomb, and the girl herself, Chryseis of the fair cheeks,*
*and let there be one responsible man in charge of her,*
*either Aias or Idomeneus or brilliant Odysseus,*
*or you yourself, son of Peleus, most terrifying of all men,*
*to reconcile by accomplishing sacrifice the archer.'*
    *Then looking darkly at him Achilleus of the swift feet spoke:*
*'O wrapped in shamelessness, with your mind forever on profit,*
*how shall any one of the Achaians readily obey you*
*either to go on a journey or to fight men strongly in battle?*
*I for my part did not come here for the sake of the Trojan*
*spearmen to fight against them, since to me they have done nothing.*
*Never yet have they driven away my cattle or my horses,*
*Never in Phthia where the soil is rich and men grow great did they*
*spoil my harvest, since indeed there is much that lies between us,*
*the shadowy mountains and the echoing sea; but for your sake,*
*o great shamelessness, we followed, to do you favour,*
*you with the dog's eyes, to win your honour and Menelaos'*
*from the Trojans. You forget all this or else you care nothing.*
*And now my prize you threaten in person to strip from me,*
*for whom I laboured much, the gift of the sons of the Achaians.*
*Never, when the Achaians sack some well-founded citadel*
*of the Trojans, do I have a prize that is equal to your prize.*
*Always the greater part of the painful fighting is the work of*
*my hands; but when the time comes to distribute the booty*
*yours is far the greater reward, and I with some small thing*
*yet dear to me go back to my ships when I am weary with fighting.*
*Now I am returning to Phthia, since it is much better*
*to go home again with my curved ships, and I am minded no longer*
*to stay here dishonoured and pile up your wealth and your luxury.'*

## NOTE

1. Ajax.

*Source:* Homer, *Iliad.* Translated by Richmond Lattimore (Chicago: University of Chicago Press, 1951), i.53–69, 93–115, 121–171.

# DOCUMENT 14
## Zeus Contemplates the Fate of Sarpedon

*In the following passage, Achilles' retirement from battle has achieved its
desired result. The Achaeans have been beaten back, and the Trojans have
breached the wall surrounding the Greek camp and are among the ships.
In tears Patroclus approaches Achilles whom he upbraids for sitting idle
while the ships burn, and begs at least to be allowed to don his master's
armor and lead the Myrmidons against the Trojans. Reluctantly, Achilles
agrees to this plan but warns Patroclus not to pursue the fleeing Trojans
too far or attempt the walls of the city, but to return to him once he has
driven the enemy from the ships. Of course, Patroclus does not heed
Achilles warning, but after putting the Trojans to flight he pursues them,
resulting in his own death. But before Patroclus is slain, he encounters
the Trojan hero Sarpedon. Zeus is divided in mind whether to save Sarpedon or allow Patroclus to slay him, as is fated.*

But Sarpedon, when he saw his free-girt companions going
down underneath the hands of Menoitios' son Patroklos,
called aloud in entreaty upon the godlike Lykians[1]:
'Shame, you Lykians, where are you running to? You must be fierce now,
for I myself will encounter this man, so I may find out
who this is who has so much strength and has done so much evil
to the Trojans, since many and brave are those whose knees he has unstrung.'
He spoke, and sprang to the ground in all his arms from the chariot,
and on the other side Patroklos when he saw him leapt down
from his chariot. They as two hook-clawed beak-bent vultures
above a tall rock face, high-screaming, go for each other,
so now these two, crying aloud, encountered together.
And watching them the son of devious-devising Kronos[2]
was pitiful, and spoke to Hera, his wife and his sister:
'Ah me, that it is destined that the dearest of men, Sarpedon,
must go down under the hands of Menoitios' son Patroklos.
The heart in my breast is balanced between two ways as I ponder,
whether I should snatch him out of the sorrowful battle
and set him down still alive in the rich county of Lykia,
or beat him under at the hands of the son of Menoitios.'
In turn the lady Hera of the ox eyes answered him:
'Majesty, son of Kronos, what sort of thing have you spoken?
Do you wish to bring back a man who is mortal, one long since

doomed by his destiny, from ill-sounding death and release him?
Do it, then; but not all the rest of us gods shall approve you.
And put away in your thoughts this other thing I tell you;
if you bring Sarpedon back to his home, still living,
think how then some other one of the gods might also
wish to carry his own son out of the strong encounter;
since around the great city of Priam are fighting many
sons of the immortals. You will waken grim resentment among them.
No, but if he is dear to you, and your heart mourns for him,
then let him be, and let him go down in the strong encounter
underneath the hands of Patroklos, the son of Menoitios;
but after the soul and the years of his life have left him, then send
Death to carry him away, and Sleep, who is painless,
until they come with him to the countryside of broad Lykia
where his brothers and countrymen shall give him due burial
with tomb and gravestone. Such is the privilege of those who have perished.'
      She spoke, nor did the father of gods and men disobey her;
yet he wept tears of blood that fell to the ground, for the sake
of his beloved son, whom now Patroklos was presently
to kill, by generous Troy and far from the land of his fathers.

## NOTES

1. Sarpedon was the king of Lycia, an ally of Troy.
2. Zeus.

*Source:* Homer, *Iliad*. Translated by Richmond Lattimore (Chicago: University of Chicago Press, 1951), xvi.419–461.

# DOCUMENT 15
## The Death of Hector

In this passage Achilles, enraged over the death of Patroclus, has returned to battle with disastrous consequences for the Trojans. Although advised to retire within the Trojan walls on the night after Patroclus' death, Hector foolishly decides to make camp on the plain hoping to attack the Greek ships again on the following day (Il. xviii.243–313). The result is that the Trojans are driven back with great slaughter and Hector himself is caught by Achilles alone outside the city walls where he is slain. Not content, Achilles proceeds to defile Hector's body in sight of all the Trojans watching from the wall.


. . . and now [he] thought of shameful treatment for glorious Hektor.
In both his feet at the back he made holes by the tendons
in the space between ankle and heel, and drew thongs of ox-hide through
    them,
and fastened them to the chariot so as to let the head drag,
and mounted the chariot, and lifted the glorious armour inside it,
then whipped the horses to a run, and they winged their way unreluctant.
A cloud of dust rose where Hektor was dragged, his dark hair was falling
about him, and all that head that was once so handsome was tumbled
in the dust; since by this time Zeus had given him over
to his enemies, to be defiled in the land of his fathers . . .
. . . but the wife of Hektor had not yet
heard: for no sure messenger had come to her and told her
how her husband had held his ground there outside the gates;
but she was weaving a web in the inner room of the high house,
a red folding robe, and inworking elaborate figures.
She called out through the house to her lovely-haired handmaidens
to set a great cauldron over the fire, so that there would be
hot water for Hektor's bath as he came back out of the fighting;
poor innocent, nor knew how, far from waters for bathing,
Pallas Athene had cut him down at the hands of Achilleus.
She heard from the great bastion the noise of mourning and sorrow.
Her limbs spun, and the shuttle dropped from her hand to the ground. Then
she called aloud to her lovely-haired handmaidens: 'Come here.
Two of you come with me, so I can see what has happened.
I heard the voice of Hektor's honoured mother; within me
my own heart rising beats in my mouth, my limbs under me
are frozen. Surely some evil is near for the children of Priam.
May what I say come never close to my ear; yet dreadfully
I fear that great Achilleus might have cut off bold Hektor
alone, away from the city, and be driving him into the flat land,
might put an end to that bitter pride of courage, that always
was on him, since he would never stay back where the men were in numbers
but break far out in front, and give way in his fury to no man.'
So she spoke, and ran out of the house like a raving woman
with pulsing heart, and her two handmaidens went along with her.

But when she came to the bastion and where the men were gathered
she stopped, staring, on the wall; and she saw him
being dragged in front of the city, and the running horses
dragged him at random toward the hollow ships of the Achaians.
The darkness of night misted over the eyes of Andromache . . .
But she, when she breathed again and the life was gathered back into her,
lifted her voice among the women of Troy in mourning:
'Hektor, I grieve for you. You and I were born to a single
destiny, you in Troy in the house of Priam, and I
in Thebe, underneath the timbered mountain of Plakos
in the house of Eëtion, who cared for me when I was little,
ill-fated he, I ill-starred. I wish he had never begotten me.
Now you go down to the house of Death in the secret places
of the earth, and left me here behind in the sorrow of mourning,
a widow in your house, and the boy is only a baby
who was born to you and me, the unfortunate. You cannot help him,
Hektor, any more, since you are dead . . .

*Source*: Homer, *Iliad*. Translated by Richmond Lattimore (Chicago: University of Chicago Press, 1951), xxii.395–404, 436–485.

## THE ODYSSEY

# DOCUMENT 16
## Odysseus' Visit to Hades

In Book 11 of the Odyssey, Odysseus must visit Hades, the land of the dead where he will learn from the shade of the seer Teiresias how he can appease Poseidon and find his way back home to Ithaca. Once there he summons the dead by digging a pit into which he pours the blood of sacrificed sheep. The blood attracts hordes of ghosts that lap the blood eagerly. After consulting with Teiresias, he spies the ghost of Agamemnon.

But when pure Persephone dispersed the shades
Of the delicate women now this way, now that
The mournful shade of Agamemnon, son of Atreus, came forward.
About him had gathered all the other shades, who at the same time
Fell to their death and doom in the very hall of Aegisthus.
He immediately recognized me, since he had drunk the dark blood.
He cried out piteously, shedding warm tears

And, stretching out his arms, he struggled to reach me.
There was no longer any strength or force
Such as that which had once filled his supple limbs.
I wept on seeing him and felt pity in my heart
And addressed him uttering winged words.
"Glorious son of Atreus, lord of men, Agamemnon
What fate subdued you with death that lays men low?
Was it Poseidon who broke you on shipboard
By stirring the dreadful blast of harsh winds
Or did violent men slay you on dry land
While you were rustling cattle or fair flocks of sheep
Or at a citadel fighting over women?"
So I spoke and he answered replying quickly,
"God-like son of Laertes, cunning Odysseus,
No, Poseidon did not break me on board ship
By stirring the dreadful blast of harsh winds
Nor did violent men slay me upon the land.
But Aegisthus plotted my death and doom
And with the help of my hateful wife, killed me.
They called me into the hall, and feasted me,
Just like someone would slaughter an ox at the feeding trough.
Thus I perished in pitiful death. My other companions
Were slaughtered without pause, like white-toothed swine
Who are slain in the house of a wealthy lord
Either for a marriage or fête or banquet.
You have come face to face with the slaughter of many men
Killed singly or in heavy battle.
But seeing these sorts of things in particular your heart would ache
As we lay among the drinking vessels and heaped tables
In the megaron, the entire floor flowing with blood.
I heard the most wrenching voice of Priam's daughter,
Cassandra, whom the wily Clytemnestra killed
Right beside me. But I raised my hands and beat the ground
As I died spitted on the sword. But that dog-faced woman
Turned her back nor did she have the heart
To close my eyes with her hand nor to close my mouth as I went to the house
    of Hades.
Thus there is no woman more shameless and impudent
Than one who plots such a deed in her mind
And this woman contrived just such a deed, ruin for her wedded husband
I expected to be welcomed by my children and servants

*When I returned home. But she, scheming gruesome plots,*
*Poured shame on herself and on all delicate*
*Women henceforth, even one who acts blamelessly."*

*Source: Odyssey, xi.387–434, translated by Carol Thomas and Tristan Goldman.*

## VIRGIL: THE AENEID

*While both Virgil (70–19 B.C.E.) and his masterwork, the Aeneid, have been called by their detractors the tools of imperial Roman propaganda, these charges should not be allowed to diminish the status of this work, which by any measurement is a great epic. After Homer, Virgil is the greatest of the surviving epic poets of antiquity. As for the poem itself, it is both inspired by Homer's poems and is in some sense an answer to them. The Aeneid presents the matter of Troy, both the siege and destruction of the city and the subsequent wanderings of the hero Aeneas, from the Trojan viewpoint.*

*The following selections are from Book II which tells of the destruction of Troy, beginning with the entry of the Trojan Horse into the city and ending with Aeneas' escape with his father and son.*

*The first selection tells of the slain Hector's appearance to Aeneas in a dream on the night of the city's destruction. Hector tells Aeneas to gather up his family and the hearth gods of Troy and make his escape. At the end of the passage, Hector's ghost utters a thinly veiled prophecy regarding Aeneas' destiny as a founder of Rome.*

# DOCUMENT 17
## Hector Appears to Aeneas in a Dream (Aen.ii.268–296)

*That time of night it was when the first sleep,*
*Gift of the gods, begins for ill mankind,*
*Arriving gradually, delicious rest.*
*In sleep, in dream, Hector appeared to me,*
*Gaunt with sorrow, streaming tears, all torn—*
*As by the violent car on his death day—*
*And black with bloody dust,*
*His puffed-out feet cut by the rawhide thongs.*
*Ah god, the look of him! How changed*

*From that proud Hector who returned to Troy*
*Wearing Achilles' armor, or that one*
*Who pitched the torches on Danaan ships;*
*His beard all filth, his hair matted with blood,*
*Showing the wounds, the many wounds, received*
*Outside his father's city walls. I seemed*
*Myself to weep and call upon the man*
*In grieving speech, brought from the depth of me:*

*'Light of Dardania, best hope of Troy,*
*What kept you from us for so long, and where?*
*From what far place, O Hector, have you come,*
*Long, long awaited? After so many deaths*
*Of friends and brothers, after a world of pain*
*For all our folk and all our town, at last,*
*Boneweary, we behold you! What has happened*
*To ravage your serene face? Why these wounds?'*

*He wasted no reply on my poor questions*
*But heaved a great sigh from his chest and said:*
*'Ai! Give up and go, child of the goddess,*[1]
*Save yourself, out of these flames. The enemy*
*Holds the city walls, and from her height*
*Troy falls in ruin. Fatherland and Priam*
*Have their due; if by one hand our towers*
*Could be defended, by this hand, my own,*
*They would have been. Her holy things, her gods*
*Of hearth and household Troy commends to you.*
*Accept them as companions of your days;*
*Go find for them the great walls that one day*
*You'll dedicate, when you have roamed the sea.'*

---

# NOTE

1. Aeneas' mother was Aphrodite, or Venus in the Roman pantheon.

*Source:* Virgil, *Aeneid*, translated by Robert Fitzgerald, copyright © 1980, 1982, 1983 by Robert Fitzgerald. Used by permission of Random House, Inc.

## DOCUMENT 18
### Aeneas Contemplates Killing Helen

*Aeneas leads out a body of warriors to make what defense they can, but although they make a valiant effort, they are overwhelmed by sheer numbers. His men having fled, Aeneas stands alone when he spies Helen, the author of all their misery. He contemplates making a quick end to her, when Venus, his mother, appears to stay his hand. (Aen.ii.569–631)*

It came to this,
That I stood there alone. And then I saw
Lurking beyond the doorsill of the Vesta,
In hiding, silent, in that place reserved,
The daughter of Tyndareus. Glare of fires
Lighted my steps this way and that, my eyes
Glancing over the whole scene, everywhere.
That woman, terrified of the Trojans' hate
For the city overthrown, terrified too
Of Danaan vengeance, her abandoned husband's
Anger after years—Helen, that Fury
Both to her own homeland and Troy, had gone
To earth, a hated thing, before the altars.
Now fires blazed up in my own spirit—
A passion to avenge my fallen town
And punish Helen's whorishness.
               'Shall this one
Look untouched on Sparta and Mycenae
After her triumph, going like a queen,
And see her home and husband, kin and children,
With Trojan girls for escort, Phrygian slaves?
Must Priam perish by the sword for this?
Troy burn, for this? Dardania's littoral
Be soaked in blood, so many times, for this?
Not by my leave. I know
No glory comes of punishing a woman,
The feat can bring no honor. Still, I'll be
Approved for snuffing out a monstrous life,
For a just sentence carried out. My heart
Will teem with joy in this avenging fire,
And the ashes of my kin will be appeased.'

So ran my thoughts. I turned wildly upon her,
But at that moment, clear, before my eyes—
Never before so clear—in a pure light
Stepping before me, radiant through the night,
My loving mother came: immortal, tall,
And lovely as the lords of heaven know her.
Catching me by the hand, she held me back,
Then with her rose-red mouth reproved me:
'Son,
Why let such suffering goad you on to fury
Past control? Where is your thoughtfulness
For me, for us? Will you not first revisit
The place you left your father, worn and old,
Or find out if your wife, Creusa, lives,
And the young boy, Ascanius[1]—all these
Cut off by Greek troops foraging everywhere?
Had I not cared for them, fire would by now
Have taken them, their blood glutted the sword.
You must not hold the woman of Laconia,[2]
That hated face, the cause of this, nor Paris.
The harsh will of the gods it is, the gods,
That overthrows the splendor of this place
And brings Troy from her height into the dust.
Look over there: I'll tear away the cloud
That curtains you, and films your mortal sight,
The fog around you.—Have no fear of doing
Your mother's will, or balk at obeying her.—
Look: where you see high masonry thrown down,
Stone torn from stone, with billowing smoke and dust,
Neptune is shaking from their beds the walls
That his great trident pried up, undermining,
Toppling the whole city down. And look:
Juno in all her savagery holds
The Scaean Gates, and raging in steel armor
Calls her allied army from the ships.
Up on the citadel—turn, look—Pallas Tritonia[3]
Couched in a stormcloud, lightening, with her Gorgon!
The father himself empowers the Danaans,
Urges assaulting gods on the defenders.
Away, child; put an end to toiling so.
I shall be near, to see you safely home.'

*She hid herself in the deep gloom of night,*
*And now the dire forms appeared to me*
*Of great immortals, enemies of Troy.*
*I knew the end then: Ilium was going down*
*In fire, the Troy of Neptune going down,*
*As in high mountains when the countrymen*
*Have notched an ancient ash, then make their axes*
*Ring with might and main, chopping away*
*To fell the tree—ever on the point of falling,*
*Shaken through all its foliage, and the treetop*
*Nodding; bit by bit the strokes prevail*
*Until it gives a final groan at last*
*And crashes down in ruin from the height.*

## NOTES

1. Also called Iulus elsewhere in the poem. Iulus was the ancestor of Julius Caesar, Augustus' uncle.

2. Laconia is another name for Sparta.

3. Tritonia is Athena.

*Source:* Virgil, *Aeneid*, translated by Robert Fitzgerald, copyright © 1980, 1982, 1983 by Robert Fitzgerald. Used by permission of Random House, Inc.

## DOCUMENT 19
### Quintus of Smyrna: *The Destruction of Troy*

*Only a little more is known of Quintus of Smyrna than of Homer. As a native of Smyrna, the modern Izmir on the west coast of Turkey, he would likely have heard the verses of Homer from childhood. Smyrna was one of a number of cities that claimed Homer as a native son. Concerning Quintus' dates, evidence internal to his poem indicates that he was writing sometime in the middle of the fourth century C.E., over a thousand years after Homer.*

*The following selections are from Book 10 in which Paris is mortally wounded by Philoctetes. Early in the book, in one of Quintus' finer passages, Eris or Strife, whose actions at the wedding of Peleus and Thetis*

led eventually to Troy's doom, has grown to a monstrous figure, as she
whips the opposing armies into a frenzy of destruction.


To one place Strife incarnate drew them all,
The fearful Battle-queen, beheld of none,
But cloaked in clouds blood-raining; on she stalked
Swelling the mighty roar of battle, now
Rushed through Troy's squadrons, through Achaea's now;
Panic and Fear still waited on her steps
To make their father's sister glorious.
From small to huge that Fury's stature grew;
Her arms of adamant were blood-besprent,
The deadly lance she brandished reached the sky.
Earth quaked beneath her feet: dread blasts of fire
Flamed from her mouth: her voice pealed thunder-like
Kindling strong men. Swift closed the fronts of fight
Drawn by a dread Power to the mighty work.
Loud as the shriek of winds that madly blow
In early spring, when the tall woodland trees
Put forth their leaves—loud as the roar of fire
Blazing through sun-scorched brakes—loud as the voice
Of many waters, when the wide sea raves
Beneath the howling blast, with thunderous crash
Of waves, when shake the fearful shipman's knees;
So thundered earth beneath their charging feet.
Strife swooped on them: foe hurled himself on foe.


*Source:* Quintus of Smyrna, *The Destruction of Troy.* A. S. Way Translation (London: Heineman and New York: Macmillan, 1913), x.59–81.

# GLOSSARY

Asterisks (*) are placed before terms appearing elsewhere in this Glossary.

**Agon, agonisma:** This Greek word meaning *contest* or *struggle* has entered the English language as *agony*, referring to extreme discomfort or distress, either physical or psychological. For the Greeks, the term had the more neutral meaning of struggle, both physical and psychic. *Agon* could be used to describe either athletic contests or warfare. The warriors of Homer's time or later Macedonian warriors under Alexander, were apt to view life as an *agon* through which one achieved honor, *\*arête*, and in this way a meaningful immortality. Both the physical and psychological or spiritual forms of *agon* are present in Homer in the person of Hector. Watching the fatal approach of Achilles, Hector holds an interior debate, *agonizing* over whether he should confront the Achaean or dash to safety behind Troy's walls. Deciding on the former course results in a physical *agon*, or battle, with Achilles which Hector ultimately loses.

**Apollonius of Rhodes (third century B.C.E.):** Apollonius is one of the best known and respected of the scholar-poets of Hellenistic Alexandria. Like the Alexandrian elegiac poet Callimachus under whom he studied, much of Apollonius' work, now lost, appears to have consisted of scholarly poems recounting Egyptian legends (*Canobus*) or the foundations of cities. Fortunately for us, his greatest work, the *Argonautica*, survives nearly extant. Except for Homer's works and Quintus of Smyrna's *Destruction of Troy* the

*Argonautica* is the only ancient epic in the Greek language to come down to us. As its title indicates, the epic, written in four books of nearly 6,000 lines, recounts the legend of Jason and the Argonauts in their quest for the Golden Fleece guarded by a fearful dragon in far-off Colchis on the Black Sea. In the adventure, Jason is aided decisively by Medea, a sorceress and the niece of Circe, in stealing the Fleece from her father, King Aeëtes of Colchis.

**Arête:** This is a Greek word denoting goodness, virtue, manliness, or prowess. The latter connotations are particularly relevant for describing the qualities of honor and excellence after which the warriors of Homer strove. One gained *arête* by performing well in an *agon whether it be in an athletic contest or in combat. Significantly, *arête* could also be achieved through demonstrations of eloquence or sound, logical thinking in counsel or the law courts.

**Ashlar:** In architecture *ashlar* refers to squared or dressed stonework in walls. The word *ashlar* derives from the Latin *axillarium*, which in turn is an extension of *axis*, a wood beam or plank. The term *ashlar* was applied to dressed stone because of its resemblance to closely fitted wood planks. Whereas the walls of Mycenae were *cyclopean, that is, undressed, rough stone, the walls of Troy VI are of dressed ashlar stonework.

**Bronze Age (Early, Middle, Late):** This truly revolutionary age of human history is named for the common use of this alloy, composed of tin and copper, in tools and weapons. Just as the term *stone age* fails to adequately describe the increasing level of complexity of *Palaeolithic*, *Mesolithic*, and *Neolithic* culture, so too the term *Bronze Age* says nothing of the development of complex urban civilizations during this period. Like the Stone Age, archaeologists and historians have divided the Bronze Age into three long periods: Early (c. 3000–2000), Middle (c. 2,000–1680), and Late (c. 1680–1100 B.C.E.). This 2000-year epoch witnessed the rise of powerful city-states in Sumeria and Akkad in southern Mesopotamia, kingdoms in Egypt and in Assyria in northern Mesopotamia, and the empires of Egypt, Babylonia, Assyria, and Hatti. Although Troy was a sizable community displaying at times considerable wealth and power during much of this period, the Mycenaean kingdoms developed later, achieving their greatest power between 1550 and 1200 B.C.E.

**Cartouche:** A cartouche is an oval figure inscribed on objects and monuments; it contains the formal or throne name of an Egyptian pharaoh, or sometimes of a god. The finding of cartouches in association with artifacts not only within Egypt but throughout the Near East, and as far afield as Greece and the Aegean, has provided important clues in establishing chronology.

**Cyclopean:** This term derives from the Greek word *kuklops* meaning *round-eye*, in reference to the single eye possessed by the mythological *Cyclopes*. The best known of the *Cyclopes* was the giant Polyphemus, the son of Poseidon, who was blinded by Odysseus. In architecture, the term refers to the construction of walls out of massive, undressed stone. The walls of Mycenae and Tiryns were thought to have been constructed by *Cyclopes* from Lycia in southwest Anatolia. The hero Perseus enlisted them in this effort because only they were capable of lifting such heavy stones.

**Dendrochronology:** This is a technique in dating by means of tree rings. The annual growth rings that most trees produce vary in size owing to the tree's maturity and to fluctuating climatic conditions. For example, inordinately cool or dry conditions may result in little growth, producing narrower rings. Comparison of rings from living trees and old timber produces long sequences reaching back centuries or even millennia.

**Eratosthenes (c. 285–194 B.C.E.):** Eratosthenes of Cyrene (in Libya), like *Apollonius of Rhodes, was a student of the Alexandrian poet Callimachus, and succeeded Apollonius as Royal Librarian at Alexandria. Even his contemporaries knew him as a polymath who was interested in and wrote extensively on a broad range of topics from mathematics to literary criticism. One of his chief interests was in the establishment of a secure chronology of Greek history founded not on legendary lore but on what he considered actual events. His chronology appears to have been anchored on the destruction of Troy which he calculated to have occurred in 1184 B.C.E.

**Herodotus (484–425 B.C.E.):** Herodotus chose as his subject the *Persian Wars against the Greeks from c. 525 to 479 B.C.E. Born in Halicarnassus in southwest Anatolia, then within the Persian Empire, he emigrated to Athens in 447 where he wrote his history. Although he was faulted by scholars, both ancient and modern, for putting too great a credence in folktale and local legend, his highly entertaining writing style and his relentless curiosity about the Persians, Egyptians, and the many peoples of Anatolia make his book invaluable. His ability, even willingness, to rationally examine the motives not only of his Greek protagonists but of the Persian enemy as well make his title *father of history* one that was well earned.

**Hesiod (fl. c. 700 B.C.E.):** After Homer, Hesiod is the earliest Greek poet of whom we have extant works. He is best known for the *Theogony*, a genealogy of the gods and major heroes written in an epic style, and the quite different *Works and Days* which, in its cataloging of chores and duties incumbent on the successful farmer, is closer in spirit to the Near Eastern wisdom literature of the Late Bronze and early Iron Ages. In *Works and Days* (109–201) Hesiod sets out a quasihistorical scheme of five ages of man: an age of Gold, Silver, Bronze, Heroes, and Iron. Each succeeding age is characterized by the increasing misfortunes of mortals and by an ever growing separation from the gods. For Hesiod his fourth age, the Age of Heroes, was the last period in which men were capable of behaving in an honorable or godlike fashion. But in this age, like the preceding Age of Bronze, men were too warlike and their numbers were depleted through ruinous assaults on Thebes and Troy.

**Hexameter:** In poetry the term *hexameter* refers to a verse or line consisting of six metrical feet. Typically used by the Greeks and Romans in writing epic poetry, the first four feet were either *dactyls* (a three-syllable measure, the first long and the other two short) or *spondees* (a foot of two long syllables). The fifth foot of a hexameter line was a dactyl, and the sixth was either a spondee or a *trochee* (a two-syllable foot, the first long and the second short).

**Ice core sampling:** This is the process of deep drilling into ice glaciers to retrieve cylinders, or cores, of ice many meters in length. Samples of these cores can be examined to reveal historical fluctuations in climate or the presence of foreign substances such as ash at certain times in the past. Finding ash in ice cores has been critical to the dating of explosive volcanic eruptions such as the Thera volcano in the second millennium B.C.E.

**Indo-European:** This is a large and widespread family of languages. Nearly all the languages of modern Europe and a number of west and south Asian languages are Indo-European and hence exhibit broad morphological and syntactical similarities. Indo-European is divided into a number of subfamilies, two of which are Hellenic, from which Greek is derived, and Anatolic, a now extinct branch that included Hittite and *Luwian, possibly the language spoken at Troy.

**Land and Sea Peoples:** This was a loose coalition of tribes and peoples who made two massive assaults on numerous cities in Syria–Palestine and on Egypt. These two attacks, occurring during the late thirteenth and the first third of the twelfth centuries B.C.E., respectively, brought ruin to Bronze Age Cyprus and the Levant and may have been instrumental in the toppling of the Mycenaean states and the Hittite Empire. Egypt, first under Pharaoh Merneptah (c. 1213–1204) and then under Ramses III (c. 1185–1154), succeeded in repulsing these attacks. The coalitions in both instances seem to have been comprised of Libyans and a number of Aegean and Anatolian peoples. Among those listed are the *Ekwesh* or *Akhaiwasha*, perhaps Achaeans, the *Danyen*, perhaps Danaoi (Argive Greeks), and the *Tjakker*, identified by a number of scholars as Teucrians, that is, inhabitants of the Troad.

**Lawagetas:** This archaic Greek title appears in the *Linear B tablets from Pylos as *ra-wa-ke-ta*. Although this word did not survive into later Greek, its meaning is clear: *leader of the host*. The first syllable, *law*, becomes *laos* in later Greek and refers to the people in arms, or an army. The remainder of the word, *agetas*, is related to the verb *āgéomai* meaning to lead. Thus, the holder of the title *lawagetas* was originally very likely a war leader. However, by the time the Pylos

Linear B tablets were inscribed (c. 1230 B.C.E.), the *lawagetas* appears to have taken on some religious functions.

**Linear B:** This syllabic script is inscribed on clay tablets fortuitously preserved in the destruction fires of Knossos and Pylos and dating to around 1200 B.C.E. (It was long thought that the Knossos tablets dated to 1400 B.C.E., but this is increasingly doubted.) Although Sir Arthur Evans began collecting specimens of Linear B on Crete as early as 1900, it was not until 1952 that the British architect and architect-classicist Michael Ventris succeeded in deciphering the script. Although Evans had long thought Linear B to be the expression of a pre-Greek, even pre-Indo-European Minoan language, the script turned out to be an archaic form of Greek. Other syllabic scripts found on Crete, some of the Aegean islands, and on Cyprus show similarities to Linear B. Linear A, for instance, shares many of the same signs but is probably not Greek. The latest Linear A evidence seems to indicate a connection with an Anatolian language, perhaps *Luwian. In Linear B each sign represents a syllable, that is, a vowel, or a consonant plus a vowel. Such a script is a good deal more cumbersome than an alphabet and would be of little use in the composition of lengthy documents whether of prose or poetry. The script seems to have been used almost exclusively for tax accounting and other administrative purposes. Linear B consists of around eighty syllabic signs that are combined with another system of numerical signs and pictograms representing the objects listed.

**Luwian:** Luwian is an *Indo-European language of the now extinct Anatolic subfamily spoken from the early centuries of the second millennium down to the last centuries B.C.E. in western and southern Anatolia. Presently, Luwian is a leading candidate for the language of the Trojans, at least during the second millennium. It is also possible that it, or a dialect of it, was spoken on Crete during the same period. Other Anatolian languages include Palaic in northern Anatolia and Hittite, originally spoken in central Anatolia, but expanding outwards with the growth of the Hittite Empire. Some Luwian words are: *tati* (father), *tiwaz* (sun/day), and *mallit* (honey, related to Greek *mellissa*, or *melitta*).

**Magnetometer:** Magnetometers use electric currents to reveal items below the earth's surface, producing a subterranean map of the configuration.

**Međedović, Avdo (c. 1870–1955):** Međedović was a Muslim from eastern Montenegro, although his family was by origin Serbian Orthodox Christian. He was one of the last, and by many accounts one of the greatest, of Yugoslavia's oral epic poets. Međedović was considered a genius by *Milman Parry who recorded a number of his epics during the 1930s. Međedović is reported to have had fifty-eight epics, some quite long, in his repertoire and was capable of learning and elaborating on new ones after a single hearing.

**Minoan:** The term *Minoan* was coined by the British excavator of Knossos, Sir Arthur Evans, who named the Bronze Age civilization he discovered on Crete after the legendary King Minos of Knossos. Although the roots of Bronze Age culture on Crete reach back to c. 3000 B.C.E., it is the Middle and early Late Minoan periods from c. 2000 to 1400 that display the greatest brilliance and wealth. Indeed, so great was the wealth of Late Minoan Crete and so widespread were its cultural contacts that Evans and many other scholars thought Knossos to be the capital of a great, sea-borne empire, or *thalassocracy. Many scholars have now come to doubt this assertion while retaining the notion of a Minoan culture with wide trading contacts, including Egypt, Syria, and western Anatolia. From the mid-fifteenth century on, Knossos, and perhaps other parts of the island, appears to have been occupied by a Greek-speaking dynasty.

**Mycenaean:** In archaeology this term refers to the Late Bronze Age culture of Greece from c. 1680 to c. 1100 B.C.E. The term is derived from Mycenae, which appears to have been the most powerful Greek state during much of this period. Although Mycenaean culture owed much to the older Minoan culture of Crete, there were substantial differences. The Mycenaeans appear to have been more warlike, as was demonstrated by their expansion during the fifteenth and fourteenth centuries into the Aegean and to Crete itself with their occupation of Knossos. If the Trojan War actually took place, it is quite likely that Mycenaean Greeks were responsible for the city's destruction.

**Nostos, Nostoi:** *Nostos* is a Greek word meaning a return home. Specifically, *nostoi* are the returns of the Homeric warriors after the destruction of Troy. There were many *nostos* legends which told of the difficulties endured by a number of the Achaean leaders on their return from the war. Chief among these legends were the tales told of Odysseus, Agamemnon, Menelaus, Diomedes, Philoctetes, and Neoptolemus. These tales soon became the subject of epic poetry, the greatest of which was the *Odyssey* of Homer.

**Parry, Milman (1902–1935):** Parry was an American Classical scholar who conceived of an idea to perform a cross-cultural study between Homeric epic and the then contemporary oral epic of Yugoslavia. His studies of South Slavic epics revolutionized Homeric studies by concluding that Homer was an oral poet who combined great powers of memorization in terms of plot and action with a fund of stock formulas, creative and elaborate use of simile, and an undeviating *hexameter rhythm in performing his epics. At the same time that Parry was making substantial changes to Homeric scholarship, he almost single-handedly founded the new field of oral or nonliterate studies.

**Pausanias (c. 110–c. 180 C.E.):** The writer of a Guide to Greece, Pausanias lived at least for a time in Magnesia in western Anatolia. His Guide was written specifically for wealthy Roman travelers in search of a little culture. The Guide's lengthy and meticulous cataloging of Greek monuments and shrines gives the book something of the "if it's Tuesday, it must be Thespiae" quality common to tourist guides. Still the Guide is invaluable for presenting a picture of Greece under Roman rule, for its retelling of countless local myths and legends, and for its lengthy histories of the Messenian wars and the Olympic Games. Heinrich Schliemann wisely relied on Pausanias' Guide during his excavations at Mycenae and Tiryns.

**Peloponnesian War (431–404 B.C.E.):** This was the great and ruinous war, which some have called a civil war, between Athens and Sparta and their allies. The root cause of the war (really two wars, the first being fought between 461 and 446) was the establishment, particularly after the *Persian Wars, of two powerful but quite different hegemonies within Greece. Even before the Persian Wars, Sparta had acquired a dominant position in the Peloponnese. The rise of the Athenian-dominated Delian League following the Persian defeat at Salamis and Plataea was viewed with jealousy and suspicion by Sparta. The war was not, however, simply a matter of power politics between two incipient empires. There were also deep ideological differences between Athenian democracy and Spartan aristocratic oligarchy. The great tragedy for Athens and Sparta was that these divisions were capable of neither political nor military solution. Athens could not defeat Sparta on land, but even Sparta's occupation of large parts of Attica could not stop Athens from being re-supplied by its fleet. So the war continued for decades with neither belligerent capable of gaining a decisive advantage. Even Athens' catastrophic Sicilian Expedition of 415–413 was not enough to force the city to sue for peace. It was only through the carelessness of the Athenian commanders that their fleet was finally destroyed by the Spartan Lysander at Aegospotami (405), which brought an end to conflict (404). The result of the war was the long-term exhaustion of both Sparta and Athens, leading to the ephemeral rise in the fortunes of Corinth and Thebes, and finally to a revival of tyranny in Sicily and the domination of Greece by Macedonia.

**Persian Wars (490–479 B.C.E.):** After the Persian king Cyrus I defeated Croesus of Lydia (546), the Persian Empire proceeded to expand westward, and by 525 they held the Ionian Greek cities of the Anatolian coast in dominion. When the Ionians rose in revolt in 499, the Athenians as fellow Ionians sent them aid but the combined force was defeated at Lade in 494. Upon learning of the Athenian aid sent to the rebels, Herodotus states that the Persian king at the time, Darius I, ordered a servant each day to say to him, "Master, remember the Athenians (*Hist.* v.106)." In 490 Darius sent his general Mardonius with a force to Greece but was defeated by the Athenians at Marathon. A second, larger force was sent ten years later by Xerxes I, Darius' son and successor. After dislodging the small Spartan force contesting the pass at Thermopylae (480), their fleet was destroyed by the Athenians at Salamis. The combined Greek land force delivered the *coup de gras* to Mardonius and his army at Plataea (479). The result of the Persian Wars was to instill among the Greeks, but particularly among the Athenians, a pride and confidence in their culture and institutions. Unfortunately, this confidence soon soured into ideas of Greek superiority over the Persians, who along with most other Asiatic peoples came to be thought of as barbarians.

**Phaeacia:** Phaeacia was kind of a Homeric never-never-land of boundless wealth and good order ruled over by the wise and open-handed king Alcinous on the island of Scheria. It is here that Odysseus was washed up after leaving the nymph Calypso. Nausicaa, Alcinous' daughter, leads Odysseus to her father's hall where he is treated royally as one who witnessed the destruction of Troy. Odysseus relates his adventures over the course of several books of the *Odyssey* to his Phaeacian hosts who are duly impressed. It is the Phaeacians who finally take Odysseus back to Ithaca heavily laden with parting gifts including thirteen bronze *tripod cauldrons. Many Greek traders and colonists of the late Dark Age and Archaic periods came to identify Scheria and Phaeacia with the island of Corcyra, or modern Corfu, off the coast of Epirus.

**Radio carbon dating:** Carbon is an element present in all living matter. The most common carbon isotope, carbon 12, interacts with cosmic radiation from nitrogen in the atmosphere to produce the radioactive isotope carbon 14. The carbon 12 in the living organism continues to be impacted by this radiation and thus continues to produce carbon 14 until it dies. After death, carbon 14 decays at a known rate, thus making the remains of the organic material datable within fixed limits. This dating technique and the related potassium/argon dating method for much older specimens are just two examples of how archaeology has successfully allied itself with chemistry, geology, and nuclear physics for achieving more secure chronologies since the mid-twentieth century. Other new dating methods include *dendrochronology and *ice core sampling.

**Retrograde script:** Semitic scripts, both today and in antiquity, are written from right to left—the opposite of how this book was written and how the reader has been reading it. For example, modern Hebrew is written right to left, as was ancient Phoenician. The earliest examples of Greek alphabetic writing, based ultimately on the Phoenician script, were also commonly written right to left. Since this writing progresses in the opposite direction of later Greek scripts, it is called *retrograde*.

**Rhyton:** This is a vessel often of conical shape, although others are in animal form such as the famous Bull's Head Rhyton from *Shaft Grave IV at Mycenae.

**Shaft Graves:** Shaft graves are essentially deep pit or cist graves capable of accommodating several burials. Such graves were commonly lined with stone and roofed over before being filled in with soil. The best known examples are the two grave circles, Grave Circles A and B, from Mycenae dating to the sixteenth to fourteenth centuries B.C.E.

**Sons of Heracles (*Heraclidae*):** According to legend, after the death of Heracles, his sons were banished from the Peloponnese by Eurystheus, king of Mycenae and Heracles' sworn enemy. Their leader Hyllus went to Delphi to inquire of the Pythia when they might return. "After the third crop," was her reply. Consequently, Hyllus led his forces back into the Peloponnese after the third year, but they were defeated and Hyllus was slain. What the Pythia had meant by "the third crop" was after the third generation. Thus, the Heraclidae took to wandering and eventually struck up an alliance with the king of Doris in north-central Greece. In the third generation after the death of Hyllus, the sons of Heracles led by Temenos, Cresphontes, and the twins Prokles and Eurysthenes reentered the Peloponnese and with their Dorian allies sacked Mycenae, slaying Tisamenes, the grandson of Agamemnon. They conquered Sparta and Pylos as well. Speakers of the Dorian Greek dialect dated their rise to power in the Peloponnese from this event. Later historians dated the return of the Heraclidae to sixty years after the sack of Troy. That would be c. 1190 B.C.E. by *Herodotus' reckoning and 1124 B.C.E. by that of *Eratosthenes.

**Symposion, Symposium:** This term literally means a *drinking together*, that is, a drinking party. This semiritualistic, aristocratic gathering seems to have been an institution of some antiquity in Greece with roots reaching back into the Dark Age, if not earlier. The *symposion* may have begun as a ritual, competitive feasting not unlike the potlatch ritual feast held among the northwest Native American tribes until early in the twentieth century. In such a celebration, a local chieftain, or *basileus* in Dark Age Greece, would have feasted his chief warriors to win honor, *\*arête*, and popular support. Such feasting is recounted in the medieval English epic *Beowulf*. In King Hrothgar's great hall, Heorot, the great warriors of Denmark feasted until Grendel cast a pall on the festivities (*Beowulf* 64–125). The *symposion* of the Archaic period in Greece would have been less ritualistic and more festive, and often featured games of extemporaneous eloquence in which one reveler would quote or invent a line of poetry, a second adding another line topping the first, then a third adding a line, and so on. Some of these verses were written down on drinking cups used at the *symposion*, a likely origin of the hexameter lines on the Cup of Nestor found at Pithecoussae.

**Thalassocracy:** A compound of the Greek words *thalassa*, sea, and *kratos*, rule or dominion, thalassocracy means rule, or dominion by sea. As such, this term has often been used in the past to describe a supposed Minoan sea empire during the seventeenth to fifteenth centuries B.C.E., first suggested by Sir Arthur Evans. Since Evans' death, however, the idea of a Minoan *thalassocracy* has declined in popularity. Although it cannot be denied that Minoan culture, and the outward trappings of that culture from ceramics to styles of dress gained wide currency in the Aegean and in mainland Greece, there are no indications that this phenomenon is owing to anything other than a dynamic and attractive culture carrying on a brisk trade. There is as yet no evidence that the spread of Minoan style and practices was imposed by force. It has been suggested, however— this time with more solid evidence—that the Mycenaeans may have been at the center of a thalassocracy over the Cyclades, Crete, and some of the islands off the coast of Anatolia from the middle four- teenth to the mid- to late thirteenth centuries B.C.E. Miletus/Milla- wanda may have been an outpost of this sea empire.[1]

**Theogony:** This is a long poem of just over 1,000 lines in epic style by the Greek poet *Hesiod, a younger contemporary of Homer. The *Theogony*, as the name indicates, recounts the origins of the gods from the world's beginning, born of *Chaos*, *Nux* (Night), and Ere- bus, darker and deeper than Hades, through the first generation of elemental deities—Gaia (Earth) and Ouranos (Sky); to a second generation of gods and titans ruled by Kronos and Rheia; and fi- nally to the third generation of the Olympian gods ruled by Zeus. *Theogony*, together with Homer's portrayal of the gods in the *Iliad*, and the *Homeric Hymns* written mainly in the seventh and sixth centuries, supply the reader with the closest thing to a holy text ever achieved by the ancient Greeks.

**Thucydides (c. 455–c. 400 B.C.E.):** If *Herodotus is the Father of His- tory, then Thucydides might be called the Father of Rational His- tory, that is, historiography pursued as a reasoned, dispassionate inquiry into past events. He stands today as the model of the ob- jective, "scientific" historian who engages in the enterprise of re- counting the past, not out of chauvinist sentiment or antiquarian curiosity, but because of the sure knowledge that people must know what happened and why. Some of Thucydides' zeal for presenting a "true account" may be explained by who he was and the nature of the subject about which he wrote. Thucydides was an Athenian who lived through, and took part in, the *Peloponnesian War. In 424 he was appointed *strategos*, or general, and charged with re- lieving the allied city of Amphipolis in Thrace. His failure in this venture resulted in his exile from Athens. Never was failure so for- tunate an occurrence for the discipline of history. His sudden en- forced retirement gave Thucydides time and perspective to write his great work about an event that he believed "would be great and noteworthy above all the wars that had gone before" (I.i.4–5).

**Tripod cauldron:** These large, bronze vessels supported by three massive, bronze legs were used as aristocratic dedications to the gods. Although most of our examples were produced during the eighth and seventh centuries B.C.E. and have been found for the most part at such important pan-Hellenic sanctuaries as Olympia and Delphi, thirteen cauldrons were found in 1954 in the Cave of Polis on the out-of-the-way island of Ithaca. These tripod cauldrons appear to have been placed in the cave as a dedication to the hero Odysseus, perhaps in memory of the thirteen cauldrons given him by the *Phaeacians. This find is impressive not simply because of the large number of cauldrons discovered, but also for the age of some of them. The earliest appear to date to the late tenth or early ninth century. Also, the ornamentation on the legs of some of them match closely the ornamentation found on tripod leg molds from Lefkandi on Euboea. These molds were also found in a tenth-century context. These cauldrons were too large to serve any practical purpose and served an almost exclusively dedicatory function. That so much metal could be put to so nonutilitarian a purpose is a measure of the increasing wealth of at least some Greeks by the late tenth century.

***Works and Days:*** This long poem of just over 800 lines is the second work attributed to the early Greek poet *Hesiod. This poem is quite unlike the *Theogony, for it treats of such seemingly mundane matters as wise and efficient farm management. Recently, the work has been compared to Egyptian and Syrian wisdom literature which was popular in the late second and early first millennia. In presenting his opinion of how best to be self-sufficient and prosperous in farming, Hesiod addresses his ne'er-do-well brother Perses, upbraiding him for his laziness. Instead of gaping at the proceedings in the law courts, Perses should be busy about the farm mending fences or sowing a crop. The poem gives us an invaluable glimpse into rural life in Greece in about 700 B.C.E.

## NOTE

1. See in particular C. Mee, "A Mycenaean Thalassocracy in the Eastern Aegean?," in E. B. French and K. A. Wardle, eds., *Problems in Greek Prehistory* (Bristol, 1988), pp. 301–305.

# ANNOTATED BIBLIOGRAPHY

## *Iliad* and *Odyssey*

There are numerous translations of the epics in both prose and poetry. Since the Homeric epics were poems, a poetic translation is closer to the original. Many scholars recommend Richmond Lattimore's translation of the *Iliad* (University of Chicago Press, first published in 1951). Lattimore also translated the *Odyssey* (currently published by Perennial Press, 1999). Both epics have also been translated by Robert Fitzgerald: the *Iliad* (New York, 1979, repr. Oxford University Press, 1984) and the *Odyssey* (Doubleday, 1961). Also highly successful is Robert Fagles' translation of the *Odyssey* (Viking, 1996).

Another way to experience the poetry is by listening to it, as did the early Greeks. Fine tapes of both have been produced: *Homer: The Odyssey*, translated by Robert Fagles, read by Ian McKellen (Penguin Audiobooks, 1996) and *Homer: The Iliad*, translated by Robert Fagles, read by Derek Jacobi (Penguin-Highbridge Audio, 1990).

For an introduction to basic features of the poems, it is useful to consult the two concise guides in the series Landmarks of World Literature published by Cambridge University Press:

Michael Silk, *Homer: The Iliad* (1987; 2nd ed., 2004)

Jasper Griffin, *Homer: The Odyssey* (1997)

Mark W. Edwards offers a fuller companion to an understanding of the *Iliad* in his *Homer: Poet of the Iliad* (Baltimore, MD: Johns Hopkins University Press, 1987). In this work he examines the characteristics of

Homeric poetry and then turns to a commentary on the poem itself. Ian Morris and Barry Powell have jointly edited *A New Companion to Homer* (Leiden: Brill, 1997).

The Inaugural Issue of *Archaeology Odyssey* (1998) was largely devoted to Homer and includes the following articles:

Birgit Brandau, "Can Archaeology Discover Homer's Troy?"

Carol G. Thomas, "Searching for the Historical Homer"

Jasper Griffin, "Reading Homer after 2,800 Years"

Barry Powell, "An Odyssey Debate: Who Invented the Alphabet?"

The list of books focused on Homer and Homeric poetry is impressive in its quantity and diversity. We mention only a handful.

Carpenter, Rhys. 1958. *Folk Tale, Fiction and Saga in the Homeric Epics.* Berkeley and Los Angeles: University of California Press. This is a discussion of the Homeric poems and their relation to folk tale and saga. Carpenter is a conservative critic of those scholars who, in his opinion, are too eager to find Mycenaean references within the poems. Carpenter believes there is only one Mycenaean relic to be found in Homer—the boars' tusk helmet of Odysseus. This little book is also valuable for its distinction between the Mycenaean cultural *reference* and the Dark Age cultural *context* of the poems.

Carter, Jane B., and Sarah P. Morris, eds. 1995. *The Ages of Homer. A Tribute to Emily Townsend Vermeule.* Austin: University of Texas Press. This collection of thirty-one essays examines three aspects of Homeric studies: Homer and the Bronze Age: Memory and Archaeology; Homer and the Iron Age: History and Poetics; After Homer: Narrative and Representation. Many contributions concentrate on physical evidence, Homeric poetry is the main theme of six others, historical context is a primary concern of five other essays, four treat cultural interaction, and others are directed toward interpretation of concepts.

Finley, M. I. 1965. *The World of Odysseus.* New York: Viking. In this seminal work in early Greek studies, Finley argues that the world described in the Homeric poems is one with which Homer himself would have been familiar—the world of the late Dark Age and early Archaic (c. 900–700 B.C.E.).

Havelock, Eric A. 1963. *Preface to Plato.* Cambridge, MA: Harvard University Press. What the title of this book does not reveal is the centrality of Homeric poetry to its goal of describing the Homeric and the Platonic states of mind and of contrasting the two attitudes. The first is conditioned by the nonliteracy of the age, whereas the second is that of a literate culture. Plato's view that poets must be removed from the ideal Republic is not a personal vendetta but an appreciation of the different qualities of oral and literate cultures.

Kirk, Geoffrey S. 1976. *Homer and the Oral Tradition*. Cambridge: Cambridge University Press; and 1965. *Homer and the Epic*. Cambridge: Cambridge University Press. The first book ranges widely over subjects related to Homeric studies: warfare, topography, language, and style. In the prefatory words of the author, however, its central theme is "the nature and effects of the oral tradition in ancient Greece." Kirk identifies the core of the book as Chapter 4, "The Oral and the Literary Epic." The second study examines the relation of the *Iliad* and *Odyssey* to the oral heroic poetry of the Greek Dark Age and beyond. It is the author's view that two accomplished bards cast the legendary tales as monumental poems in the eighth century B.C.E.

Lord, Albert Bates. 1991. *Epic Singers and Oral Tradition*. Ithaca, NY: Cornell University Press. This is a compilation of articles and lectures by Milman Parry's student and collaborator. The book treats the nature of oral epic, touching on various aspects of the methods and artistry of oral poets from Homer to the Serbo-Croatian epics.

Luce, J. V. 1975. *Homer and the Heroic Age*. London: Thames and Hudson. Combining the evidence of archaeology, epic poetry, and places, the author concludes that the inherited tradition is inherently sound, a valid memory of the Age of Heroes. An epilogue traces the Homeric tradition.

Page, Denys L. 1959. *History and the Homeric Iliad*. Berkeley and Los Angeles: University of California Press. This series of lectures opens with a summary of the archaeology of Troy from Schliemann and Dörpfeld through Carl Blegen's work in the 1930s. The catalog of artifacts and architecture is enlivened by a rich analysis of the varying fortunes of the settlement from Troy I (c. 3000 B.C.E.) to Troy VIIb (c. 1150 B.C.E.). Both in this summary and in the following chapter dealing with the historical grounding of the Trojan War, Page insists that Ahhiyawa is not mainland Greece, nor is it in the Troad. Page posits a theory that Ahhiyawa is to be found on the island of Rhodes off the southwest coast of Anatolia. In succeeding chapters, Page examines the question of how much light the Linear B tablets shed either on the Trojan War in history or on Homeric poetry.

Scott, John A. 1925. *Homer and His Influence.* New York: Longmans Green and Co. Reprint, New York: Cooper Square Publishers, 1963. This compact study by a major Homeric scholar explains Homeric poetry and then sketches "the reach of his genius" from antiquity into the twentieth century. The author dares to state that Homer's influence is permanently in place in far more areas than poetry. He maintains that drama, literary criticism, history, philosophy, public speaking, and even medicine are all indebted to this great bard.

West, M. L. 1988. "The Rise of the Greek Epic." *Journal of Hellenic Studies* 108: 151–172. This article demands some knowledge of Greek and linguistics. Even in the absence of such knowledge, however, the article makes for fascinating reading as West argues not only for connections between Homer and Mycenaean epic, but goes on to examine possible relations with Vedic Indian epic, positing along the way an original Proto Indo-European epic tradition giving rise to both Indian and Homeric poetry.

## Troy

Allen, Susan Heuck. 1999. *The Walls of Troy: Frank Calvert and Heinrich Schliemann at Hisarlik.* Berkeley, Los Angeles, and London: University of California Press. The focus of this study is the Troad where the English-born Frank Calvert lived during the late nineteenth century, at the time that Heinrich Schliemann was seeking the site of ancient Troy. The author's view is that Calvert has as strong a claim to the honor of discovering Troy as Schliemann does.

Barber, R.L.N. 1987. *The Cyclades in the Bronze Age.* Iowa City: University of Iowa Press. This is an archaeological study of the Cyclades islands during the Bronze Age, c. 3000–1100 B.C.E. Chapters 6–9 are especially valuable for the examination of the increasing Minoan influence during the Cycladic Middle and early Late Bronze periods, followed by growing Mycenaean dominance throughout the period c. 1500–1250. See also his 1987 article "The Late Cycladic Period: A Review." *Annual of the British School at Athens* 76: 1–21.

Blegen, Carl W. 1963. *Troy and the Trojans.* London: Thames and Hudson. This is an account by the archaeologist who directed the second major excavation at Troy in the 1930s. Using newer archaeological methods than had been available to Schliemann, Blegen refined the understanding of the site's many levels and their chronology. As in all the volumes in the Peoples and Places series, the book is easily readable by nonspecialists.

Boedeker, Deborah, ed. 1997. *The World of Troy: Homer, Schliemann and the Treasures of Priam*. Proceedings from a Seminar sponsored and published by the Society for the Preservation of the Greek Heritage. Essays by major scholars include examination of the character and accomplishment of Heinrich Schliemann, the relationship of Troy to the larger Aegean and Mediterranean sphere, a summary of the most recent investigation of the site by the director of the project, the historical implications of the Homeric account of the Trojan War, and the ongoing significance of the Trojan War legend.

Deuel, Leo. 1977. *Memoirs of Heinrich Schliemann: A Documentary Portrait Drawn from His Autobiographical Writings, Letters, and Excavation Reports*. New York: Harper & Row. Deuel's account is a readable story of Schliemann's life told through an interweaving of Schliemann's own writings and the author's commentary.

Easton, Donald. 1985. "Has the Trojan War Been Found?" *Antiquity* 59(227): 188–196. Drawing upon physical evidence, Hittite materials, and chronology, the author concludes that the Trojan War cannot be proved. However, "for those who wish to believe—faith is once again possible" (195).

Foxhall, Lin, and John K. Davies, eds. 1984. *The Trojan War: Its Historicity and Context*. Bristol: Bristol Classical Press. Originally papers of a conference, the essays examine the evidence of historical accounts, archaeological data, topographical information, and oral tradition in a broad sweep that includes the Anatolian and Mycenaean perspectives. Another essay investigates the Trojans in the *Iliad*.

Luce, J. V. 1998. *Homer's Landscapes: Troy and Ithaca Revisited*. New Haven, CT: Yale University Press. The author does not simply describe the Homeric landscapes of Troy and Ithaca in text and illustrations, but he peoples the places with figures from the poems. Other major issues appear in the study, such as the character of Schliemann. Both general readers and scholars of the classics, archaeology, and the classical tradition will find much to admire.

Mellink, Machteld J., ed. 1986. *Troy and the Trojan War*. Bryn Mawr, PA: Bryn Mawr College; printed by Science Press. This collection draws together seven essays and a postscript that originated as presentations at a symposium. Subjects include descriptions of Troy and the Troad by Manfred Korfmann; discussions of Troy in the Hittite texts by Hans Güterbock; the language of the Trojans by Calvert Watkins; the physical identity of the

Trojans by J. Lawrence Angel; and a thousand years of Trojan memories by Emily Vermeule.

Morehead, Caroline. 1996. *Lost and Found: The 9,000 Treasures of Troy.* New York: Viking. Two themes intertwine in this study: the odd life of Heinrich Schliemann and the fate of the Trojan treasures from the time of their discovery through the rediscovery of 259 of the artifacts fifty years after they disappeared from Berlin at the end of World War II.

Peters, Elizabeth, 1987. *Trojan Gold.* New York: Tom Doherty Associates. Accomplished mystery writer Peters, who is fond of the ancient world, has woven a modern tale of detection around the lost "Treasure of Priam."

Schliemann, Heinrich, 1881. *Ilios: The City and Country of the Trojans.* New York: Harper & Brothers. The first account of Schliemann's excavations at Troy recounts his earliest exploration at the site. It also includes an autobiography. A second publication, *Troja: Results of the Latest Researches,* was published in 1884. In addition to description, the books are very well illustrated.

Sherratt, E. S. 1990. " 'Reading the Texts': Archaeology and the Homeric Question." *Antiquity* 64: 807–824. The student would do well to read this article in conjunction with Rhys Carpenter, Sarah P. Morris, and Denys Page (*supra*). Sherratt's examination of the use of spears, shields, helmets, and iron in the *Iliad* suggests that elements of this poem date to the fifteenth, rather than the thirteenth, century. Although Sherratt makes no claims for an historical Trojan War, he feels that if such an event did happen it would most likely have occurred c. 1400 rather than c. 1250.

Skutsch, Otto. 1987. "Helen, Her Name and Nature." *Journal of Hellenic Studies* 107: 188–193. This brief article is a fascinating study of the character of Helen, who was long thought to have originally been a goddess. Skutsch presents linguistic evidence that connects the name of Helen and the stories surrounding her to a Vedic Indian solar deity. In India her name was Saraṇyu, and she was the mother of the twin horsemen known as the Aśvins. In Greece Helen was the sister of the Dioscouroi, also twins famed for their horsemanship.

Thomas, Carol G. 1993. *Myth Becomes History: Pre-Classical Greece.* Claremont, CA: Regina Books. This is one of the publications of the Association of Ancient Historians whose purpose is to further the teaching and study of ancient history through succinct accounts describing basic directions in the field and proving basic bibliography. This pamphlet uses Troy to examine a possible war and also as a metaphor for the larger dimensions of pre-Classical Greece.

Tolstikov, Vladimir, and Mikhail Treister, eds. 1996. *The Gold of Troy.* New York: Henry N. Abrams. The newly rediscovered treasures from Troy are gloriously displayed in this study, which grew out of the exhibit held in the Pushkin State museum of Fine Arts in Moscow. After a brief biography of Schliemann, a longer essay describes the history of Troy and its excavation. Much of the book is a beautifully illustrated catalog. The hotly debated issue of the treasures' authenticity is discussed, with a positive verdict given.

Wood, Michael. 1985. *In Search of the Trojan War.* New York and Oxford: Facts On File. Also available on BBC video. This deservedly popular detective story manages both to present the history of Anatolian and Mycenaean archaeology and to weigh fairly all of the arguments for and against accepting the Trojan War as historical fact.

## Mycenaeans

Betancourt, Philip P. 1976. "The End of the Greek Bronze Age." *Antiquity* 50: 40–47. Many believe that there is no single cause for the collapse of the Mycenaean civilization. On this line of reasoning, the author suggests that the kingdoms may have become too specialized to adjust to economic difficulties. Basic crop failures—a regular occurrence in Greece—would have upset all aspects of the economic picture, with serious political ramifications.

Chadwick, John. 1967. *The Decipherment of Linear B.* 2nd ed. Cambridge: Cambridge University. This is the story of the decipherment of the Linear B script employed in Late Bronze Age Greece and Crete from the discovery of the tablets a century ago by Sir Arthur Evans to their decipherment in 1952 by Michael Ventris. It is a well-written and exciting tale of the solution of a major linguistic mystery. The last two chapters provide a brief overview of Mycenaean and Minoan culture in light of the Linear B documents. The book also contains a handy list of the then known eighty-seven signs with their phonetic values.

Chadwick, John. 1976. *The Mycenaean World.* Cambridge: Cambridge University Press. Acknowledging the existence of a number of studies revealing the nature of the Mycenaean civilization through its archaeological evidence, John Chadwick undertook to reveal other aspects through the recently deciphered Linear B tablets. With this evidence, he presents the geography, people, administrative system, religion, and economic and military structure of this first civilization of Greece.

Hooker, J. T. 1980. *Linear B: An Introduction*. Bristol: Bristol Classical Press. An introduction to Linear B Greek, this book requires some knowledge of Classical Greek. Even those interested students who have no Greek should read this text, however, for its introductory essay, which places the script in its historical context.

Hooker, J. T. 1976. *Mycenaean Greece*. London: Routledge and Kegan Paul. Concentrating primarily on the Mycenaean culture, the author traces the historical development of Aegean cultures during the Bronze Age beginning with the situation before the Mycenaean Age and carrying through the collapse of the Mycenaean civilization.

McDonald, William A., and Carol G. Thomas. 1990. *Progress Into the Past: The Rediscovery of Mycenaean Civilization*. 2nd ed. Bloomington and Indianapolis: Indiana University Press. *Progress Into the Past* provides the reader with two books in one. It delineates the archaeology and history of the Aegean Bronze Age by recounting the history of Bronze Age Aegean scholarship from Heinrich Schliemann's first excavations at Hissarlik and Mycenae through Carl Blegen's work at Hissarlik and Pylos to the 1980s and the rise of new archaeological techniques such as survey and underwater archaeology.

Mylonas, George E. 1966. *Mycenae and the Mycenaean Age*. Princeton, NJ: Princeton University Press. This is an overview of major sites and features of Mycenaean culture by an archaeologist who participated in major excavations in the mid-twentieth century, including three campaigns at Mycenae between 1952 and 1954 together with Dr. John Papadimitrious, then director of the Greek Archaeological Services. The book is richly illustrated with plans and photographs.

Schliemann, Heinrich. 1976 (1880). *Mycenae: A Narrative of Researches and Discoveries at Mycenae and Tiryns*. New York: Arno Press. Schliemann describes his excavations at Mycenae and briefly examines his excavations at Tiryns as well. The presentation is accompanied by copious illustrations of finds. Unlike the situation at Hissarlik, there were visible remains from the Bronze Age site, and the ancient travel guide written by Pausanias assisted in identifying specific areas.

Taylour, Lord William. 1983. *The Mycenaeans*. Revised ed. London: Thames and Hudson. This book has become the standard survey of Mycenaean Greece.

Not nearly as heavy on the archaeology as Oliver Dickinson (*infra*), it is a lively introduction for the nonspecialist.

Webster, T.B.L. 1964. *From Mycenae to Homer.* New York: W. W. Norton. This is a masterful, if now somewhat dated, study of Mycenaean art and the likely forms that would have been assumed by its poetry. Of particular interest is an account of the debt of Homeric epic both to the Mycenaean past and to other Bronze Age poetry in Anatolia and Syria–Palestine.

## Thera Frescoes

Doumas C., ed. *Thera and the Aegean World I.* London: The Thera Foundation, 1978. A compilation of articles examining the archaeology of Thera and Akrotiri, which attempts to relate this important site to neighboring Cycladic cultures as well as to the Mycenaean and Minoan cultures to the north and south. See particularly the articles by M. Cameron and Lyvia Morgan Brown for varying interpretations of the Akrotiri frescoes.

Marinatos, Nanno. 1985. "The Function and Interpretation of the Theran Frescoes." *Bulletin de correspondance hellénique Suppl. XI*, pp. 219–230. This article describes and interprets the frescoes of Akrotiri quite differently than either L. Morgan Brown (see previous entry, Doumas) or Sarah P. Morris. In these famous works Marinatos finds clues to Bronze Age Cycladic religious ritual and belief.

Morris, Sarah P. 1989. "A Tale of Two Cities: The Miniature Frescoes from Thera and the Origins of Greek Poetry." *American Journal of Archaeology* 93: 511–535. Morris argues that the South and North Wall frescoes of the West House at Akrotiri have a narrative aspect. That is, they tell a story, and the story they tell bears close relation to elements in the Homeric epic. The frescoes, in Morris' opinion, are pictorial versions of Bronze Age epic poetry current at the time they were painted. Furthermore, she argues that this epic material, though predating Homer by 800 years, provided a narrative framework for both the *Iliad* and *Odyssey*.

Wachsmann, S. 1980. "The Thera Waterborne Procession Reconsidered." *International Journal of Nautical and Underwater Exploration* 9.4: 287–295. This is yet another attempt to interpret the famous Akrotiri fresco from the West House. In this article, Wachsmann proposes that the scene represents a festival boat race to mark the beginning of safe sailing weather. He compares the scene to such nautical festivals as those held in Hong Kong until recent times.

## Hittites

Bryce, Trevor. 1985. "A Reinterpretation of the Milawata Letter in the Light of the New Join Piece." *Anatolian Studies* 35: 13–23. In 1981, a new fragment of Hittite text was found to belong to a previously identified document known as the *Milawata Letter*. (In this book we have referred to this letter as the *Millawanda Letter*. Both *Milawata* and *Millawanda* appear in the Hittite archives, and today many, perhaps most, scholars identify Milawata/Millawanda as Bronze Age Miletus.) This new join clarified a number of issues arising from the previously fragmentary nature of the document. The document could now be more securely dated to the reign of Tudhaliya IV in the latter half of the thirteenth century B.C.E. More importantly, the document seemed to imply the establishment of a shared sphere of influence in western Anatolia between the Hittites and the king of Milawata/Millawanda. Bryce's order of events in this early article is somewhat different from that followed in his later book, *The Kingdom of the Hittites*.

Bryce, Trevor. 1998. *The Kingdom of the Hittites*. Oxford: Clarendon Press. This is a fine, up-to-date survey of the Hittite Empire from its rise in the seventeenth century to its collapse in the late thirteenth or early twelfth century B.C.E. A study of this great state is extremely important for our subject for its dealings with such shadowy powers as Ahhiyawa, Wilusa, and Millawanda, which an increasing number of scholars identify as Mycenaean Greece, Ilios, and Bronze Age Miletus, respectively. Special attention should be paid to Chapters 3, 8, 9, 11, and 12 for references to Ahhiyawa and Wilusa. The final chapter (14) discusses the possibility of an historical Trojan War in light of these references.

Ceram, C. W. 1956. *The Secret of the Hittites: The Discovery of an Ancient Civilization*. New York: Alfred A. Knopf. A deservedly popular account of the discovery of the Hittites as a great Bronze Age power. Though dated, it is still valuable as an introduction to the Hittites as a culture, but particularly for its retelling of the archaeological and linguistic work which raised the popular conception of the Hittites from an obscure tribe referred to in the Old Testament to a great power of the Bronze Age on a equal footing with Assyria and Egypt.

Cline, Eric. 1991. "A Possible Hittite Embargo Against the Mycenaeans." *Historia* 40.1: 1–9. Archaeological evidence has demonstrated that, although the Hittites carried on a lively trade with Assyria, Babylonia, and Egypt, there is little evidence of such trading relations with the Aegean. In the Aegean world very few Hittite artifacts have been discovered, although much evidence has been found for trade with Egypt, Syria–Palestine, and even distant Babylonia. Cline suggests that this anomaly can be accounted for by a possible trade embargo imposed by the Hittites on Mycenaean goods. That such embargoes existed is demonstrated by the *Šaušgamuwa Treaty* in which the Hittite king Tudhaliya IV instructs his client, King Šaušgamuwa of Amurru, not to allow Ahhiyawan shipping into his ports. If the Ahhiyawans are Mycenaeans, the possibility of a long-term embargo is strengthened owing to the ever strained relations between Ahhiyawa and Hatti.

Güterbock, Hans G. 1983. "The Hittites and the Aegean World: Part 1. The Ahhiyawa Problem Reconsidered." *American Journal of Archaeology* 87: 133–143. This brief article has served as the opening salvo in a renewal of the old debate concerning whether Ahhiyawa as referred to in the Hittite archives may be identified with Mycenaean Greeks. The article is based on new interpretations of the Hittite documents and argues strongly for such an identification.

MacQueen, J. G. 1975. *The Hittites and Their Contemporaries in Asia Minor*. Boulder, CO: Westview. Although this is another highly accessible survey of the rise and fall of the Hittite Empire, it differs from Bryce in one signal feature. As MacQueen states on page 40, he is an unapologetic "anti-Mycenaean"—meaning he does not accept the Ahhiyawans = Mycenaeans equation. See Chapter III for his argument. Further on in the book, in Chapter 5, MacQueen seems to indicate a belief that Ahhiyawa was in the Troad and was thus a neighbor of Troy.

## Larger Context

Braudel, Fernand. 2001 (English translation by Allen Lane). *Memory and the Mediterranean*. London: Penguin. This is a sweeping study by the historian who has been called *the* outstanding historian of the mid-twentieth century. It tracks the *longue durée* of the Mediterranean from the Paleozoic era to the Roman encirclement of its shores, interweaving places with people and people with one another.

Dickinson, Oliver. 1994. *The Aegean Bronze Age*. Cambridge: Cambridge University Press. This book is the most recent survey of the archaeology of the entire Aegean area. Not for the faint of heart, this book is heavy on description of the architectural and ceramic evidence from c. 3000 to 1100 B.C.E., with little in the way of analytical evaluation until the final chapter. Before examining Dickinson, the reader may wish to first consult McDonald and Thomas' *Progress Into the Past*, which is more accessible.

Drews, Robert. 1993. *The End of the Bronze Age: Changes in Warfare and the Catastrophe ca. 1200 B.C.* Princeton, NJ: Princeton University Press. This is a well-written account of the collapse of the Mycenaean civilization and the contemporaneous attacks of the Sea Peoples on Egypt and the cities of Syria–Palestine. Drews proposes the hypothesis that new fighting tactics featuring highly mobile, lightly armed raiding parties—rather like the Vikings of the ninth and tenth centuries C.E.—helped bring about the demise of the great Mycenaean citadel centers.

Erskine, A. 2001. *Troy Between Greece and Rome*. Oxford: Oxford University Press. The author tracks the endurance of the Trojan association from its Greek origins into Roman tradition. He looks at the myth in Roman context as well as in the Archaic Age, the period of the Persian Wars, and in the western Greek colonial setting.

Fitton, J. Lesley, 1996. *The Discovery of the Greek Bronze Age*. Cambridge, MA: Harvard University Press. Beginning with "A Past That Never Was Present," the author summarizes the ancients' own view of their past and the renewed interest in Greece from the eighteenth century through the first half of the nineteenth century. She then turns to "The Heroic Age of Excavation" and, finally, sketches certain current theories and problems.

Grimal, Nicholas. 1992. *A History of Ancient Egypt*. Oxford: Blackwell. Translated from the French by Ian Shaw. A relatively detailed discussion of ancient Egypt from prehistorical times to the final phase associated with Persia and Greece. In addition to the narrative of periods, the book includes detailed treatment of aspects of culture and larger connections, including the Aegean world.

Hornung, Erik. 1999. *History of Ancient Egypt: An Introduction*. Ithaca, NY: Cornell University Press. Translated from the German by David Lorton. This concise basic history is well illustrated by a distinguished professor emeritus of Egyptology at the University of Basel.

Knapp, A. Bernard. 1988. *The History and Culture of Ancient Western Asia and Egypt*. Belmont, CA: Wadsworth. This book is useful as a brief survey of the Near Eastern Bronze Age societies to the east and south of Troy and the Aegean world. It is recommended particularly for those readers who have little or no acquaintance with these ancient societies.

Malkin, Irad. 1998. *The Returns of Odysseus: Colonization and Ethnicity*. Berkeley and Los Angeles: University of California Press. This is a most interesting study of the spread of Homeric poetry, and the legends on which it was founded, out of Greece and into the lands bordering the Adriatic and Ionian seas. It is a fascinating account of the uses to which these tales were put, not only by Greek traders and adventurers, but by the Epirote, Italian, and Sicilian peoples who heard, adopted, and adapted them as their own.

Mee, Christopher. 1978. "Aegean Trade and Settlement in Anatolia in the Second Millenium B.C." *Anatolian Studies* 28: 121–156. This important article examines the evidence of Mycenaean trade and dominance in this region, suggesting the development of a naval hegemony centered at Mycenae.

Powell, Barry. 1991. *Homer and the Origin of the Greek Alphabet.* Cambridge: Cambridge University Press. 1989. "Why Was the Greek Alphabet Invented? The Epigraphical Evidence." *Classical Antiquity* 8.2: 321–350. The long-established argument concerning the beginnings of the Greek alphabet says that at some time in the late ninth or early eighth century the Greeks borrowed a variant of the Phoenician consonantal alphabet for use in their trading activities. Somewhat later, this alphabet was modified with the inclusion of vowel symbols that made it usable for longer texts. Powell's article suggests that, since no examples of a rudimentary Greek consonantal alphabet are attested, it is possible that the Greeks did more than simply borrow an alphabet, but reinvented it. The article also states that this was done primarily for the reproduction of poetry of which there are a number of early examples.

Raubitschek, Anthony. 1989. "What the Greeks Thought of Their Early History." *Ancient World* 20: 39–45. A scholar with a deep understanding of ancient Greece argues that the ancient Greeks themselves had a "reasonably comprehensive view of the mythical period. Not only did ancient historians calculate the number of generations between themselves and their heroic past, but they also provided names of people and accounts of events of those earlier years." The historical mileposts for a fifth-century Athenian might have been the exploits of Theseus, the Voyage of the Argo, the expedition of the Seven Against Thebes, the Trojan War, the invasion of the Heraclidae, and the Persian Wars.

Thomas, Carol G., and Craig Conant. 1999 and 2003. *Citadel to City-state: The Transformation of Greece, 1200–700 B.C.E.* Bloomington and Indianapolis: Indiana University Press. This account for the nonspecialist treats the Mycenaean collapse, the ensuing Dark Age, and the Greek renaissance of the eighth century. Of special interest to the reader are Chapters 3 and 4, which contain material regarding the Aeolian and Ionian Migrations to Anatolia and the activities of Euboean traders and colonists in Italy and Sicily.

Tyldesley, Joyce. 2000. *Ramesses: Egypt's Greatest Pharaoh*. London: Penguin Books. An introductory survey of the long reign of Ramses II, this book also contains much material on Egyptian art, architecture, and general culture. Chapters 2 and 3 are especially valuable for an account of the disastrous end of the Eighteenth Dynasty and the rise of the Nineteenth Dynasty. Chapter 3 contains a fine account of the Battle of Kadesh.

Ward, J. W., and M. Joukowsky, eds. 1992. *The Crisis Years: The Twelfth Century BC*. Dubuque, IA: Kendall/Hunt Publishers. This collection of twenty-three papers examines the disruptions of the late Bronze Age in a wide geographical context—from the Danube to the Tigris—in five categories: the problem defined; Eastern Europe and Anatolia; the Aegean World; Syria–Palestine and Egypt; and Western Asia.

# INDEX

## About the Authors

CAROL G. THOMAS is Professor of History at the University of Washington and the coauthor of *Citadel to City-State: The Transformation of Greece, 1200–700 BCE* (with Craig Conant), *Makedonika* (with Eugene N. Borza), and *Progress into the Past: The Rediscovery of Mycenaean Civilization* (with William A. McDonald).

CRAIG CONANT is the coauthor (with Carol G. Thomas) of *Citadel to City-State: The Transformation of Greece, 1200–700 BCE.*